ROBERT PLANT

ROBERT PLANT

The Voice That Sailed the Zeppelin

Dave Thompson

Backbeat
Books

An Imprint of Hal Leonard Corporation

Published in 2014 by Backbeat Books
An Imprint of Hal Leonard Corporation
7777 West Bluemound Road
Milwaukee, WI 53213

Trade Book Division Editorial Offices
33 Plymouth St., Montclair, NJ 07042

Printed in the United States of America

Book design by John J. Flannery

Library of Congress Cataloging-in-Publication Data

Thompson, Dave, 1960 January 3-
Robert Plant : the voice that sailed the Zeppelin / Dave Thompson.
       pages cm
Includes bibliographical references and index.
ISBN 978-1-61713-572-9
1. Plant, Robert. 2. Led Zeppelin (Musical group) 3. Rock musicians–England–
Biography. I. Title.
ML420.P58T46 2014
782.42166092–dc23
[B]
                            2014027917

www.backbeatbooks.com

Contents

Author's Note

There is a debate that raises its beastly little head every time Robert Plant releases a new album. Every time a new piece of footage surfaces on YouTube. Every time, in fact, his name is mentioned in a room where three or four people might be standing. And it goes something like this:

"He doesn't need the money. Now he's just out there singing oldies for the fun of it."

"No, he's singing old songs because he hasn't written any new ones."

And why hasn't he written any new songs?

"Because he doesn't have the need anymore. He just wants to enjoy himself."

Or: "Because he can't cut it on his own. He can't do it without Led Zeppelin."

Both sides of the argument might, conceivably, have something going for them. At the same time, both are so simplistic as to be utterly contemptible. To suggest a musician is "past it" because he no longer wants to run with the same gang he hung with forty years ago is to be absolutely ignorant of the things that make a band a band in the first place. And to suggest that a love of singing other people's songs is in some way easier than writing your own is to make a mockery of every interpretative singer from Billie Holiday to Rod Stewart, from Frank Sinatra to Elvis Presley.

Yet it's an argument that won't go away, and in a way it's the argument that inspired this book. Biographies of Robert Plant and Led Zeppelin (how easily the two names go together) are ten-a-penny today; with the exceptions of the Beatles and the Stones, and possibly Presley and Bowie, more books have been written and published about Zeppelin than any other band or performer of the rock 'n' roll era.

The need for one more is probably not the most pressing concern facing twenty-first-century rock, all the more so as two more or less definitive tomes hit the bookshelves while this one was being written: Paul Rees's *Robert Plant: A Life* and Barney Hoskyns's *Led Zeppelin: The Oral History of the World's Greatest Rock Band*. Indeed, taken together, these two books lay out the lives and times of their subjects in almost forensic detail, not only through the pages of written history, but also through that most precious of all the commodities that lie at the historian's disposal: the first-hand accounts of the people who were there while the history itself was being written.

Precious, but also misleading.

Ex-bandmates, ex-colleagues, ex-whatevers are very much like ex-wives. They see a lot, they remember a lot. And then they shape those memories, first through the prism of their own experiences with the person at the center of them, and then through their interpretations of the requirements of the person asking questions ten, twenty, forty years later. Reiterating, in other words, the same shallow sentiments as the fans we were introduced to earlier: betrayal, on the one hand, because a favored performer will no longer perform their favorites; weary acceptance on the other, because he's rich enough now that he doesn't have to bother.

It is often said by new divorcees that you can live with someone for years and years and never really know who they are. So it is with former bandmates. Early on, before fame and fortune come along, and you're still sharing the same toilet roll between four musicians and two roadies, you can say that you have few secrets from one another. But once fame does arrive, and everyone's traveling in his or her own separate limo, each equipped with its own private bathroom (we're speaking figuratively here, not literally), that's when you start to notice things. Bad things. Cruel things. Spiteful things. The things that stick in your craw and stick in your mind. There's a reason why the vast majority of tell-all (or even tell-quite-a-lot) biographies seem to show their subjects in the worst possible light. And that's a big part of it.

This is not a tell-all biography. Frankly I could care less how many women Robert Plant might have slept with, how many he allegedly penetrated with recently acquired marine life, how many times he may have gotten high. And you should feel the same way. Welcome to rock 'n' roll in the '70s. And the '60s. And the '80s, '90s and noughties too. It's what bands did, and what they still do today. It's called being young and bored and on the road, and you could take any account of one band's backstage misdemeanors, cross out their name and write in someone else's, and the stories would remain just as true. Or not.

Under any reasonable criteria, what matters is not what "fame" allows an artist to get away with. It is what the artist had to do in order to achieve that fame in the first place. That is what this book is about, and that is why the story takes the shape that I have given it. Life is chronological. But unless an artist is so single-mindedly one-dimensional that nothing can knock him off his musical course (in which case, he will be so boring that most people would have given up listening after the first two albums), a career is constructed from a series of loops, circuits, and sudden shifts, some of which follow a preordained course . . . a, b, c; but others of which apparently have no logic whatsoever . . . m, d, i.

This book follows that latter course.

It can, of course, be read as in a conventional, linear fashion. The even-numbered chapters, for the most part, trace Plant's life from childhood until the end of Led Zeppelin; the odd-numbered chapters follow his subsequent solo-and-otherwise career. Thus rearranged, a life and career will spool out as straightforwardly as you could wish. But they will do so without the internal twists and integral turns that have enabled Plant to maintain the career as intriguingly as he has, and it is those twists and turns that are the real subject of this book, as they resolve themselves into an "a, b, c" of their own.

It is a fascinating journey, rendered all the more so by the knowledge that it still has a long way to go. Perhaps alone of the musicians who have survived from his generation, certainly over the past fifteen years or so, Robert Plant is unique in that he has never allowed his audience to second-guess his career; that every move he has made—from the dissolution of the Page-Plant partnership in 1998 to his one-off album with Alison Krauss a decade later, from the Priory of Brion to the Sensational Space Shifters—has apparently taken him by surprise almost as much as it has caught his audience off guard.

Which, in turn, returns us to the squabbling acolytes we met at the beginning, and the reason their arguments can never be resolved. Because Robert Plant is not following a career course. He is following his dream. And dreams, as everyone who has ever had one can tell you, are rarely as straightforward as reality.

INTRODUCTION

The Only Sound That Matters
(2013–2014)

Late in 2013, Robert Plant announced that his next album, *lullaby and . . . The Ceaseless Roar*, rumored to have been gestating for at least the past eighteen months, was finally nearing completion—and that it was all about moving forward, instead of looking back. The following June, talking to the *New York Times*, he elaborated, "It's really a celebratory record, but it's very crunchy and gritty. . . . There's a lot of bottom end, so it might sound all right at a Jamaican party, but I'm not sure it would sound all right on NPR."

What it would not sound like was ancient history. Which some people might think is an odd thing for him to say when his last decade-plus has been spent singing covers of the songs he enjoyed in his youth, but it does not alter one basic truth.

His own past, he was saying, was the past. Not the songs, not the music, not what it meant to him, but the mechanics, the delivery and the circumstances of that past. They were behind him. Meaning, it was rather ironic that he should make that observation at precisely the same time as Jimmy Page was putting the finishing touches to the latest repackaging of the old Led Zeppelin catalog, bolstering the familiar old albums with all the odds-and-ends bonus material that the modern market has come to expect. That is, the stuff that wasn't good enough to release at the time the album was made, that wasn't worthy of inclusion in any subsequent reissue campaign, and that will now be talked up to Tomb of Tutankhamen proportions because it gives us all something new to look forward to.

Jimmy Page's assertion that he, too, has been working on some new material, also for release in 2014, was barely a footnote in the accompanying news stories. Because that is how a lot of people regard everything that the surviving members of Led Zeppelin have done since the band dissolved: as footnotes.

Two out of three times, they're probably right. No matter how far messrs Plant, Page, and Jones may have traveled, both chronologically and creatively, there is no denying the fact that the three of them are guaranteed a far more impressive payday, both critically and commercially, when their names are attached to that of Led Zeppelin, than they could ever hope to achieve beneath their own steam. Not because the music they make is in any way inferior to that they played forty-plus years ago. Indeed, a dispassionate ramble through Zeppelin's own back catalog can unearth any number of space-fillers, placeholders and "Wow, I'd completely forgotten they even recorded that" drifters.

No, Led Zeppelin are bigger because that is always the way it is, and it doesn't matter who you are. From four ex-Beatles to sundry solo Stones; from the mid-'70s madness that permitted every single member of Yes, Kiss, and the Moody Blues to take time out for their own LPs to the shattered remnants of countless other headline acts, it is rare indeed that the one-man show can ever eclipse the renown of the full-strength band. Which is why many folks don't even bother to try, and many more go scampering back to the security of the brand name at every opportunity they're given. How many times can an old album be remastered before they finally get it right? Or at least, get it sounding the way it did back in the days of vinyl, before ears were replaced by computer graphics and notes were translated into numbers? A lot more than we'd like to think.

Of course, when Robert Plant made his brief pronouncement, he probably *wasn't* taking a poke at the people who have been waiting since 1980 for Led Zeppelin to re-form on a permanent basis. But he didn't really need to.

His entire solo career had already done that for him.

Sixty-seven years old on August 20, 2015, Robert Plant is still instantly recognizable today. Not for him, it seems, the ravages of hair loss; his mane, though shorter and stragglier than it was in its prime, remains a distinctive tangle. Maybe his (comparatively) newly grown beard is showing distinct shades of gray, and the lines and folds that crease his face remain in place regardless of whether or not he is straining out one more mighty note. Disheveled of dress and insouciant of air, blessed with that aura of distracted involvement that only original hippies can pull off with such conviction, he looks good all the same, certainly when compared with the cadaverous visages of so many of his peers, or the gone-to-pot-and-then-Botoxed-back-again horror of so many others.

Vanity has never felt like a comfortable bedmate for Plant, not even when every magazine on the planet seemed to be describing him as an Adonis for the ages, his bare torso was winning the Chest of the Year, and the fan club was bitterly divided over whether he was best referred to as a Viking warrior or a Greek god. Such things never mattered to him because he has never lost sight of the reason why they mean so much to other people. It is the music that drew them to him in the first place—the music he makes, the music he listens to, the music he grew up with, the music he wants to hear—and everything else is just window dressing. More than one journalist, and many fans too, have walked away from an audience with Robert Plant having learned far more about, say, Robert Johnson and Sonny Boy Williamson than they have about Plant himself, and that is the way he prefers it.

Even his own children accuse him of being "this big kid." Alison Krauss told the *Daily Mail*, "He is crazily enthusiastic when it comes to music. He's very passionate and excited about a wide variety of obscure artists, which is what makes him so much fun to work with." You do not go into the studio with Robert Plant to find out how Zeppelin pulled off this or that track. You go in to find out how Plant wants to do it.

Not for him, the endless self-aggrandizement of the superstar machine. Even when Led Zeppelin were on the top of the world, Plant was more likely to turn up at the Roxy Club in London than Studio 54 in New York City, was photographed more frequently in the kind of clothes that David Bowie wouldn't even wear to do the gardening in than the finery of a rock star. And when first rumor and then sundry associates and employees began bolstering Zeppelin's legend with tales of the on-the-road debauchery that hallmarked their American tours—including many of the greatest excesses in the entire rock 'n' roll canon, if some tales are to be heeded—it was rarely Plant who took center stage in them. There may have been a Bacchanalian King in the court, but it wasn't Robert Plant.

This is one of the reasons he has proved so reluctant to even discuss something more than the occasional one-off reunion with his old bandmates and band name. "You've got to have a lot in common with the people you're working with at this time in your life," he told the *Daily Telegraph* in 2010. "Everything has to move on and forward, in all relationships."

Look to your own life. Social media has made it so very, very easy for us to reconnect with old school friends, old lovers, or simply old compatriots, names that were central to our very existence back in our late teens and twenties. Twenty, thirty, forty years on, however, how strong do those old ties remain? How many times can you ask "Do you remember?"; how many IMs really ping back and forth before you return to your own present day and they return to theirs, and the great reunion has fizzled out before the champagne has even stopped bubbling? Ray Davies of the Kinks even wrote a song about it, "Do You Remember Walter," back in 1967, before Facebook and MySpace and Twitter were even dreamed of. "If I talk about the old times, you'll get bored," he mourned. Then he snapped, "I bet you're fat and married and always back at home by half-past-ten."

Old bandmates are a lot like old school friends. And the more time that passes, the greater the chance that they will be fat and married and not just home but tucked up in bed by half-past-ten.

"I know that bands that haven't put out a record for ten years are playing to 20,000 people a night," Plant continued in that same 2010 interview. "But that's not the achievement. The achievement is to knock yourself out. It's a very selfish thing. The tail must never wag the dog."

But of course it does, because it's easier that way. The discographies of the world are positively lousy with the sordid stains of dried-up creative juices, album after album cut in the shadow of the purple patch, and each one greeted with less applause than the last, because all the audience really wants to hear are the songs that created that audience in the first place. It is a rare talent indeed, then, that can sustain the initial impetus and spread it over much more than four albums; a rarer one still that can keep it going for four decades; and even Robert Plant will admit that there have been times throughout his solo career when the roar of the crowd became more of a murmur, and the plaudits that once popped like corks were suddenly plopping instead.

On those occasions, it would have been the easiest thing in the world to make a few phone calls, rehearse a few songs, reprise an old band name . . . and once, that is precisely what he did. But when the headlines announced back in 2012 that Robert Plant was re-forming the group he used to play with, it was a revamped Strange Sensation that roared out of the garage, and the slate was swept clean overnight.

It is reinvention, not reincarnation, that is the true mark of the survivor, and the only reason it's David Bowie, and not Robert Plant, who is most frequently described as the chameleon of rock is that Bowie changed his hairstyle more often, signposting new sounds with the sweet release of his latest eight-by-twelves, to give the audience a clue as to what they might expect next.

Whether at the helm of Led Zeppelin, where it was generally Plant's lyrics that set the mood of the music; alone with his own band; or drifting through the welter of side projects that have occupied him throughout the intervening years, Plant has rarely stood still for any longer than he needed to—and on the occasions he has, he just leapt a little further the next time around. But it is not the dilettante shuffling of rock's other shapeshifting skipjacks that sustains him. A straight line drawn from Plant's first recording will always lead to his latest, no matter how many technical, sonic, or cultural advances might separate the sessions, and no matter what caliber of musician he may choose to work with next.

For Plant, reinvention means reignition: rediscovering the impetus behind the songs that make him happiest and then setting out from the same initial starting point, confident that whatever he ends up with will stand alongside its predecessor, no matter how many years and cheers divide them.

The historical record seems unanimous that "Stairway to Heaven" remains his greatest lyrical composition, and Plant himself has acknowledged as much over the years, albeit with a weariness that suggests he is tired of arguing rather than wholeheartedly agreeing. Certainly it is his best known and most loved. But is it the song or the overall arrangement that is responsible for the acclaim? From the same album (Led Zeppelin's fourth), "The Battle of Evermore" is at least its lyrical equal; it is the accompaniment (stark, Spartan, and according to Jimmy Page, "made up on the spot . . . never having played a mandolin before") that clouds its epic qualities—that and the fact that it never became an anchor within the band's live set.

That notion—the belief that greatness is conferred by popularity and familiarity—is another element within Plant's personal conflict with his past. Notably when he performs live, even today, the oldies that he chooses to exhume are far more likely to be someone else's entirely than excerpts from his own past, and when he does bring out a Zeppelin crowd-pleaser, it's very often one that scarcely pleases the crowd at all. "Hey Hey What Can I Do," a 1970 B-side. "Houses of the Holy." Something from *Coda*, the 1982 tombstone that rounded up a few stray oddities to mark the final passing of the band. "Yes," he seems to be saying, "I know you want to hear 'Whole Lotta Love.' But really, how boring would that be?"

And then the next time you see him, he *will* play it, because the sterility of the scheduled set list has always been anathema to him. Live music is not about hitting the right notes, playing the right chords. It's about living in the moment, grasping the personal spirits that every concert invokes, and dancing to the tune that they demand.

That *is* something that he learned, or at least perfected, during Led Zeppelin's heyday, and the fact that the sheer enormity of the band and the absolute rigidity of their organization effectively penned those spirits into the improvisational segments that pockmarked the set—Page's "Dazed and Confused" showcase, Jones's "No Quarter," and John Bonham's "Moby

Dick"—should not obscure that. Though their onstage repertoire was never as fluid as the solo Plant's has been, still, Led Zeppelin seldom played the same concert twice, which is why their live albums are never as magical as they ought to be and their reunions are memorable more as art installations than as living, breathing beasts.

No matter how wild the response to the band's 2007 performance at London's tumorous O2 Arena, the band onstage was no more Led Zeppelin than it was a reconvening of the reunion of just Page and Plant in the 1990s. True, they were the same people, mostly. They played the same songs, unanimously. And they were witnessed by the same audience, partially. But three more-or-less sexagenarians and their late drummer's son, playing a one-off set of thirty-year-old favorites in memory of their record company's recently deceased founder, could and should never compare with a working band at the height of its powers, scouring the concert halls of the Western world and knowing that *every* night they need to be at their best, because they owe that much to the people who are buying their latest album—and hopefully already own the ones that came before it.

That, more than any of its myriad other attributes and ambitions, is the true spirit of rock 'n' roll, and it is that which continues to fire Robert Plant. It's about pleasing the crowd with something more than the crowd-pleasers; it's about competing with the rest of the pack, but most of all with yourself. It's about being honest with your own intentions, and placing that honesty on a higher pedestal than any of the so-called rewards of rock success.

It is for others (publicists and pressmen, management and roadies, groupie girls and fan boys, photographers and pharmacists) to weave the legends that, from outside the circle, might sometimes seem to obscure that honesty—and can certainly chip away at it, which is why so many so-called superstars wind up believing their own press. And generally they wind up either on the scrapheap or appending the old band name to a bunch of sad-sack sessionmen, and marching out onto the oldies circuit, insisting that because they still have the same roadie in their employ, they are still the same stars we once knew and loved.

The artists that avoid that final fate are the ones that sidestepped its temptations in the first place, and it's interesting that all three surviving members of Led Zeppelin have taken that same journey.

Jimmy Page may spend much of his time curating the old catalog, but he also knows that if *he* doesn't do it, then some whiz-kid engineer who wasn't even born when the band broke up will have the master tapes on his laptop tomorrow, giving every note a nice modern sheen. And you can ask Marc Bolan about *that*.

John Paul Jones has meandered down some absolutely fascinating avenues, in an apparent quest to place a well-timed finger into every musical pie that has ever taken his fancy. Asked whether he would be interested in a Led Zeppelin reunion sometime in 2014, he told Red Carpet TV News that he wasn't. "2014 is full of opera for me at the moment," he explained, and it looks likely to remain that way. He was writing an opera based around Swedish playwright August Strindberg's *Spöksonaten* (The Ghost Sonata), and he was still "only halfway through the first act."

And Robert Plant has his own album to take care of, together with a host of the activities that may or may not play out in the same kind of spotlight but are just as important to him. Such as the May 2013 evening when he turned up at his old alma mater, Kidderminster College, for a concert for autistic performers organized by twenty-year-old student Jordan Statham.

Plant was already patron of the MAS record label that operated out of the college; back in 1989, as one of his earliest bandmates, Kevyn Gammond, was first setting it in motion, Plant even agreed for a demo recorded by his pre-Zeppelin group Band of Joy, a song called "Adriatic Seaview," to appear on the label's maiden release, a cassette compilation titled *In the Forest*. It was Gammond again who tipped him off to this latest event, telling him "about Jordan's ambition and his unique achievement in producing a music showcase like this. I think it is great that he is able to let go and express himself in public." As Plant informed the 240-strong audience when he introduced Statham to the stage with the recommendation, "[He's] a very special guitarist." He continued, "I was the same person as Jordan is now, sadly too many years ago. I've tried to advise him as he goes out into the circus that is the world."

None of which rules out a reunion; none of which closes the door one final time on what, now that there are so few Beatles left alive, remains the No. 1 revivification on every classic rock fan's list. But as Robert Plant reminds us every time the subject is raised in his hearing, the past has always looked after itself. It's the future we should all be focusing on, because the future's where we have to live, and God knows the present is already grim enough.

His current band is called the Sensational Space Shifters.

It's a role he has played all his life.

1

No Regrets
(1980–1981)

After John Bonham, there was nothing.

After John Bonham, there was a void.

After John Bonham, there was no going back.

The rumor mill was already grinding. Cozy Powell, the powerhouse force behind Ritchie Blackmore's Rainbow and, before that, the beast that was Bedlam, was one of the first names pushed forward as a suitable replacement for the recently deceased percussionist.

So were Phil Collins, Carmine Appice, Queen's Roger Taylor, Jethro Tull's Barriemore Barlow, Bad Company's Simon Kirke, and ELO's Bev Bevan. While Zeppelin grieved, without even a thought for the future, the music press and the media grapevine positively hummed with suggestions, rumors, and I-heard-this-from-someone-who's-really-close-to-*whoevers*— not one of which emanated from the Zeppelin camp, not one of which had any chance of happening.

A great band is not simply four people in a van. It is four spirits in tandem, a unique chemistry that demands they create the music they make and that will never be swayed from that course. It is why the fans of a band that has undergone a significant membership change will assign to it a "classic line-up": a golden age whose musical output can never be eclipsed.

The Stones without Jones, the Who without Moon, 10cc without God-ley-Creme. All continued on, all continued having hits. Sometimes, they even became bigger. But the music they made when they were together was derived from a chemistry that can never be duplicated.

Genesis without Gabriel, Roxy without Eno, Bowie without the Spiders from Mars . . . Led Zeppelin without John Bonham. It was unthinkable.

So, of course, it became all that a lot of people *did* think about.

It is insulting to say that Robert Plant felt Bonham's loss the most. Bandmates Jimmy Page and John Paul Jones, manager Peter Grant—everybody in the extended Zeppelin family was reeling too. But from the moment Plant's personal assistant, Benji LeFevre, discovered the drummer's lifeless body in its bed on September 25, 1980, the singer had not simply lost a bandmate. He had lost one of the oldest and closest friends he had ever known.

Both were just sixteen when they first met: Robert Anthony Plant was a former grammar school boy slumming it in a blues band called the Crawling Kingsnakes; John Henry Bonham was a working class lad, already married to a girl named Pat, already drinking, and already possessed of a ferocious reputation around their native Black Country.

At school, Bonham's headmaster predicted that the boy would end up becoming either a garbageman or a millionaire. The bands he'd played with so far suggested the former: local club and pub acts that were most comfortable opening someone else's show, and that only once bothered the world at large, when the Senators cut a single called "She's a Mod."

But Bonham had ambitions far beyond that, a point he proved when he buttonholed Plant as the singer came offstage that day in 1966. A vision resplendent in an orange ostrich-skin bomber jacket, echoing precisely the same sentiment as Keith Moon declared when he first pitched to join the Who, Bonham didn't even bother introducing himself. He just announced that the Crawling Kingsnakes' drummer was crap, and that he could do better himself.

Plant responded in the same way Pete Townshend had: "Okay then, prove it." But first he asked where the interloper was from.

"Redditch," replied Bonham, naming a town that lay fifteen miles away. Plant laughed. "I don't care if you're Buddy Rich, I'm not picking you up from Redditch."

But he would.

Bonham did not remain with the Crawling Kingsnakes for long. Pat was expecting the couple's first child, and his previous band, the Way of Life, had earned far more money than his new group ever could. He quit, but he and Plant remained in close contact. So close, says Bonham's sister Deborah, that Robert used to describe Bonham's mom as his own "second mother." And years later, when the pair met up, "they were just engrossed in stories: mum holding court, [telling] stories of Robert and John when they were young." When, three years and a few more groups later, the singer's latest band found itself in need of a drummer who could offer the bulldozing barrage that their first discussions demanded, "Bonzo" Bonham was the first name he called.

And the only name Led Zeppelin would ever consider.

It is ironic, then, that Bonham's last days should also have been the first days of a whole new phase in that band's existence. On September 24, 1980, the quartet convened to commence rehearsals for their first American tour in three years, on the heels of their first new LP in almost four.

It was a tighter, more economical band than before. A recent tour of Germany saw Led Zeppelin perform without any of the bombast that had hitherto been their stock-in-trade. No extended solos, no thirty-minute noodle fests. Just the tightest, hardest-hitting rock 'n' roll you could imagine, as played by the tightest, hardest-hitting rock 'n' roll band there was. It should have been a whole new beginning, the dawn of another decade-long dominance of the music scene.

The drummer was already in poor shape, though. He had recently abandoned a heroin habit, and was still taking drugs to fight the anxiety and depression that accompanied his withdrawal. He was also drinking heavily, hitting the vodka that he had specifically been warned against because it would only counteract the pills. Still, when he told Plant that he really didn't want to be rehearsing—that the singer should play drums and Bonham would handle the singing—it was easy to think he was kidding. Until the rehearsals got underway and Bonham continued drinking, pushing himself toward unconsciousness. Finally, the session was abandoned, and everyone went back to Jimmy Page's house in Windsor, where

Bonham continued sinking the Russian potato. Finally he did pass out, and someone carried him up to one of the spare rooms, tucked him into bed, and left him to sleep it off.

By morning he was dead, suffocated by his own vomit.

The band broke up there and then. Nobody said as much; they were all too numb. But Plant spoke for everyone when he reflected, years later, "It was so . . . final. I never even thought about the future of the band or music."

Jimmy Page, the workaholic whose vision Led Zeppelin had been in the first place, was the first to recover—or at least, the first to consider moving on. Shortly before Christmas, just three months after Bonzo's death, Page was at a Christmas party when he bumped into Chris Squire, bassist with Yes. The pair got talking, and by the new year had convened what can only be described as a supergroup—the first of a decade that would ultimately creak beneath the weight of such conceits. With Squire's fellow Yesman Alan White sitting in on drums and Greenslade's Dave Lawson on keyboards, the quartet was named by Squire's father: ex-Yes and Zeppelin; XYZ.

They had already recorded a handful of songs by the time Page called Plant into the situation. With the bassist on vocals, two Squire compositions titled "Telephone Secrets" and "Can You See" had been joined by a couple of instrumentals—one of which, "Mind Drive," would later be recorded by Yes. None of which impressed Plant in the slightest when he heard them at an XYZ rehearsal on the last day of February 1981. Complex slabs of unabashed prog, they might indeed, as Page explained, have been immeasurably improved by a stronger vocal. But Plant wanted nothing to do with the project, either musically or personally.

Because after Bonham, there was nothing.

Until the day he ventured out to that rehearsal, Plant had more or less spent the last six months at Jennings Farm, his secluded property in Blakeshall, a small community out in the fields near Wolverley and Kidderminster. It had been his home for the past ten years but a part of his landscape for even longer, overlooking the same range of hills that he had stared at from his bedroom at his parents' home in nearby Hayley Green.

The farm had been all but derelict when he purchased it for £6,000 in 1969, an abandoned shell that had not even been hooked up to the electricity. He, wife Maureen, and daughter Carmen stayed with Maureen's parents while the workmen labored to render Jennings Farm livable; Plant himself worked to transform an old barn into a music room, and when John Bonham purchased a similar property just a couple of miles away, the local pub frequently found itself hosting one half of the biggest rock band in the world. Although neither of the pair ever gave much evidence of that. For both, their farms were where they went when they needed to escape their day jobs, and where they turned to escape their nightmares as well.

Three years earlier, on July 26, 1977, Plant was in New Orleans with Led Zeppelin when he learned that his five-year-old son, Karac, had died from a viral infection. It was John Bonham who sat next to him on the hastily arranged flight back to London, and then for the drive up to the farm. There the boy was buried, at a funeral where Bonham was the only one of the singer's bandmates or management to even bother attending. There, too, Plant came as close as he ever had to swearing off rock 'n' roll forever.

His lifestyle, he knew, had already placed his marriage under incredible strain—the months he spent away touring, leaving Maureen to raise two children on her own. Now there was just one, and Plant could not help but wonder whether things might have been different if he had been at home.

Friends speak of the stygian darkness that engulfed Plant then, how he even considered applying for a teacher training college. Almost a year would pass before he met again with his bandmates, in May 1978 at Clearwell Castle, a gorgeous mock-Gothic manor house in the heart of the Forest of Dean on the fringe of the Welsh borders. Longer than that would elapse before he forgave them for not attending Karac's funeral.

But slowly he pieced himself back together. By August, vacationing in Spain, he was even feeling good enough to join Dr. Feelgood onstage, a band with whom he'd been friends since the mid-1970s. Now, the very person who had stood alongside him throughout that terrible night, providing much of the glue with which he repaired his shattered psyche, had himself been taken away.

Interviewed in the mid-1980s, Peter Grant made it clear that he had no intention of trying to put the band together again. Their last album, *In Through the Out Door*, had been a struggle from the outset, recorded with Plant still mourning Karac and Page apparently undergoing some form of writer's block; the singer, said Grant, was astonished to discover that Page had barely written a note of new music throughout the band's layoff. Even before Bonham's death, all four members were in desperate need of new challenges, be they musical or personal, and now the surviving three needed a fresh start even more. Beyond the occasional call just to check in and say hi, Grant said, he barely spoke to Plant for another year.

Nor did Plant call him. Instead, he lost himself in a life stationed somewhere between a gentleman farmer and a wealthy recluse. Both of which he was. His assistant Benji LeFevre, a permanent resident of the farm, was put to work around the place—everything from clearing up outbuildings to handling the mail—and when LeFevre got it into his head to start building a four-track studio in the music room/barn, Plant just let him get on with it.

Later, with Plant back in action, it became common belief that the outfitting of this modest little studio was the biggest of the tiny steps that pulled the singer out of his funk, and so it probably was. At the time, however, LeFevre was doing it as much for his own amusement as any hope of repotting Plant.

A couple of years before, during the terrible months following Karac's death, the pair of them had taken a local band, Dansette Damage, under their wing, producing a single for them at the Old Smithy Studios in Worcester. In keeping with the punk-drunk spirit of the times, Dansette Damage were very much rooted in the Mach 10 province of the one-chord wonders, in an age when punk rock itself was seen as both the antidote to the rocking dinosaurs of the past and the waste-disposal unit that would suck them into oblivion. The session was fast and furious: two songs—"The Only Sound" and "New Musical Express"—cut for release on the equally local Shoestring label.

Posting a video of "New Musical Express" on YouTube, keyboard player Eddie Blower recalled, "We made this record in early 1978 and were lucky enough to get Robert . . . and Benji . . . to twiddle the knobs in the studio for us. Robert put all needles in the red, which is why it sounds so raw! Also, we couldn't sing and you can hear Robert's high falsetto at the top end, trying to keep us lot in tune!"

It was all low budget, low expectation, low profile—Plant did not even demand a credit on the record, insisting instead that his contributions be assigned to the mysterious Wolverhampton Wanderer. As he worked on the new studio, LeFevre could only wonder if the Wanderer might one day venture out again.

Friends dropped around—old friends, from long before Plant became a star, some from a time before he even started to perform. Robbie Blunt had been an aspiring guitarist at the same time as Plant was an aspiring singer, and although they had never really placed those aspirations together on the same stage, they frequented one another's homes, disappearing to the bedroom to listen to records and talk. Since that time, Blunt had carved his own career in music, alongside other local lads made good— Jess Roden and past-and-future-Robert-Plant-bandmate Kevyn Gammond in Bronco, and Stan Webb in Chicken Shack—and had even had a stab at glam-rock superstardom as one-fifth of showman supreme Michael Des Barres's Silverhead.

But now he was back to being plain old Robbie, an anchor from the early days, as Plant decided that that was what he needed most. He'd been a superstar, he'd toured the world, he'd made his million dollars and then some. But the things he'd lost were far more precious, and these were not only his son and his best friend. He'd lost sight of the reason he was in the music industry in the first place. The simple joy of making music.

Andy Sylvester went way back too, a friend from the Seven Stars blues club in Stourbridge, where the band he'd formed with Chris Wood and Stan Webb, Sounds of Blue, was one of the attractions that drew Plant through the door in the first place. A few years later, Sylvester and Webb formed Chicken Shack, and Wood was a co-founder of Traffic—sterling indications of the sheer tumult and fervor with which the towns and cities that surrounded Jennings Farm embraced rock, the blues, and folk, and of the careless, wild enthusiasm that Plant now found himself reaching back toward. A time when he was unknown, a time when he was happy. A time when his friends and family didn't die.

Other players dropped by, local guys, nobody anyone outside of the area would have heard of. A sax player named Keith Evans, a harmonica player called Ricky Cool, drummer Kevin O'Neil, bassist Jim Hickman. And together, they just played. Their diet was oldies, precisely the same kinds of songs they'd all grown up with. Pop numbers, blues belters, R&B shakers. "Got My Mojo Working," "Born Under a Bad Sign," "Just Can't Be Satisfied"—songs that were the staple diet of every British blues band of their youth, from Alexis Korner to John Mayall, from the Rolling Stones to Cream.

At first, they were content simply to play in the barn to an audience of whoever else might have dropped by. But just as the young Plant had quickly grown out of singing along with his record player with a hairbrush for a microphone, so the band started looking across at one another and wondering whether they were ready for the big time. The local pub. A nearby university. An occasional club.

Plant gave the band a name. The Honeydripper was boogie-woogie blues pianist Roosevelt Sykes's nickname and the title of one his albums, purchased by the teenaged Plant from the Diskery record shop on Hurst Street, Birmingham. It had a great cover, too, white with a partial checkerboard of photographs; King Curtis on sax and Robert Banks on organ; and a love song to Sputnik, "Satellite Baby." *The Honeydripper* was one of the records that had set Robert Plant on his way. The Honeydrippers would be the band that put him back on course.

Plant took his lead from Paul McCartney. A decade earlier, on the run from the Beatles, Fab Macca had bought a van, gathered a band, and then piled in with his wife and kids and set off up the motorway, stopping off at every college they passed to ask if they could play. Wings took flight from those first guerrilla workouts, and Plant intended to follow a similar path.

Of course the nature of the industry had changed somewhat since then, so he did need to involve a few outsiders. Promoter Roy Williams was one, instructed to book the Honeydrippers a handful of local shows, with just two unbreachable conditions. First, that they should stay as far from London as possible (Plant pinpointed Watford as the furthest south he would countenance playing), and second, that Plant's own name be kept firmly out of the public eye. Anybody going along to see the Honeydrippers should expect nothing more than they conjured from that name, an unknown R&B band adrift amid a sea of such things. Bands like Dr. Feelgood, Nine Below Zero, the Inmates, the Dirty Strangers, and S.A.L.T. had done much in recent years to revitalize the old R&B circuit, playing hard and nasty with old and new material alike, and when Williams was asked by bookers what to expect from this latest name, that's the direction he pointed them in. And he was telling the truth.

On March 3, 1981, the Honeydrippers made their official live debut at Keele University, a few miles from the midlands city of Newcastle-Under-Lyme, and nobody could have failed to be impressed. Down and dirty, gritty and grimy, the Honeydrippers dripped with conviction and authenticity.

They put on a great show, sets extending to eighteen songs long, marching through a virtual crash course in primal blues, rock, and R&B. Elvis, Gene Vincent, Muddy Waters, Albert King, Otis Rush, Buddy Holly, Carl Perkins . . . classic stuff! Maybe their singer did go a little over the top, raising his voice toward the occasional scream, especially when they hit into Sonny Boy's "Bring It On Home." But a lot of singers sounded like Robert Plant in those days, and this guy even looked a bit like him. Shorter hair, maybe. Less of a showoff, but a cock-of-the-walk all the same. But, you know? Catch him in the right light . . . watch him from the right angle . . . and slowly the whisper went around. *You do know who that is, don't you?*

With Roy Williams operating as the band's driver, further shows followed. Few went too far afield; Sheffield's Limit Club, Derby's Blue Note, and Bradford University were all close enough that the band could be back in their own beds that same evening, or at least home for the following morning. Once they journeyed as far as Kirklevington Country Club, in Yarm, near Middlesbrough, right up on England's northeasternmost shore. Other nights they were so close to home they could have used their own kitchens as dressing rooms. The Porterhouse in Retford, the Club Lafayette in Wolverhampton, and naturally, Birmingham—all of them venues that were most accustomed to hosting unknowns, or at least bands still awaiting their first minor hit; few of them the kind of place where even local journalists trod too often.

Precisely the environment the Honeydrippers were looking for.

Offstage and on, things were kept simple. Plant traveled in the Transit van with the rest of the band, their gear trailing behind them in a three tonner piloted by Benji LeFevre, the band's road crew and sound guy all in one. There was no private jet, no limousine, no vast entourage—nothing whatsoever to compare with any of the tours Plant had undertaken across the previous thirteen years. Except for one thing. Like Peter Grant before him, he still demanded 90 percent of the door money. He had always had a sharp eye for money.

The band didn't even book hotels ahead of time, preferring just to park themselves wherever they could find the room—or if they were close enough, driving back home once the show was over. Which is what they did on June 15, 1981, following what would prove to be the Honeydrippers' final show, at the Golden Lion in Birmingham. No end-of-tour party, no Bacchanalian bean-feast in an unsuspecting hotel room. Just home to the telly and bed.

The Honeydrippers' anonymity had long been blown by then, of course. The moment Plant appeared on stage at the Keele University show, those members of the audience who did recognize him gave a collective sigh of disbelief that was as loud as their applause for the gig. When they played Manchester Polytechnic on May 11, Plant even walked past the queue of people waiting to get in, resplendent in Hawaiian shirt and newly shorn locks, unrecognized by almost all who saw him until he hit the stage, still clad in that same garish shirt.

But everyone who was there would have told a friend what they'd witnessed; those friends would tell others; and soon, even the most secretly staged show was cluttered by the growing coterie of in-the-know onlookers, hoping against hope that tonight would be the night when Plant might play

"Stairway to Heaven," "Whole Lotta Love." Something they recognized, anything they knew, anything from his back catalog at all. Sometimes they even shouted out requests, but Plant ignored every call, cry, or demand. And afterwards, when those same fans filed up with Led Zeppelin covers for him to autograph, he'd turn them away as well. Occasionally, though, he would catch a glimpse of an old photograph of the band or a magazine cover being thrust forward by a fan, and he would have a moment's pause.

"Who *is* that guy?"

On August 20, 1981, Robert Plant would be turning thirty-three. For just a few weeks that spring, however, he felt as though he'd shed fifteen years, to a time when he was just another unknown singer in another unknown band. And further back than that, to a time before he even had band.

But he was singing, even then.

2

Early in the Morning
(1948–1961)

obert Anthony Plant was born on August 20, 1948, in the town of West Bromwich, in the midst of the English Midlands—so named because they sit more or less in the middle of the country.

It is a lie, perpetrated by the ease with which a few dropped aitches can transform the plummiest tones into working-class roughage, to claim that British rock 'n' roll was the sound of the streets. Well, it was, but they tended to be nice streets. Where nice people lived. The kind of people who would look upon rock music with a sneer of disgust and then scrape it off the sole of their shoe. Which might explain why their children loved the music so much. Because it annoyed their parents.

Or it might not. Either way, with so few exceptions that the real things really needed to work at it, the vast majority of rock 'n' rollers who arose out of the British 1960s and beyond came from comfortably middle-class or better environments. Who else could afford all the gear, for a start? They may not have been born with the proverbial silver spoons in their mouths. But they weren't queuing up for the workhouse either.

Robert Plant was no exception. His mother, Annie Celia Cain, claimed a Romany bloodline. But father Robert left nobody in doubt of either his background or his aspirations. A talented violinist and a member of the local cycling club, he was a civil engineer who had served in the Royal Air Force during the recent World War II. Peace broke out just three years before Robert A. was born, and much of the elder Plant's time now was spent on projects aimed at repairing the damage that his counterparts in the German air force, the Luftwaffe, had wrought upon his hometown and its surroundings.

West Bromwich lies in the heart of England's Black Country, an area so-called for the preponderance of industry that made its home in the environs. The *black* in Black Country refers to the smoke that hangs like a permanent pall over everything, the soot that adheres to every surface, the industrial dirt that is worn like a second skin. The city of Birmingham, just five miles down the road, was very much the center of the entire country's industrial output, but its manifold operations were largely fed by the vast coal deposits that had been discovered beneath West Bromwich during the nineteenth century.

Everything from staples and nails to guns and aircraft had their origins in the grim and grimy brick factories of the Black Country, and as early as June 25, 1940, more than three months before the London Blitz began, Birmingham heard its first air-raid siren. It would be almost exactly four years before the last, by which time Birmingham had been bombed seventy-seven times, including one ten-day period in November 1940 when almost eight hundred people were killed and over twenty-three hundred injured.

The bombs did more than devastate the region. They also undid much of the work that the local authorities had been engaged upon in the years since the end of the last war, in 1918. Like its neighbors, West Bromwich had grown quickly during the Industrial Revolution two centuries before—so quickly that much of the accommodation built to handle the earliest influx of settlers had been thrown up as hastily as possible, and then maintained with nothing more than quick fixes for major problems.

By the early 1920s, great swathes of West Bromwich had been condemned as unfit for human habitation, leading to a major boom in replacement-house building—much of which was then flattened during World War II. Robert Plant Sr. was one of the many men employed in rebuilding the shattered town and country as swiftly as possible—and his son was one of the many children for whom the bomb sites that lay all around were the earliest playground they knew.

The Plants were fortunate. Their own house, built before the bombs rained down, survived the war intact, and it would remain their home until 1957, when little Robert was nine. By which time, three lifelong passions had already infiltrated his soul: music, engendered not only by his violin-playing father but also by a grandfather (also named Robert) and great-grandfather who themselves were accomplished musicians; football (soccer), inculcated into him by his father, a staunch supporter of the Wolverhampton Wanderers side (the Wolves, as they were popularly known); and storytelling, in the shape of the myths and legends with which the Black Country abounds.

Holy rocks and ancient stones, haunted mines and phantom beasts — all stalk the region, and the young Robert voraciously devoured their stories. The Night of the Dead, when the townspeople of Bilston kept a vigil in the churchyard; the derring-do of Aynuch and Ayli, rebel colliers who rose up against the dire working conditions of the early nineteenth century and who were said to be responsible for every misfortune that struck the pit and factory owners; the sacred well in Endon; the Wych Elm in Hagley Woods, scene of one of Britain's most baffling ritual murders; the fairies who still called the Clent Hills their home.

Mother Celia (few people called her Annie) fed further fuel to this juvenile fire. As a Romany, a gypsy, her own upbringing was itself alive with ancient traditions and beliefs that seemed all the more precious for their links with a past that had long since been swept away by modernity and industry, but lived on regardless, in the very landscape that surrounded her.

At night, standing gazing into the darkened sky, the factories and workshops belching their smoke and flames into the atmosphere, it was as if the entire world was afire — afire, or poised teetering on the very precipice of hell. By day, the air simply hung thick and heavy, alive with the myriad particles and pollutants thrown out by manufactories that had never even dreamed of "clean air acts." The darkness, however, was the preserve of the flames, by whose bloody red glow it was possible to imagine all manner of demons and devils cavorting through the night.

Football, too, seemed the preserve of the superhuman, if not the supernatural. When his father took young Robert to his first-ever game, at

Wolves' stately Molineux stadium in 1952, it was to witness a team that was on the brink of establishing itself as the predominant power in the English game. Captained by Billy Wright, a player whose gifts are still spoken of in hushed tones today; managed by Stan Cullis, a former Wolves player and a master tactician; and with names like Bert Williams, Ron Flowers, Roy Swinbourne and Johnny Hancocks already established as household names around the country, the Wanderers had already given notice of their intention by finishing second in the First Division in 1950.

That first game has remained with Plant ever since. In 2010 he recalled for the *Express & Star*, "Billy Wright waved at me. Honest he did! And that was it. I was hooked from that moment." As he told *FourFourTwo* in 2002, "I met him later. Nice bloke, liked a G&T, told me his daughter was making a record. But I couldn't get over the fact that here I was talking to Billy Wright."

Soon, Wolves were pushing even harder for the game's premier English honors, and the season after Robert's first game—by which time he was firmly established as a regular on the terraces, where upwards of forty-five thousand people gathered every game—they took the first of the three League Championships they would collect that decade.

Wolves were not the only top team in the area. West Bromwich had the Albion; Birmingham had its City, and Aston Villa too. But Wolves were the biggest and the best, and with the press declaring them to be the best team on the planet after a string of victories against the cream of European soccer, the 1950s were a great time to be a Wolves supporter. The Plants relished every fresh success, particularly those that delivered more silverware to the Molineux trophy room, and every Saturday evening, Robert would pore over the pages of the local "pink 'un," the weekly newspaper dedicated to bringing the day's results into every home, committing the results and the scorers to memory and still able to recollect them years, even decades, later. The 8–1 demolition of Chelsea in September, 1953, and the 5–0 defeat of Charlton in April the following year. The team parading the Championship trophy through the town at the end of the month. The 103 goals they scored four seasons later, as they brought the trophy back to the

Black Country, and the night they played the German side Schalke in their first-ever European Cup match.

Home or away, the Wolves devoured their foes with net-bursting ruthlessness. Six goals against Bolton one week, five against Sunderland the next. Four against Tottenham, five against Birmingham, and then another five a few weeks later, just to rub their local rivals' noses in it. Nobody was safe against the marauding Wolves, and their invincibility was contagious. Ten years old now, and taking Wolves' success for granted, Plant learned courage and confidence from the best masters imaginable. The eleven men (and in those days, there was just eleven; no substitutes or squad rotation to rest tired legs) whose own courage and confidence was on display every weekend.

It didn't last, at least for Wolves. A new decade brought change to both the dressing room and management, and through the 1960s, Wolves' once unchallenged omnipotence first faltered, then failed. In 1965, they succumbed to relegation to the second division, and although they bounced back up in 1968, things could never be the same.

Nevertheless, by the time Plant reached adolescence, the black and gold colors of Wolves were firmly, and irrevocably, in his blood. He couldn't have stopped supporting them, no matter how low they sank, and when the 1970s saw him jetting off to all four corners of the world, instead of filing his way through the crowds to watch Wolves, he even arranged to have British newspapers flown out to wherever he might be so he could keep up with their results. Finally, in August 2009, Plant's devotion to the side was rewarded by his being elected one of the club's vice presidents.

In 1957, the Plant family, soon to be swollen by the arrival of Robert's sister Allison, finally escaped the choking environs of West Bromwich for Hayley Green, one of the up-and-coming suburban communities to which white-collar England was then being enticed. A modern development on the southern reaches of the ancient town of Lutley, on the road to Kidderminster and Stourbridge, the town was surrounded by farmland, and the new family home, 64 Causey Farm Road, had its own magical view.

"When I was little, I dreamed heroic dreams," Plant reflected later. "Most of the time I was the hero . . . the odds were always pretty much against me. Sort of like . . . Robin Hood."

Sherwood Forest, Robin Hood's famous haunt, was too far away. But Uffmoor Wood was a mere walk away, an ancient woodland that houses not only the source of the river Stour but also one of England's oldest Christian legends, that of the spring that gushed miraculously forth when Kenelm, the boy king of the Anglo-Saxon tribal kingdom of the Hwicce, was beheaded by his sister in 821 AD. The waters swiftly became known for their curative powers, a church was erected to the newly canonized Saint Kenelm, and the wood became a focal point of medieval pilgrimage.

This was also Tolkien country. The author of *Lord of the Rings* and so forth had grown up in these parts, and students of the fantasy writings that would establish his genius would recognize so many local landscapes and features when they stepped out onto Clent Hills. Looking out from his bedroom window, the young Robert could pause in his own voracious consumption of Tolkien's books, and it was as if he could actually *see* the places he was reading about. And maybe he could.

The story cycle, when Plant discovered it, was still some years away from the cultural all-encompassment with which it met the late 1960s and early 1970s; indeed, the publishing world was still chuckling at the possibly (but hopefully not) apocryphal tale of the day Tolkien read passages from the then-work-in-progress to his fellow members of the Inkling Club, a society of fantasy authors who regularly met at the Eagle and Child pub in Oxford. Tolkien had barely begun to read when C. S. Lewis loudly declaimed, "Dear God, not another fucking story about elves." Neither he nor even Tolkien could ever have imagined a day when *The Lord of the Rings* might inspire rock and pop lyrics—and neither, though he would be writing some of the best of them, could Robert Plant.

Plant hiked to the summit of the hill to visit the Four Stones, a seventeenth-century folly designed to replicate the ancient standing stones of elsewhere, and positioned so that each stone stood in a different county. Warwickshire, Worcestershire, Stafford, and Shropshire all met in this spot, and the stones marked each one. Yet the stones were not without their mystery, for local legend still insists that come Midsummer Eve, the four will uproot themselves and make their ways to nearby Walton Pool to drink. But no man has ever been foolish enough to wait and watch, for to see the stones walk is to invite a ghastly death before another year has passed.

An Iron Age fort stands on Wychbury Hill, surrounded by rings and ditches and the folk memory of a battle fought here between invading Romans and woad-clad Britons. Harry-Ca-Nab, the Devil's own huntsman, leads a wild hunt across the hills, astride a ghostly white bull.

Plant read of, and watched for (almost) each of these mystic sites, but other haunts captured the boy's imagination, too. The Welsh borders were not so far from home, with their own panoply of history and heritage, centuries of conflict between the warring tribes that left both physical and psychic scars on the landscape. The Britons, pushed into what is now Wales, first by the Romans and then by the Angles and Saxons, fought ferociously to protect their lands, and the history of the era is littered with the names of the battles fought—even though many of the actual battlefields have long been forgotten.

It was these histories, in years to come, that Plant would draw from as he composed "The Battle of Evermore," a highlight of the fourth Led Zeppelin album and still one of the most impressive lyrics he has ever written, despite Plant himself admitting that perhaps "it suffered from naïveté and tweeness." There was no historical battle of this name; rather, Plant drew his imagery from Tolkien and his account of the Battle of Pelennor ("The drums will shake the castle wall/The ring wraiths ride in black"); from the Arthurian legends, and their encapsulation of pre-Christian belief and practice; and from another period of British history, the Anglo-Scottish wars of the fifteenth and sixteenth centuries. A mishmash, then, but—as *lullaby*'s "Up on the Hollow Hill" reminded us in 2014—an insight into youthful fascinations that still impinge upon his lyricism today.

Further inspiration was drawn from the family's regular summer holidays in Snowdonia, the craggy, mountainous corner of Wales from which any number of legends come tumbling. At home, Plant would bury his nose in collections of Welsh mythology; on holiday, he was forever in search of those places from whence the myths emerged in the first place.

Frequently, the family would holiday in Machynlleth, the medieval town poised in the shadows of the mountain Cadair Idris, named for a giant who used to lie on its slopes and gaze up at the stars. The town itself has a long and proud history; the self-proclaimed "ancient capital of Wales," it was here that the Welsh leader Glyndŵr established his Parliament in 1404, at the height of his rebellion against the English King Henry IV—here, too, that he was crowned Prince of Wales, in the presence of dignitaries from Scotland, France, and Spain. His rebellion was eventually crushed, and the Prince went into hiding; local legend abounds with tales of his escape and even his immortality. No matter how great the rewards that were offered for his capture or the hardships imposed on the people by his vengeful enemies, Owain Glyndŵr was never betrayed, never captured. The history books say he died around 1415, but mythology places him alongside King Arthur as a deathless figure and the personification of Welsh nationalism.

He became a hero, too, to Robert Plant, and in 2004, now a permanent resident of Machynlleth, the singer contributed generously toward the erection of a £5,500 bronze statue of Owain Glyndŵr in the churchyard of St. Peter ad Vincula (St. Peter in Chains) in nearby Pennal, the village where Glyndŵr raised his final parliament. (Plant would also work with singer Julie Murphy, of the Welsh traditional band Fernhill, after hearing her perform the ballad "Marwnad Yr Ehedydd" [The Lark's Elegy], a recounting of Glyndŵr's final battle.) Likewise, Plant has raised funds for other historical projects and commemorations in the area, including a slate carving of Glyndŵr's coat of arms at the Celtica museum in Machynlleth.

A fascination born in childhood remains a consuming passion today, and no matter what other interests would take root in the growing boy's mind—and as the 1950s progressed and he approached his teens, there were plenty—his love of Welsh mythology would never be shaken. In 1972, he would even name his first son after two of the great legends of the land: Karac Pendragon was so-called for the warrior king Caradoc (more familiarly Anglicized as Caractacus), who led the Celtic tribes against the invading Romans around 50 AD, and for the father of King Arthur, Uther Pendragon.

The quiet study of legend, myth, and history was not, however, the young Plant's sole outlet. Indeed, by the time his family moved to the neatly ordered suburbia of Hayley Green, with its red brick homes and manicured backyards, another obsession had taken hold—one that might initially appear wholly opposed to the dreams of his reading, but which, in the young boy's heart, seemed inextricably linked regardless.

Rock 'n' roll hit Britain in 1955, in the forms of Bill Haley, Elvis Presley, Little Richard and so forth—howling, yowling, absurdly costumed imps sent to shatter the calm reserve and gentle politeness of what had hitherto passed as the local music scene.

Their impact was necessarily profound. Britain, ten years out of the Second World War but just a few beyond the strictures of wartime rationing and privation, was still a country desperate to relocate its place in the world. Victory in the war had come at a hefty price: a shattered economy needed rebuilding, a battered people needed rewarding, and of course, both things cost money. Money the country did not have.

Successive political and military shocks knocked the national morale back further, culminating in the embarrassment of the Suez campaign, when British attempts to prevent Egypt's takeover of the Suez Canal ended in ignominious defeat. For the generation of kids brought up in the aftermath of the Second World War, raised on tales of their parents' wartime exploits and heroism, there was a growing sense of disbelief and betrayal. So what if you won the war? You didn't win the peace.

Rock 'n' roll was not a solution to that. But it was a distraction. For the first time, a cultural force had emerged that was not beholden for its thrills on pomp and circumstance, hope and glory, flags and monarchy. Instead, like a horde of invading barbarians, it swept in from over the ocean, from the American land of plenty, to demolish all that the old guard held holy.

The BBC, sole repository of Britain's cultural education, reeled in horror. Rock 'n' roll was never banned outright by the country's only broadcaster, but it wasn't given much airtime either. Listeners tuning in to the Light Programme, as the BBC's "pop" arm was called, were more likely to hear refined orchestral renderings of popular parental favorites than anything as subversive as rock 'n' roll, and when a new song did make it onto the airwaves, likely as not it was a pallid cover version, recorded by a middle-aged English singing star or again rendered Muzak by light-orchestral sessionmen.

Still, parents shivered, revolted; newspaper editorials shrieked in dire warning. A lot of the people who most loudly opposed rock 'n' roll, therefore, had never actually heard it. But they read about it in the tabloid newspapers, quaked at the imagery that the songs seemed to advocate, and swore that they would fight it till their last dying breath. Rock 'n' roll was degenerate, disgusting, debilitating. It sapped moral fiber and it crushed obedience. Prolonged exposure to the music not only aroused criminal tendencies, it encouraged them.

And the more the oldies complained, the tighter the music grasped the hearts and minds of the country's youth. The more the media insisted that rock 'n' roll was just a passing phase, the more it began to look like a permanent revolution. Because it was more than a mere musical happenstance. Rock 'n' roll was the voice of the people—young people, anyway—raising itself above the tumultuous hubbub of everyday mundanities in precisely the same manner as folklore and mythology cling on in the heart, even as the head becomes absorbed by the preoccupations of the modern world.

Mythologies are the beliefs that politics and religion try to suppress; folklore is the story of the people, not their leaders. Rock 'n' roll filled that same space and served that same purpose. Beyond the guitars and the clothes and the haircuts and the often-meaningless lyrics, it was an insurgence of independent thought and action, shrugging off the strictures and structures that "society" erected around its youth, and demanding freedom on its own terms.

Not, of course, that many of its adherents actually thought of it in those terms. Nine or ten years old when he discovered Elvis Presley, Robert Plant simply enjoyed the sound, was enslaved by the excitement. "When I was a kid I used to hide behind the curtains at home at Christmas and I used to try and be Elvis," he once said. But Elvis was quickly followed, for Plant and for every other kid of his generation, by Buddy Holly, Eddie Cochran,

Gene Vincent—wave upon wave of American invaders hurling themselves through Britain's increasingly fragile cultural defenses to sweep up the hearts and minds of youth. And slowly, the authorities came to recognize that not all of it was as bad as it was painted.

In 1958, a visiting Buddy Holly—a bespectacled singer-songwriter who really could sing, really could write songs—became a star turn on television's weekly ritual of *Sunday Night at the London Palladium*. By the following year, both BBC radio and television were devoting precious weekly air time to shows aimed directly at teenagers. The British music industry, caught completely off guard by the American explosion, had even commenced the hunt for its own rock 'n' rollers, and 1958 also saw the emergence of Cliff Richard, Britain's first truly credible rock idol—and almost sixty years on, still going strong today.

Neither was rock 'n' roll the only game in town. Dig deep enough into teenaged culture, and all manner of musical currents were beginning to swirl. Trad jazz was making a comeback, a blues boom was taking its first uncertain steps, and the skiffle movement—homemade instruments pounding American blues and folk songs—was in full swing, and this time, it was readily available via radio and television.

It is true. The majority of the kids who listened and sung along with Lonnie Donegan, Wally Whyton, and Chas McDevitt as they told of the "Rock Island Line," "Cumberland Gap," and the murderous occupant of the fast rolling "Freight Train" had no idea whatsoever of the musical lineage that lay behind such hit records as these. Few of them, even in London, were making a beeline for Collett's record shop on the Charing Cross Road, seeking out the original renderings of the skifflers' smashes. But their elders were beginning to, and so, with that evangelical fire that lay at the heart and soul of rock 'n' roll's early years, an entire generation slowly found itself being educated into the history of the blues, folk, and R&B. And a couple of years later, the resultant hybrid would come sweeping out of the underground, as fiercely and unstoppably as the original rock 'n' roll in the first place.

≈

In September 1959, just three weeks after his eleventh birthday, Plant took up his place at King Edward VI Grammar School for Boys, on the Lower High Street in Stourbridge—an indication of just how comfortably well-off the Plant family now was.

Perhaps King Edward VI lacks the cultural gravitas of some of England's other "great" seats of learning: Eton, Charterhouse, and so forth. But in terms of its own sense of self, and its confidence in its place within the fabric of upper-class British culture, it compares with any of them.

KEGS, as it was known, could trace its origins back over five hundred years, to the foundation of the Chantry School of Holy Trinity in 1430. A century later, in 1552, the reigning King Edward VI granted it a charter as a grammar school, and since that time, KEGS had been firmly in the business of turning out smart, prepared, and most of all, responsible young men.

Doctor Samuel Johnson—creator of the English language's first-ever dictionary, among so many other literary achievements—was a schoolboy there in the early 1700s, and according to legend, the autograph that he carved into one of the classroom desks was still there to be found. Robert Plant, on the other hand, carved Dion DiMucci's name into the headboard of his bed. Different times. . . .

More recently, KEGS had been responsible for supplying the British Empire with Squadron Leader Mike Cooper-Slipper DFC, one of the Battle of Britain's most distinguished pilots; the justice Sir Michael Davies; politicians Sir Ian Kennedy and Terry Davis; scientist Basil Lythall CB; mathematician Professor David Trotman; aeronautical engineer Dr. Richard Stanton Jones; and many more. A roster within which an aspiring rock 'n' roll singer stands out like the proverbial sore thumb.

The very fabric of the place breathed history and tradition, centuries that permeated the ancient buildings with their fine stained-glass windows, the schoolrooms that would have still been recognizable to students of one hundred years before (Johnson's desk was not the only survivor from antiquity), the standards of discipline and cleanliness that were ingrained into the pupils from the moment they first donned their regulation uniform of gray shorts, green blazers, green caps, and red and green ties.

The school had its mysteries and its secrets, too, including the network of seventeenth-century English Civil War–era tunnels that spread out from beneath the school to become a labyrinth of passageways and hidey-holes honeycombing the streets beneath the town. Although they were out of bounds to the pupils, and indeed to the general public, a few lads knew of their existence nevertheless, and knew how to infiltrate them as well. Particularly the one, or so a whispered rumor insisted, that led in the direction of the girls' school on the other side of the town.

Indeed, amidst all this finery and class, there was just one major drawback. Immediately behind the school, some careless past planner had permitted the erection of an abattoir and a tanners' yard. When the wind was in the right direction—which, for the boys and staff, meant the *wrong* direction—the entire KEGS campus was choked in the thick stench of sliced meat, old blood, and fresh death. There was no use complaining about it, though. More than one past master simply shrugged that the cloying odor was character forming—probably as he held a scented handkerchief to his own olfactory organ.

KEGS demanded discipline, and meted it out, too. Saturday-morning attendance was compulsory through Plant's first year at the school. Latin was on the curriculum, and sports were mandatory too: cricket in the summer, rugby in the winter, both played on Saturday afternoons. Plant's beloved soccer was prohibited from the grounds, and soccer balls were outlawed altogether. Maybe the masters would tolerate the occasional scratch match at break time, blazers for goalposts, and a tennis ball for kicking as an outlet for any stray high spirits, but even conversations about the game were perforcedly conducted in whispered tones.

Girls, too, were verboten; hence the allure of the tunnels. A boys-only school, KEGS's gown-and-mortar-clad masters kept a ferocious eye out for any indication whatsoever that their charges were mixing with the female of the species, with detention the least of the punishments in store for any lad caught breaking the rule.

Rob Plant, as he styled himself in those days, passed with comparative anonymity through those revered halls of learning, at least for his first few years. He was seldom one of the boys held back after school. Neither did he often come to the attentions of the headmaster, the fiercely accoutered Richard Chambers, all horn-rimmed glasses and viciously hooked nose, a man who was perfectly aware that his charges mocked his inability to pronounce the letter R, but was content to allow them that little victory in the knowledge that it kept them from greater mischief.

As did the cane that he was wont to introduce to the most incautious behinds. In those glorious days before political correctness (and maybe a touch of humanitarian mercy) decreed that corporal punishment had no place in the halls of education, a summons to Old Beaky's office, every former pupil remembers, was divided into three very separate acts.

First, there was the punishment for the crime, in the form of an early-morning lecture, followed by four sharp swishes of the beating instrument. Then there were the hours spent contemplating both the pain and the foolishness of the original transaction. And then there was a second visit to the office, where another whacking would be administered, to make sure that the lesson had sunk in all the way.

Small wonder, then, that Plant kept his head down. His love of history, a keen eye for English, and the general politeness inculcated into him by his parents kept him firmly within that middle rank of boys who were neither so gifted nor so delinquent that they were constantly coming to the attention of the authorities. He threw himself into rugby and relaxed with his stamp collection, and the only thing that really marked him out was the gentle quiff haircut that he styled after Eddie Cochran, but managed to train to remain just the right side of the school dress code. That and his penchant for turning up his shirt collar in emulation of old Elvis photos, a look that gave him enough of a swagger to draw all eyes in his direction, but again, not enough to merit more than a disapproving glare. By his second year as a KEGS student, he had even been raised to the giddy heights of class monitor, charged with cleaning the blackboard, refilling the ink wells, and generally serving as the tutor's eyes and ears when he had need of an extra pair.

It was a position that a boy could use to either his own advantage or that of his classmates. A monitor who fulfills all the requirements of the job, and ensures that the masters are kept fully apprised of all that takes place behind their backs, might be rewarded with the approval of the faculty, but will swiftly find his classmates turning against him. Whereas one whose own behavior could occasionally be as reproachable as that he was meant to be informing on — well, he would become something of a hero to his peers, and that is the direction in which Plant chose to move. Even after his mother finally tired of the quiff and demanded its removal.

His closest friends, hardy surprisingly, were those who shared his love of music, who would have the radio on from the moment they woke up to the moment they left for school and then turn it on once again when they got home, no matter how daunting the daily routine of three hours' homework might be. With Paul Baggott, John Dudley, and Gary Tolley, Plant could while away hours talking either about old favorites or new discoveries, and once they discovered that the BBC was not the only broadcaster in the world, every night would be devoted to listening to Radio Luxembourg, the all-pop station that beamed across the English Channel on waves of static, hiss, and interference, for the enterprising ear to then decode into the latest releases by a host of heroes.

Years later, in a 2010 interview with Showbizspy.com, Plant would declare, "I was looking for a way out [of] grammar school. . . . You had Elvis telling us of another world. I don't know how much more expressive you can get than being a rock and roll singer." In reality, however, he was scarcely any different from any other thirteen- or fourteen-year-old kid whose love of music exceeded his love of learning; who schemed imaginary bands in class with his friends, assigning the instruments they intended to play — regardless of whether or not they could actually play them — and fashioning set lists of the songs they most wanted to perform.

Besides, music didn't take up all of their time. Twice-monthly visits to Molineux remained a consuming passion, even as Wolves commenced their downhill spiral. Inheriting his father's love of cycling, Plant stripped down his racing bike and took off on marathon treks around the local countryside or hurtling around the local velodrome, his mind's eye mapping out a career as a professional racing cyclist. 1960 was the year that the Italian cycling teams swept the golds at the Rome Olympics, and the names of Livio Trape and Sante Gaiardoni were on every tongue. Their example gave cycling an enormous boost that year, and with his father's involvement in the local cycling club to further his ambitions, the adolescent Plant found another possible future beckoning to him.

His world continued to expand. He began making regular journeys into Birmingham, just to look around the shops, hang around the streets—all the things that kids enjoyed doing in those days when, as the old cliché puts it, you had to make your own entertainment. Stamp collecting was a major hobby in those days, and Birmingham boasted several stores where he could browse through albums of unaffordable treasures and pick up cheaper specimens for his collections. There were book shops, too, where he could at least look at the volumes he wanted to read before ordering copies from his local library. And there were record shops, where he could commence delving into the American roots of the music that he found himself increasingly drawn to.

The early 1960s—1961, 1962—saw Britain moving into a period of avid fascination with the blues. It was the era in which performers like the Rolling Stones, John Mayall, and the Yardbirds took their first steps into something approaching daylight, although their existence would have been no more than rumor to a thirteen-year-old boy in Stourbridge. His education remained the radio, and whatever music the elder brothers of his school friends might be playing when he went round to visit. But slowly and surely, he found himself growing curious to learn more.

It wasn't all the blues. "Cathy's Clown" by the Everly Brothers was a juvenile favorite; Billy Fury, another of England's primal rockers, another. The youthful Bob Dylan, just an album old on the Columbia label. But one day a book dropped into Plant's lap, which he still cites as perhaps the most formative of all his early influences. *Blues Fell This Morning: Meaning in the Blues* was published in 1960, a study of American blues written by an Englishman, Paul Oliver, and concerned not with the lives of the bluesmen themselves but with the existence that they detailed in their songs.

It was a scholarly tome, as the literary stands of the day demanded. Beyond its capacity to be listened to and enjoyed, music in the 1950s and early 1960s was there to be analyzed as a cultural and societal force, and Oliver fulfilled that brief. But he wrote with a rare, contagious passion, and while it probably isn't true to say that everybody who read his book went on to form a blues band, the converse is very likely: everyone who formed a blues band had read his book. And having done so, set about putting sounds to the names that they gleaned from its pages.

For Plant, that entailed making regular pilgrimages to the Diskery, his favorite record store in Birmingham, just around the corner from main railway station. There, as was the case with a host of similarly minded record stores elsewhere around the country, the very act of opening the door immediately exposed the listener to a nonstop soundtrack of blues and R&B, while the racks were stuffed not with the standard fare of the other record shops in town—the latest releases by Cliff, Alma, Eden, and Adam—but with impossibly glamorous-looking American imports, stack upon stack that would devour a lifetime just to listen to.

Plant got a job delivering newspapers, up at the crack of dawn every morning and cycling around his sleeping town, dropping newspapers and comics through the letterboxes, just to feed his growing vinyl habit. When his birthday or Christmas saw him come into extra money, even his stamp collection was starved as he instead took his cash up to the Diskery. Then, back in his room, he would painstakingly catalog his latest purchases before sitting down to transcribe the lyrics of every song into a series of notebooks.

He did not fall in love with every record he heard, or even every one purchased. As in every other genre, there is good blues and there is bad blues; as with every other artist, there are good songs and there are bad ones. So he learned which performers to avoid, which labels to eschew, and as his appreciation of certain artists increased, he slipped free of the early dilettantism from which all young listeners forge their musical taste and began racking up his favorites.

Sonny Boy Williamson was one, but it was Robert Johnson, perhaps the epitome of the live fast, die young ethos that rock 'n' roll itself would subsequently hijack, who swiftly moved to the top of the pile. "When I first heard 'Preaching Blues' and 'Last Fair Deal Gone Down,' I went 'this is it!'" Plant told the *Guardian* newspaper.

There's a moment in Mick Jagger's movie debut, *Performance*, that probably says all you need to know about Robert Johnson. It's short, just a couple of minutes long, and it's essentially a throwaway when compared to some of the other scenes in the movie. It didn't even make the soundtrack album, and there's probably nobody who would rate it among Jagger's most memorable performances. But the whispered, fractured medley of "Come On in My Kitchen" and "Me and the Devil Blues" that the reclusive pop star Turner scratches out of his acoustic guitar is as dangerously dark as any mood in the movie, a sibilant, shivered hiss of malevolence that transports the listener away from even the half-life reality of *Performance* and out to the same desolate midnight crossroads where Johnson himself is said to have met with the devil. And then bartered away his soul, in return for the ability to play guitar and write songs.

Johnson was not the first person to make that deal, not even in the annals of the blues. Almost ten years earlier, in 1924, Clara Smith was singing "Done Sold My Soul to the Devil (And My Heart's Done Turned to Stone)," while a browse through the writings of folklorist Harry M. Hyatt, writing around the same time as Johnson was singing his songs, makes you wonder how the devil had the wherewithal to make any mischief anywhere else in the world, so much time did he spend hanging around the American South, signing contracts with itinerant blacks. He certainly lived up to his side of the bargain with Robert Johnson, though. Over the next two years, the last of his life, Johnson recorded a total of twenty-nine songs for release across a dozen 78s—and every one of them destined to become a blues archetype.

Plant first encountered Johnson on a various-artists compilation album, one of the many that were being released on both sides of the Atlantic at that time. But he quickly graduated to Johnson alone, the 1961 *King of the Delta Blues Singers* collection of sixteen songs that the Diskery imported from the United States.

All of Johnson's best-known compositions were there. "Preaching Blues" and "Last Fair Deal Gone Down," "Crossroads Blues" and "Me and the Devil Blues," "Hellhound on My Trail" and "Come On in My Kitchen." And "Traveling Riverside Blues," a song so raw, so primal, so down-and-dirty disgusting, that the first time Plant heard it, he could not believe his ears. And he prayed that his parents, downstairs in the living room, wouldn't believe theirs either. "Squeeze my lemon 'til the juice runs down my leg," sang Johnson. "Squeeze it so hard, I'll fall right out of bed . . ." and then, so lascivious, lewd, and crude, "I wonder if you know what I'm talkin' about?"

Plant's parents probably knew, but for now they kept their own counsel. They had already lived through their son's rock 'n' roll phase, confident that passing time and changing fashions would swiftly sweep him into more mature musical pastures. The blues, they assumed, would prove to be another such passing craze. Their own tastes were firmly in the classical realm, and they were of a generation that firmly believed everybody came around to the classics eventually. They started with pop, flirted with fads, and then one day Beethoven captured their hearts.

Still it is ironic that the night Robert Sr. finally cracked and declared the boy's tastes had gone too far off the rails, it wasn't Johnson's deals with the devil that did it, or his sinister welcome into his kitchen; it wasn't even him getting a hand job from a long-ago blues babe. It was the night Junior came home with a London records pressing of Chris Kenner's pounding knockabout boogie "I Like It Like That," and proceeded to play it seventeen times without even a break for the B-side.

Scissors in hand, the elder Robert Plant marched up the stairs, threw open the bedroom door, and snipped the plug off the Dansette record player. Then, without a word, he walked out again, leaving his son staring wide-eyed in shocked disbelief.

If he had been just a few years older, Plant told his friends at school the next day, he'd have packed his bags and left home that night. Instead, it simply strengthened his resolve to get out as soon as he could.

3

Other Arms
(1981)

Leaving home.

It is a recurring motif in Robert Plant's life: leaving home or, at least, leaving the past behind him, fractures that sometimes only become apparent with hindsight but that are resolute regardless.

By the time the Honeydrippers came off the road, the news that Led Zeppelin had irrevocably split was already six months old, a terse statement delivered on December 4, 1980, following the band's first-ever meeting as a Bonhamless trio at the Savoy Hotel in London. "We wish it to be known that the loss of our dear friend and the deep respect we have for his family, together with deep sense of undivided harmony felt by ourselves and our manager, have led us to decide that we could not continue as we were."

For the optimists among the band's following, this was open-ended enough to suggest that the surviving trio could carry on if they wanted to. Maybe not as Led Zeppelin (and certainly not as XYZ). But they could.

It quickly became apparent, however, that they wouldn't.

With the Honeydrippers now in abeyance, Plant and guitarist Robbie Blunt alone returned to the studio at Jennings Farm to work up what would become the singer's official return to action. His mojo, as they say, had risen again: the Honeydrippers tour had reawakened his love of playing music, and now he was rekindling his love of making it.

The radio was constantly playing, tuned to the BBC's Radio One and pumping out the records that would define 1981. The Specials' "Ghost Town," an eerie soundtrack to the urban riots that turned so many English cities, including nearby Birmingham, into virtual no-go areas for a few weeks that summer. The dying breath of the old punk hierarchy, as the Clash and the Jam turned to tunes far removed from the raw adrenaline of their earliest recordings. And a new sound, synthesizers bleeping and burbling their way out of what, during Plant's own apprenticeship in the rites of rock 'n' roll, had seemed nothing more than a dead-end novelty, the supplanting of musicians with electronics and machines.

Fueled by influences that the average over-thirty might never have heard of, encouraged by a sudden and dramatic crash in the cost of synthesizers and drum machines, the New Romantics were suddenly headline news. Bands that in many cases could scarcely even be called a band: one voice, one machine, and a seemingly endless succession of piping keyboard confections whose innate pop sensibilities were only amplified by their makers' penchant for ambitious haircuts and performance art. Orchestral Manoeuvres in the Dark. A Flock of Seagulls. Soft Cell.

Of course Plant had no intention of traveling down the same musical paths as them. With the best will in the world, he was scarcely going to butt heads with the new darlings of the teenybop world, even if he was once spotted checking out local boys Duran Duran when they played a Birmingham club one night. But he picked up a Roland drum machine, and with Blunt's guitar raw beside him, he began picking at the bones of some fresh song ideas.

It wasn't going to be easy. He and Plant knew one another inside out, an instinctive understanding that even the best intentioned newcomer could not hope to equal. Even when their songwriting process had been interrupted by drugs and sundry other distractions, and relations between Plant and Page became "a bit twitchy," as Plant described it to Q magazine in 1988, it remained a comfortable place. The pair understood each other. "To start again with anyone else was a very, very odd feeling."

But it was a feeling Plant welcomed, the sound of a door being closed behind him as he stepped into a new room. The sound of leaving home, which he amplified with the insistence that anything that even suggested Led Zeppelin should be thrown out of the window. Even his vocals were placed under the fiercest scrutiny. His voice, of course, was his voice, and there wasn't much he could do to change that. But there was still a handful of trademarks that were indelibly associated with the past—the power-yelp that reviewers liked to describe as a "banshee-like wail," for example. With all but the most essential exceptions, that sound was banished from the room.

Plant wanted to begin again. Newly shorn hair gave him a very different appearance from the Valhalla-bound warrior of recent renown, and his listening habits reinforced the break. He even told Q magazine's Tom Hibbert, "I . . . hadn't played or listened to a Zeppelin record for two years," and admitted that the prohibition would have lasted even longer if his daughter's boyfriend hadn't riled him up one day, insisting that there was an error in "Black Dog"—"a bar of 5/4 in the middle of some 4/4. . . . I pulled the record out and plonked it on. I said, 'Listen, you little runt, that's no mistake.'"

The pair worked on, with LeFevre sitting in to add his own thoughts and notions to the percolating brew, and Plant was ready to begin embellishing their skeletons by introducing a Moog Synthesizer to the brew. Or so he said. But he returned from his shopping trip with a keyboard player too.

Gerald "Jezz" Woodroffe was one more in that seemingly bottomless supply of Birmingham musicians to whom Plant always seemed to gravitate. The son of a 1940s-era jazz musician, back in 1975, he'd toured the world with Black Sabbath as onstage keyboard player on their *Sabotage* tour, and he was on hand for their *Technical Ecstasy* album too. Now he was invited out to Jennings Farm, to the home studio that Plant had recently named Palomino for daughter Carmen's horse that was stabled next door, and he swiftly found himself slipping into place.

Plant, he told Martin Popoff of *Brave Words & Bloody Knuckles* in 2004, was leading "a kind of spiritual quest," working to find a way out of the Zeppelinesque pastures that he knew critics and fans alike would be expecting, yet without abandoning the personal musical principles that had, of course, been so much a part of that band's output. In other words, he needed to continue sounding like Robert Plant, without falling back on the sound that Robert Plant was known for. And "the nucleus of all of that," Woodroffe explained, "was Robbie and me and Robert. And it was a very special time. We were very close and we were having the most fabulous fun."

Again, the specter of past Paul McCartney drifts unbidden into the room, working up his music in a barnyard studio while his wife and children, family and friends, float in and out. Plant worked in similar surroundings, watched by his son Logan Romero, getting on for three years old; his daughter Carmen Jane, now fifteen; and a new face, a neighbor, Jason Bonham, also fifteen and already a remarkable chip off the paternal block. Bonham had been playing drums since he was four, and at ten he was filmed for Zeppelin's movie, *The Song Remains the Same*, playing away on a scaled-down drum kit. Now he was replacing the Roland machine, rolling in after class each day on the back of a school friend's scooter.

Not that the drum machine sat idle. One of the earliest songs Plant wrote, and then completed with his "band," was a tribute to Jason's father that he was adamant would be as far from the drummer's public image as possible. Where Bonham played frenetic, a force of nature, an unstoppable, pile-driving leviathan, "Fat Lip" was guided by the ruthless syncopation of technology.

Other new songs, however, reached for the most organic origins, a rushing rumble that might have been spread across a mere eight numbers but nevertheless felt as though every step moved another mile from the waiting world's preconceptions. Because, Plant knew, even those folk whom he considered his closest allies in the music business, Peter Grant, Ahmet Ertegun, and Atlantic's London chief Phil Carson, weren't at all certain whether they approved of what he had to offer, even after they heard the finished album. He didn't simply have to convince the public. He had to convince his own people.

The demos had been taken as far as they could go. It was time to start recording in earnest, and Plant began gathering a fresh coterie of players around the nucleus of Blunt, Woodroffe, and himself. An old friend, Andy Sylvester, was in the picture for a short time, but by the time the party moved to Rockfield Studios, a live-in setup parked within the green of Monmouth in Wales, Cozy Powell had been recruited to the drum seat, while the bass was handed to Paul Martinez, a gloriously rugged-looking player whose career dated back to the mid-1960s and a stint with the Downliners Sect.

A couple of years with Elmer Gantry's Velvet Opera led Martinez to a flash of notoriety when Fleetwood Mac's management hired them to tour America under the name of Fleetwood Mac, after falling out with the real thing. Horrified headlines and legal action followed, and the group returned to the UK with a new name, Stretch, promptly scoring a massive hit with the song they dedicated to Mick Fleetwood, the caustic "Why Did You Do It."

Stretch broke up, and session work consumed much of Martinez's late 1970s, a period that included a stint through the very last days of a band whose first steps had been witnessed by Robert Plant himself.

Late in 1976, while Zeppelin were rehearsing at the Cabin, a studio space in West London's Fulham neighborhood, in preparation for their next American tour, Plant's attention was caught by the sound of a band playing in the smaller space downstairs. The Adverts, he'd already surmised, were one of the groups pioneering the punk rock movement that was just getting traction on the national media, but which sounded to him more like a throwback to the frenzied adrenaline that he'd started out with. He and Jimmy Page walked down the corridor, stuck their heads round the door, and when nobody told them to fuck off out again, stepped inside to listen to them play.

Much to the Adverts' surprise.

"I like to see new bands, see what they're doing, how good they are," Plant explained later. And a few weeks after that, after catching another punk band, the Damned, in concert, he laughed when he was asked by *New Musical Express* what their performance reminded him of: "You ask me if it reminds me of when we started out, but it doesn't. It reminds me of when we were rehearsing this afternoon."

Three years later, the Adverts were on the verge of collapsing, might already have done so had they not had a new album and a British tour to complete in late 1979. Drummer and guitarist-less, vocalist TV Smith cast around for replacements, and recruited both Paul Martinez (switching from his natural bass for the occasion) and Martinez's brother Rick. Now Paul was on his way to Rockfield, as Plant was putting the finishing touches to his band.

Cozy Powell's recruitment to the line-up was never intended as a permanent relationship; "I just went along to see how things were going, and they asked me to play a few tunes," Powell explained in a 1994 interview. In fact, unreleased tapes from the Rockfield sessions contain alternate and rough takes of no less than five of the songs that would ultimately appear on the finished LP, including the B-side "Far Post," "Mystery Title," "Worse Than Detroit," "Like I've Never Been Gone," and "Slow Dancer," plus a number of other jams. Powell had not been recruited merely to play, however. He was brought in to provide another familiar face.

Another Birmingham boy, Powell had been friends with Plant for a long time, and that October, early into the album's gestation, the pair appeared together on *Tiswas*, a gloriously anarchic Saturday morning kids' TV show, in which a Phantom Flan Flinger flung flans at guests and audience alike, a dog named Spit spat, and positively nobody was immune from abuse and assault.

Plant arrived as hostess Sally James was reminding viewers of the questions posed in the previous week's competition, one of whom demanded to know, "What was Led Zeppelin called before they became Led Zeppelin?"

Speaking through a mouthful of breakfast cereal and complaining about the early hour, Plant feigned a moment of memory loss before getting the answer right the first time. He read the names and addresses of the winning competitors and then sat quietly munching his cereal until it was time for the first game of the day: a round of Pass the Pie, which pitted him against Cozy Powell and two little girls who may have looked a mere eight or nine years old, but one of whom was really, according to the voiceover, 146 and renowned as the first woman ever to climb "Everest the hard way . . . up the inside." Plant, meanwhile, was introduced as "a former farmer who used to punch cows. But he gave it up because the cows started punching back."

It was a simple game, a little like Pass the Parcel only with a pie. The music plays and the competitors pass the pie between themselves. The music stops, and the pie is thrust into the face of the next person in the line. Powell got the first taste and was eliminated from the game; Plant got the second. The 146-year-old mountaineer eventually won the game.

As for what had brought the pair of them together in the first place, Powell was just about to tell all to Sally James when Plant—all traces of his pie face now removed—reappeared, and flanned him in the face again to keep him from finishing his sentence. Neither was Plant intending to be any more revealing about his future plans, preferring instead to advertise one of his other fascinations.

"I'm playing right wing for one of the most fantastic [soccer] teams in the Kidderminster League," he declared, at which point the Phantom Flinger emerged and flanned him. The sight of Robert Plant sitting quietly—face, hair, and clothes spattered with shaving cream—is one that lived with his fans for a long time.

"Good-pie to Robert," Sally James smiled.

Goodbye, too, to Cozy Powell, whose departure from the sessions appears to have been as amicable as his arrival. In his stead, Plant turned to Bad Company's Simon Kirke, as much out of love of his playing as for the convenience of Kirke's contractual standing—Bad Company were signed to Zeppelin's own Swan Song label. For whatever reason, though, things just didn't work out, and finally another of the names put forward on the media's wish list of replacements for John Bonham was called in. Genesis's Phil Collins apparently turned up at the studio, played through the entire album in under three days, and then went home again. Six of his performances would make the finished album, only two of Cozy Powell's.

Once management and record companies became involved in the process, and such touchy areas as publishing rights became a bone of contention among Plant's advisors, the mood of the sessions began to deflate. Hitherto, Plant ran the band on the most democratic lines he could, turning to Blunt and Woodroffe for basic arrangements, then conspiring to add his own vocals when the band was down at the pub. It kept things fresh, but it also allowed him to try out some of his own ideas without anybody there to witness any failures. But then came time to play the music to the outside world: that aforementioned cabal of his closest industry confidantes, not one of whom saw its merits.

For Phil Carson, Plant was selling himself short by so wholly abandoning the sound for which he was known—an insistence that surprisingly overlooked the fact that it was very hard to say *what* a typical Led Zeppelin song sounded like.

For Peter Grant, the notion of Plant getting together with a bunch of, for the most part, no-name friends was equally absurd. As Page had proven when he tried tempting Plant with XYZ, the singer could have his pick of superstar bandmates, and the emergence on the American circuit of acts like Asia, whose 1981 launch was greeted with rabid sales in the AOR market, had left every mainstream rock manager eyeing his charges and wondering which could be press-ganged into a similar concern. Or so Grant later confessed: "I did think Robert should have come back big, and his next few albums proved that because they were nowhere near as successful as they should have been. But he had this idea in his head of starting out from scratch, or as close to scratch as he could, and it was something that he and I were never going to see eye to eye on."

Plant and Grant had often been at loggerheads in the past, the singer painfully aware that when it came to discussing Led Zeppelin's accomplishments, management habitually credited them to Jimmy Page; Grant and the guitarist had, after all, been close ever since Page began working for producer Mickie Most, Grant's then-employer, back in the mid-1960s. Together since that time, they had developed a friendship and an understanding that was always going to place Page in the spotlight to the exclusion of any other musical partners.

Plant, on the other hand, believed there was more to Zeppelin's success than the presence of a gifted guitarist. It was Grant's involvement in the XYZ project that had proved the final nail in that idea's coffin, regardless of the nature of the music. No way would Plant have acceded to Grant handling the new band's career, and while their rift never became public—either before or after Zeppelin's demise, or even following the manager's death on November 21, 1995—it was always simmering below the surface. When Grant stepped up to offer his own opinions on Plant's new music, the singer simply shrugged them off.

Plant's former bandmates were no more supportive, however, with John Paul Jones delivering the supremely sniffy verdict: "I thought you could have done something a little bit better than that, old chap." Plant thanked him for his opinion and left. With Jones, too, Plant realized, his status was as low as it could be. In 1987 he told *Guitar World*'s Steven Rosen, "Yet again, I was just the singer of the songs." Because he had always been backed by virtuoso musicians, the assumption was that he could not exist without them.

Plant was out to prove that he could. With "Burning Down One Side," a Stonesy groove colliding with an armored assault and a Blunt guitar solo as sharp as pins. With "Moonlight in Samosa," a yearning ballad that still rates among his most heartfelt performances ever. With the tripwire danceability of "Pledge Pin," riding Raphael Ravenscroft's sultry sax; with the haunted, harp-ridden barrage of "Worse Than Detroit," a song that rewrote Chuck Berry's "Memphis" with laughing intent; and with the near-anthemic "Like I've Never Been Gone," a song you could say rolled the years back a shade, but only to remind us what a great voice for bluesy laments Plant has always possessed. A straight line drawn between "Babe I'm Gonna Leave You," "Since I've Been Loving You," and "Like I've Never Been Gone" would need no other common ground than the passion of Plant's performance.

The seven-minute epic "Slow Dancer," too, if one was so disposed, could be said to look back a little, a reminder of the Arabic motifs that inspired "Kashmir" (from Zeppelin's sixth album, *Physical Graffiti*) but delving deeper into those inspirations by returning to a tape Plant had picked up while holidaying in Morocco in 1972, veteran Egyptian singer Umm Kalthum's "Leylet Hob" (Night of Love). With Blunt weaving exquisite, expressive shapes around that song's swirling guitar riff, Plant certainly did nod back to past fascinations, but only to state that they remained current ones as well.

True, the album did not maintain its standards throughout, particularly as the needle tracked through the middle of what, in those vinyl days, was called side two. But the closing "Mystery Title" dispelled any doubts, another funky mover that shook and shattered across five-minutes-plus of hyperactivity and brought *Pictures at Eleven* to a most satisfactory halt.

Yet it was not going to be an easy journey, getting the music out to Plant's audience. Almost immediately after that first meeting, Grant set about retaliating against Plant's stubbornness by recommending that Swan Song, to whom the singer was still contracted, hold back on even releasing the record. It was a stance that Phil Carson, too, threw his weight behind.

Plant was in no mood to back down though, and if the businessmen opposed him, other musicians immediately understood where he was coming from. (Phil Collins, himself no stranger to taking an established band name and completely subverting its musical direction as he helmed Genesis's shift from extended prog epics to sharp pop electro, was just one of those who were adamant that Plant had long since earned the right to dictate his own career.) And they were the ones that Plant listened to.

There would need to be compromise. Plant's original intention of releasing the album under an anonymous band name, as opposed to his own, was the first casualty. A democratic financial arrangement with co-conspirators Blunt and Woodroffe, too, was abandoned. But so were the last threads binding Plant to Led Zeppelin, as Peter Grant was eased out of the managerial picture, and *Pictures at Eleven*, as Plant titled his solo debut, made its way onto the schedule for a June 1982 release. To Plant's supreme gratification, and the certain discomfort of those self-appointed experts ranged against him, it marched into the Top 5 on both sides of the Atlantic and earned a boatload of rave reviews, most of them congratulating Plant for doing the one thing that his label begged him not to.

It didn't sound like Led Zeppelin.

For a few months after its release, visitors to Jennings Farm were greeted by framed copies of the best reviews, hung around the walls to remind Plant of his triumph. And assailed, when Plant had the record player on, by the music that he'd established as the touchstone for all that he wanted to accomplish in his reborn career. The music of his teens. Without necessarily playing the blues, he was a bluesman again.

4

Easily Lead
(1961–1965)

The British blues scene of the early 1960s, even after the Rolling Stones embarked upon their conquest of the world, was insular, intense, and ruthlessly competitive. It was a world in which dedicated fans thought little of standing in line all night, waiting for their favorite record store to unpack the latest delivery of American imports; one in which friendships were forged over a shared love of the blues—famously, Mick Jagger and Keith Richards first bonded over a Muddy Waters LP spotted across a crowded train, and they were not the only ones.

Owning a new release was special; being first to hear one was even more so. Word of mouth was as much a part of a record becoming a legend as any evidence of the ears, with singer Long John Baldry once admitting, "I got burned so many times. Somebody would tell me, 'Oh you have to hear this,' and I'd trot out and buy a copy, only to discover it was dreadful."

But Phil May, soon to find fame as frontman with the Pretty Things, continues, "People didn't have big record collections . . . big R&B record collections. You'd have a handful of albums and a few reel-to-reel tapes; someone else would have a handful more. The trick was never to buy a record that someone else had, because it wasn't about owning as many different records as you could, it was about *hearing* as many. So these records and tapes would just be passed around, and if you wanted to hear something that someone else had, but they weren't sitting in the room with you with the record, you tried to play it yourself, as close as you could get to the original."

Every urban sprawl possessed its own die-hard blues scene, but the port towns and industrial regions were by far the most dedicated. And among them, Birmingham's was especially febrile. While the vast majority of the music's English adherents were unquestionably middle class, the blues themselves were the sound of the American worker; what better soundtrack could there be to the fires and factories, sweat and labor, of the Black Country?

At thirteen years of age, Plant was younger than many of the blues' most dedicated followers, but nobody looked down on him because of it. Rather, older collectors and shop owners too would take him under their wings—encouraging and inculcating his passion, steering him toward the records that would further his education, and inching him, too, toward making the transition from passive listener to active performer.

Bands were forming constantly, for no more reason than because they could. There were no hopes of record deals, stardom, and lifelong careers; a blues band was a vocation, not a job—a handful of likeminded friends distributing the instrumental workload as the fancy took them, and then playing the songs they best agreed they loved. Few of them called themselves a "group"; fewer still went on to become one. They just got together where they could, with or without an audience of friends, and played for the love of playing.

Blues clubs began to grow up, and again the majority of them were casual, barely organized. Just a place where people could gather to talk about, listen to, and play the music, some drifting to the microphone to sing a favorite song, others content to listen. Even among those musicians who went on to greater things—and that includes the Rolling Stones, the Pretty Things, Manfred Mann, and the Yardbirds—their earliest efforts were played out as simply half-familiar faces amidst a pool of countless hopefuls.

And so it was around Birmingham. As befits its status as England's second city (behind London, of course), Birmingham and its environs were alive with live music. The legendary British TV show *Thank Your Lucky Stars* was already broadcasting out of the area, and its studio audience, if not necessarily its performers, were frequently drawn from the local musical ferment. But it was only as 1961 drifted into 1962 and beyond that things truly began to coalesce, by which time the emergence of the Beatles, in early '63, was already signaling a shift in the musical preoccupations of a generation. The sound that they spearheaded, forged around the dockyards of their native Liverpool, was called Merseybeat. So the race was on for every other city in the country to develop its own similar scene.

Brumbeat, derived from the local term for the city itself, was Birmingham's contribution to this craze, at least after Cliff Richard's producer, Norrie Paramor, arrived in town to audition regional talent for possible recording contracts. In fact, it was Paramor himself who came up with the term, once he had returned to London with six bands in his pocket and set about alerting the rest of the nation to their existence.

Jimmy Powell and the Dimensions, signed to Decca in early 1962, led the Brumbeat boom, swiftly followed by the Redcaps, one of the half dozen bands plucked from the manifold hopefuls that filed into the Old Moat House Club in Digbeth to strut their stuff for the watching Paramor. And while not one of Paramor's discoveries truly amounted to anything on a national level, the very fact they had risen far enough to cut a record for Columbia was sufficient to ignite local passions.

By early 1964, Birmingham had placed its first beat group in the British Top 10, when the Applejacks' "Tell Me When" made No. 7. The Rockin' Berries followed, and when Radio Caroline launched its pirate radio service, it looked to Birmingham for its theme tune: the Fortunes' sing-along "Caroline."

At the age of thirteen, fourteen, Plant was a witness, not a participant to all that was developing around him. Even after a few of his closest friends set out in a band of their own, Andy Long and the Jurymen, Plant seemed content merely to attend their shows, help shift equipment, and ensure that at least one pair of hands would be clapping as the band ran through its repertoire of top pop–cover versions, resplendent in the matching maroon suits and black velvet collars that conformed to the pop industry's then-established need for a band uniform.

Even the Rolling Stones took that route as they sent their first two singles into the British chart, although when Plant saw them play for the first time—at the Gaumont, Wolverhampton, on October 20, 1963—it was not the five youthful Londoners with their diet of revved-up American R&B that shook him. Nor was it the Everly Brothers or Little Richard, who also rattled the bill. Plant's attention was focused firmly on the least-known, but largest-lived, name on the stage that night, Bo Diddley. An American legend who was already past his peak by the time he arrived in the UK that fall, but whose repertoire remained the meat and potatoes of every blues band around.

Half a century on, memories of Diddley's performances remained burned vibrantly into the minds of everyone who caught them: the squat, bespectacled (and shockingly un-cool-looking) Diddley flanked on one side by Jerome Green, whacking his maracas and looking so mean; and on the other by the Duchess, Norma-Jean Wofford, in figure-hugging black and gold, a bouffant piled as high as her heels, and a Gretsch guitar that chased Bo's round the block. They had time to play just a couple of numbers, "Bring It to Jerome" and "Pretty Thing," but their effect on Robert Plant was the same as their effect on almost everyone else who saw them. It was time to say "goodbye to white music."

"Bo Diddley," "I'm a Man," "Pretty Thing," "Cops and Robbers," "Hey Bo Diddley," "Mona," "Road Runner," "Who Do You Love"—Bo was, as another of his most self-aggrandizing songs insisted, the "Diddley Daddy" to an entire generation, a Mississippi-born guitarist who moved to Chicago at age six but never let his birthplace leave his musical dreams. The guitar sound he developed was the sound of the swamps, the whack of the hambone, the percussive thwack that recalled the days when Southern slaves made prohibited music by slapping their bodies and dancing to the resultant rhythm.

"I worked on this rhythm of mine," Diddley once explained to George R. White, author of *Bo Diddley: Living Legend*. "I'd say it was a mixed-up rhythm, blues and Latin American and some hillbilly, a little spiritual, a little African, and a little West Indian calypso. And if I want to start yodeling in the middle of it, I can do that, too. I like gumbo, you dig?" It was this, though the fifteen-year-old onlooker could not yet put it into words, that made the greatest impression upon Plant. The knowledge that, behind the driving guitars and the braggadocious lyrics, Diddley never lost his sense of self.

Plant took his first step onto the stage shortly after that show, late in 1963. Andy Long and the Jurymen were now playing several shows a week, much to the chagrin of Headmaster Chambers, and to the bemusement of the local *Express & Star* newspaper, which ran a small piece on the band that noted not only the fact that they were Grammar School boys, but also that they were playing venues they would not legally be permitted to enter were they not the evening's entertainment.

Their problem right now was that Long had just been diagnosed with appendicitis and was about to go under the surgeon's knife. Six long weeks would elapse before he could return to the stage, six weeks that the band had already littered with further engagements. When Plant suggested he fill in, his bandmates didn't need to be asked twice. He knew their repertoire, he'd attended every show, he was around at rehearsals, he was practically a member of the band already. And when he stepped out on the stage at the Bull's Head in Lye, a pub owned by drummer John Dudley's grandfather, it was as if he'd been fronting the band all along. He even moved like he knew what he was doing.

All those years spent rehearsing in his bedroom had paid off.

In 2008, receiving an award from the British music magazine *Q*, Plant reflected upon this era as a part of his acceptance speech. "In 1963, most bands passing through . . . town worked off the same sheet—Chicago R&B and early Motown identikit-packed with mail order arrogance and a taste for our local girls. No social commentary, just cash and penicillin.

"One day, the singer in a school beat group got sick and I stepped in. Singing the songs was OK, [but] what do you do with yourself during the guitar solos? Stare at your shoes and think of Elvis, or preen? What a blast. I was in heaven and ignored with a vengeance."

True, the harmonica that he'd taken up playing earlier in the year did sound a little alien within the band's established sound, but it was an intriguing alien, a splash of bluesy authenticity that took the tried-and-tested covers away from the realms of familiarity and into some quite fascinating pastures of their own. At least, Plant thought they were fascinating. His bandmates, although they enjoyed working with him, were also keenly awaiting Andy Long's return—so much so that when Plant suggested he should become the band's new singer, they politely but very firmly turned him down.

His schooldays marched on, and gloriously so, at least for the moment. In November 1963, Plant was even presented with a prize for finishing top of his class in the end-of-year exams, a sure sign to all that behind the brash exterior and the apparent obsession with music there beat the heart of a keen scholar. Later in his school career, he would react violently against such expectations, by apparently, willfully, abandoning the path to academic glory in favor of slumming it with sundry musicians. But for now, the worlds of music and matriculation remained exquisitely balanced.

More shows hit town, and Plant made it his business to attend them. But the one that he was most excited about was on February 28, when the Birmingham Town Hall hosted the first-ever Birmingham R&B Festival. The opening acts alone were worth the price of admission: London's newly fledged Yardbirds, Birmingham's own fast-rising Spencer Davis Group, and Long John Baldry's Hoochie Coochie men—whose backup singer, though few people cared at the time, was a young man named Rod Stewart. But Plant's eyes were firmly on the headliner, an American bluesman named Sonny Boy Williamson II.

Williamson II was not, as the designation of "the second" makes clear, the first bluesman to ply his trade under that name. In fact, the original Sonny Boy, John Lee Williamson, was still active around the Chicago area when Howling Wolf's brother-in-law, Aleck "Rice" Miller, hijacked his name in the early 1940s and began gigging around the Mississippi Delta, insisting that *he*, and not the northern-based artist, was the genuine Sonny Boy.

It was a duplicitous feat, but he got away with it. By the end of the 1940s, Williamson II was a regular on regional radio, and an advertising icon for King Biscuit Flour, the unmistakable face of the company's Sonny Boy brand of white corn meal. He landed a recording contract and was soon pumping out the future classics: "Eyesight to the Blind," "Don't Start Me Talkin'," "Bring It On Home," "Nine Below Zero," and more. Dave Walker, another Birmingham musician who caught that same show (and who recorded his own album-length tribute to Williamson II in 2004, *Mostly Sonny*), explains, "There was a simplicity to Sonny Boy . . . the same as Jimmy Reed, it was just a shuffle, but it was a beautiful shuffle. Some of those old guys, you listen to the records and they're out of tune, or you can't understand them. But Sonny Boy's records were so warm, and so exciting."

Williamson II originally arrived in the UK simply to perform halfway up the bill at the 1963 American Folk Blues Festival in Croydon, on the outskirts of London. But audience and media alike established him as the runaway star of the show, and promoter Giorgio Gomelsky promptly set about booking him his own British tour, with almost every show introducing him to a new clutch of backing musicians. In Newcastle on New Year's Eve, Williamson was accompanied by the still-unknown Animals; other shows saw Williamson paired with the Brian Auger Trinity, to cement a relationship that grew so strong that finally, shortly before Williamson's return to the US, Gomelsky put the team (plus a teenaged session guitarist named Jimmy Page) in the studio to cut what became the *Don't Send No Flowers* album.

Williamson's most incendiary partnership, however, was with the Yardbirds, and that despite the notoriously prickly Williamson dismissing their efforts very early on: "These British want to play the blues so bad, and they play the blues *so* bad!"

"He wasn't very tolerant," Yardbirds guitarist Eric Clapton told *Rolling Stone* twenty years later. "He put us through some bloody hard paces. In the first place, he expected us to know his tunes. He'd say 'we're gonna do . . . "Fattening Frogs for Snakes,"' and then he'd kick it off and, of course, some of the members of . . . the band had never heard these songs."

The fifteen-year-old Robert Plant, too, found himself on the rough end of Williamson's infamously caustic tongue. Making his way backstage at the Town Hall, he knocked on Williamson's dressing room door and shyly said hello. "Fuck off," replied the star, and that was the end of the meeting.

Plant consoled himself by pocketing one of Williamson's harmonicas as he walked away, but his admiration for the man remained undamaged.

Plant caught the Spencer Davis Group again, a few weeks after the Birmingham R&B Festival, at the Golden Eagle, a local Birmingham pub. The same evening, he'd been to see Jerry Lee Lewis play, but the veteran American was a far cry from the fiery killer of his earliest Sun sides. It was Davis and Co. that set Plant's pulse racing this evening, not only for the ferocity with which they performed, but also for the presence in their ranks of vocalist Steve Winwood.

A mere matter of months older than Plant (he was born on May 12, 1948), Winwood already possessed a voice as seasoned and raw as any classic bluesman, yet one that was also uniquely and distinctly his own. Until now, Plant's own attempts at singing—usually alone in his bedroom, but onstage with the Jurymen too—had seen him simply ensuring that a reasonably pleasant and hopefully tuneful sound came out whenever he opened his mouth. Winwood showed him that there was a lot more to it than that. At least, there was if you wanted to make an impression. You needed to forge your own style as well, a sound that was instantly recognizable as your own. And to do that, you needed to make yourself heard.

Plant knew just the place to make that happen.

Every night after school, he would hurry home and slam through the requisite three hours' homework as swiftly (and probably carelessly) as he dared, then dress and leave the house. Invariably his destination was the same, retracing his footsteps back to Stourbridge, to the folk and blues club that had recently opened just a short distance from the school, at the Seven Stars pub.

"Everything was opening up," Plant told *Record Collector* in 2007. "New Orleans music was pumping through . . . with Jessie Hill and Allen Toussaint, they were pumping out Frankie Ford and Hughie 'Piano' Smith and the Clowns, and all of that stuff, and I'm going 'fucking hell. I'm 15—what is this music? It's got nothing to do with the youth club, it's got nothing to do with Stourbridge Grammar School.' . . . I was on fire."

The Seven Stars was one of the places where he could burn.

It is a sad truth that the passing of time has rendered the sheer variety and preponderance of British folk clubs all but indistinguishable from one another. There were hundreds of them, operating out of pubs, church halls, and youth clubs all over the country, some existing for a matter of weeks, others flaring brightly for years. Yet even among their most loyal denizens, their memory has blurred into a composite whole.

A few London venues are remembered for the ever-lengthening line of future stars who cut their hopeful teeth on those stages; Glasgow's, a few years earlier, from the presence of entrepreneur Roy Guest and the very young Bert Jansch. Others, however, are occasionally noted for birthing a future star (if they did so) and then passed over. Yet without them, the face of British folk and blues would have been unrecognizable, an informal but tightly intertwined network of venues, all reliant upon the experiences of another when it came to booking unknown talent, each dependent upon the discernment of its own loyal audience and the fairness of its organizers to maintain the ability to attract the right names.

Even Sandy Denny, by decade's end the Queen of English folk, once described her early career as time spent flitting around the country by herself, trying to find her way to one obscure pub after another, while the kind of characters that members of one club recall with such affection were also to be found in every other one.

"Folk clubs were stunning places in those days," says Richard Byers, whose Suffolk Punch harmony group was a staple of the Kent folk-club circuit. "You could go and see Bert Lloyd one Sunday, singing hard-core traditional stuff, then you'd get Roy Harper or the Alexis Korner Blues Band the next week—amazing." In and around these headline players, there would also be a slot for the club's own organizer, him- or herself usually being a musician—and then there were the floor singers, who took turns, week by week, doing songs of their own.

Byers continues:

> Floor singers could be a mixed bunch. In the '60s, there was a good deal of unaccompanied singing, solo or in groups. Most singers had some chorus songs in their repertoires, so good

clubs featured plenty of full-throated ensemble singing that the whole audience joined in with, often in harmony.

Some singers might specialize in sea songs and shanties, which offered loads of opportunities for audience participation. And clubs would have their own favorite songs (bawdy ones, lyrical ones, sentimental ones) that they got really good at singing because they were sung regularly. On a good night, these could take the roof off.

But there would be other kinds of floor singers too: the politically committed (singing Irish republican songs), the sleek and suave (imitators of Peter, Paul and Mary or Nina and Frederick), the wildly creative (people who wanted to read their own poems or sing songs they had written), and sometimes the downright awful. Folk clubs provided an outlet for it all.

Plant quickly plunged into this way of life. With a guitar-playing friend in tow, "[we] would go around the local folk clubs playing 'Corinna Corinna.' The first music which really appealed to me—even when I was still at school—was stuff like Bob Dylan's 'Corinna Corinna.' When you look deeper into that kind of music, you find that it has a lot of the feelings that exist in blues. Then, of course, you realize that the blues field is a very wide one."

Few of the clubs were more than part-time affairs, a night or two a week, operating, Byers continues, out of "back rooms or rooms upstairs, often lovely old wood-paneled rooms with a nice acoustic. And they were also places where more or less everyone smoked, so the ambience was beery, a bit dusty, and wreathed in tobacco smoke." But the dedication of staff, resident performers, and audience alike could rarely be faulted, and within their own local circle, as Ray Davies once sang, "Everybody's a star."

Plant certainly saw himself as one, descending upon the Seven Stars every week that he could, usually accompanied by the eye-catching array of kazoos that he had taken to making and the washboard with which he scratched out percussion, again in the privacy of his own bedroom.

Neither instrument would strike the modern reader as especially awe-inspiring; music history has effectively consigned both to the age of skiffle, which, by 1964, had long since had its day. But they were also integral to the British blues, particularly for would-be musicians who had no other outlet for their musical talents. So when Plant approached another of the Seven Stars regulars, the Delta Blues Band, to ask whether he could sing with them, and was asked in reply whether he played any instruments, he had no hesitation in producing his washboard. And they had no hesitation about letting him join in.

Plant did not remain with the Delta Blues Band for long. A small local circuit that included both the Seven Stars and the Stourbridge Conservative Club, but not much else, paid very little money and offered little hope of advancement. But it was a learning experience all the same, Plant spending more time jamming with other local musicians, as Chris Wood, a member at that time of the Sounds of Blue (but later to go on to form Traffic with Steve Winwood) recalled.

Interviewed in the early 1980s, Wood remembered, "He was just this big grammar school kid who was always hanging around. Very enthusiastic, very keen to play with everyone, but also very untutored; I think we all took turns with him, talking about music, just trying to educate him" (the collective *we* including the Delta Blues Band's Perry Foster; another member of Sounds of Blue, guitarist Stan Webb; and Wood himself).

All joined the chorus that counseled Plant to find his own voice and direction, but all nudged him, too, toward trying to sound at least halfway contemporary. At a time when the blues had firmly mutated into the electric soup of the Stones- and Yardbirds-style R&B, with players trying ever more inventively to bring a modern sheen to songs that were thirty, forty, even fifty years old at the time, Plant was striving not, perhaps, for authenticity, but at least for something as Spartan and scratchy as the original recordings.

And so he drifted through a succession of short-lived bands, acts whose very names were lifted directly from favorite songs—Blind Lemon Jefferson's "Black Snake Moan" (with drummer Rob Elcock) and John Lee Hooker's "Crawling King Snake"—or nudged audaciously into other people's nomenclatural territory; the New Memphis Bluesbreakers had nothing in common with John Mayall's band of the same name, beyond of course their milieu, but Plant didn't care.

Of them all, the Crawling Kingsnakes alone packed some staying power. Founded in 1963 by guitarist Johnny Pasternak, a renowned local troublemaker known for slicing cinema seats with his switchblade before he turned his attention to music; singer Al King; and drummer Nigel Knowles, they were originally known as the Javelins, becoming the Crawling Kingsnakes the following year. Based out of the Thurston Hotel in nearby Bewdlay, they swiftly established themselves among their own area's prime R&B bands, before losing Pasternak to one of Birmingham's, the Shakedown Sound. Al King quit for the Money Jungle around the same time, but the group—drummer Knowles, bassist Terry Edwards, and rhythm guitarist Roy Price—swiftly rebuilt. Ian "Inky" Watts came in on guitar; Rob Plant became the new frontman.

The Crawling Kingsnakes, by Plant's own admission, were considerably more commercial sounding than any of his previous bands, and he adapted his stage presence accordingly. No longer a weary bluesman, now he was more prone to leaping around the stage with his microphone stand held high above his head.

Not that he noticed this while it was happening. He was already a natural extrovert, and he only grew more showy once he realized how audiences responded to him: the girls were impressed, their boyfriends were jealous. For him, it was sufficient simply to be up onstage, singing his favorite songs to audiences that might have numbered in single figures, might have been calling out all night for Chuck Berry and Bo Diddley numbers, might even have laughed at the gawky school kid up on the stage. But he didn't care.

In fact, he began tailoring his repertoire toward getting even more of a reaction from the onlookers, working up a version of Robert Johnson's "Traveling Riverside Blues," in which the line about squeezing lemons and getting wet legs became a focal point for fans and foes alike. Fifteen-year-olds in the early 1960s simply didn't talk like that.

Plant's burgeoning vision of himself as some kind of outlaw bluesman extended to his schoolwork as well. He was habitually late for school now, a natural consequence of the hours he was devoting to performing and rehearsing. His homework was suffering, and his visits to either the school prefects' room or the headmaster's study were becoming more regular.

His parents, too, were growing increasingly exasperated, especially after Plant sat his end-of-school O Levels and failed every subject bar history. There was but one solution. He would stay on at school for another year, then resit his exams at the end.

Not that he had any higher hopes this time around. Time that he should have devoted to study continued to be spent circulating the clubs and pubs of the Black Country, checking out the continued explosion of new talent that was erupting onto the scene: bands like the N'Betweens, led by a raucous shouter named Noddy Holder and destined to emerge a few years later as Slade; Mike Sheridan and the Night Riders; Carl Wayne and the Vikings; the Shakedown Sound, featuring Johnny Pasternak and a young Jess Roden; Danny King and the Mayfair Set; and the Uglys, a tumultuous combo whose ever-shifting lineup constantly glittered with some of the finest players in the city, and through whose auspices Plant would meet a man destined to become another of his oldest friends, bassist Dave Pegg.

A new venue hove into view. The Ritz, in the Birmingham suburb of King's Heath, was a part of the so-called "Regan Circuit," a network of clubs owned and operated by Mary "Ma" Regan, a former schoolteacher who launched her entertainment empire with a small chain of tea shops, which led her to staging tea dances, and then, ultimately, operating full-fledged dance halls. The Plaza Ballroom in Old Hill, out on the road to Dudley; the Handsworth Plaza; the Ritz Ballroom in King's Heath; the Brum Kavern in Birmingham—all were staples of the Regan Circuit, and Ma was always on the lookout for keen young men to work as disc jockeys and emcees to warm up the evening crowd.

She hired Plant the moment she met him. Not only were the Crawling Kingsnakes regulars on her circuit, often sharing the bill with the Shakedown Sound; they were also reaching out toward a new tribe of listeners, the Mods, both musically and, though Plant's eye for fashion, visually.

With bands like the Who and the Small Faces already established as that particular movement's figureheads, the Crawling Kingsnakes were never going to be much more than a local substitute for the real thing. But Plant dressed the part anyway, seizing upon the Mod credo of smart clothes, short hair, and a frenetic dance style; pillaging songs from the Motown and James Brown catalogs; and hanging out at the Swiss Cafe, drinking coffee and playing his harp. He even changed musical direction for a time as he started moonlighting with the Banned, another KEGS-based combo, jazz-tinged firmly in the mold of the Graham Bond Organization, sweaty-keyboard and Stax-horn heavy.

He played a handful of gigs with them in between his Kingsnake obligations, although it was not only their music that appealed to him. Deteriorating relations with his parents saw Plant as often as not in need of a place to sleep so he did not have to go home and face his father's "Where've you been until this time of night"–shaped wrath. The Banned's distinctively lipstick-and-nail-varnish-graffitied van increasingly became a home away from home.

But contrary to everyone's expectations, possibly even his own, Plant's second round of O Levels landed him acceptable results in English, English Literature, Geography, and Mathematics, and while later legend (encouraged by Plant) insisted that he was rewarded for his efforts by being expelled from the school, in fact he seemed set for a most respectable future as he entered training for a career in accountancy.

5

Like I've Never Been Gone
(1981–1983)

Close to twenty years later, Robert Plant sometimes wished he had paid more attention to that particular strand of his education.

It was the accountants who stymied his dream of simply forming a new band and heading out under their name, allowing people to discover for themselves that the singer used to be in a famous group; the accountants who pointed out that, having financed the *Pictures at Eleven* sessions himself, and paid his musicians generously too, now it was time for him to recoup his outlay and make some money as well.

The name "Robert Plant" might not have literally been guaranteed a license to print money. But it certainly had a lot more commercial traction than a brand-new band name that he'd formed with his friends.

It was financing, too, that played a part in the decision not to tour the new album, and once again Plant demanded a lot of convincing before he acknowledged the wisdom behind that. He had already made clear, both privately and publicly, that the Led Zeppelin catalog remained off-limits in his repertoire. "It would be a cheap shot to visit those songs without John Bonham," he wrote later, in the liner notes for *Sixty Six to Timbuktu*. "Either with or without the remainder of the dream factory." If he was going to play, he would play his own songs.

But *Pictures at Eleven* alone would not sustain a live show, and padding the set with Honeydrippers-style covers would only focus an even brighter spotlight on the absence of the oldies. As Peter Grant reflected, "He was always walking a tightrope in that respect, and even later on you heard people complaining, 'He won't do "Whole Lotta Love," but he'll happily play a bunch of Elvis songs.'"

Neither was Plant in the mood to compete with his past. *Pictures at Eleven* was released in June 1982; *Coda*, the first in what would ultimately become a long line of Led Zeppelin compilations and repackages, was scheduled to follow it in November. Right around the time that Plant would be on the road, and serving up a major distraction for anyone who cared about what he was doing.

No matter that *Coda* was, for the most part, a hodgepodge, an assemblage of outtakes and live cuts that Jimmy Page insisted existed only because "there was so much bootleg stuff out. We thought, 'Well, if there's that much interest, then we may as well put the rest of our studio stuff out.'" The name on the cover was enough to drown any applause that its makers might individually merit.

There was only one thing to do. *Pictures at Eleven* was still fresh on the racks, and Plant was already thinking about its follow-up. The sooner it was finished (and the sooner *Coda* had run its course), the sooner he could get back out on the road.

He had already recharged his batteries, returning to his beloved Morocco with Maureen, Logan, and Carmen for a short vacation while *Pictures at Eleven* geared up for release. There, they explored the culture and legends that he had come to adore, spending time in such places as the hills and forests of Ouirghane, long before it was established as an up-and-coming vacation spot; the village of Tahanaoute; stately Marrakech—the lands that travel writer and historian Gavin Maxwell assigned to the Lords of the Atlas (in the book of the same name), and all poised at the gateway to one of the most impressive mountain ranges in the world. Lands in which, at that time at least, all you could hear on the wind was the music being made in the casbahs and souks that dot the region, drifting out of the valleys to merge with heavens and send Plant into raptures of delight.

Too soon the vacation ended. Now the quartet of Plant, Martinez, Blunt, and Woodroffe were destined for his friend Roy Harper's home studio in Hereford, to work up the songs that would become *The Principle of Moments*.

Harper had long been a part of Robert Plant's landscape, both as a friend and a musical influence. Born in Manchester, the singer-songwriter-to-be was already twenty-three when he arrived in London in 1964, part of the influx of aspiring folkies drawn to the city that season. He was rarely considered a fulcrum of the inner circle, if only because he was forever more interested in performing his own idiosyncratic compositions than voicing the traditional favorites or penning the slavish sound-alikes that were most performers' route into those charmed circles.

Nevertheless, he had his first album out by 1967, *Sophisticated Beggar*, and the following year he was in the studio with legendary producer Shel Talmy, recording *Come Out Fighting, Ghengis Smith*. He shared management with Pink Floyd, Tyrannosaurus Rex, and the Edgar Broughton Band, and he numbered Deep Purple, Kevin Ayers, and Floyd again among his labelmates.

In the early 1970s, when other purported folkies were driving toward premature musical middle age with a relentless stream of self-flagellating ballads and soft-rock future classics, Harper was conjuring side-long suites for his new LPs. At a time when there seemed to be an immovable mafia of folkie sidemen, all playing on one another's records, Harper had Jimmy Page playing on *Stormcock*. And in 1975, to the amazement of many but the disapproval of few, he supplanted all three of Pink Floyd's proven singers by taking lead vocals on their "Have a Cigar."

By which time, Harper had already been writ large in the annals of Zeppelin, via the closing track to the band's third album—a happenstance that he recalled a few years later. "I used to go up to [Led Zeppelin's] office in Oxford Street . . . and one day Jimmy was up there and gave me the [band's] new record. I just said thanks and put it under my arm. Jimmy said, 'Look at it.' So I twirled the little wheel around, and put it back under my arm. Very nice and all that. So he went, '*Look* at it!' Then I discovered 'Hats Off to (Roy) Harper.' I was very touched."

Set out in rolling fields, its closest neighbors sheep and horses, Harper's home was a natural home away from home for Plant and the band. Harper, too, owned a farm, dominated by a magnificent fifteenth-century house, and the whole place was even more delightfully rambling than Plant's own. The days when musicians had routinely traipsed off into the wilderness to "get their heads together in the country, man," were long past. But for Plant, Hereford's rural calm, mythological history, and gentle pace proved a creative panacea that even home could not.

It is, after all, one of England's loveliest cities, physically dominated by one of the country's most beautiful cathedrals, but culturally as close to Wales as you can get without leaving home turf. All around, the land speaks of the centuries of strife and uncertainty that were once waged between the two kingdoms—and following Wales's absorption into England, the two peoples—while local legend simply prickles with Anglo-Saxon saints, phantom horses, gory martyrdom, and witcheries galore.

In and around the business of making music, Plant happily meandered through town and country, and if his thoughts ever turned toward the business machinations that had strived so hard to prevent him from enjoying an idyll such as this, he ignored them. Had Grant and Co. had their way, he knew, he'd probably be writing his new album for a few hundred dollars an hour in whichever airless, whitewashed superstudio was this year's recording facility du jour. Instead, one can only be grateful that he chose to exact his revenge through his music, as opposed to the method recommended by some long-forgotten local witch, whose curse can be read alongside the effigy she made of her greatest foe in a display case in Hereford City Library Museum:

> I act this spell upon you from my whole heart, wishing you to never rest nor eat or sleep the restern part of your life. I hope your flesh will waste away, and I hope you will never spend another penny I ought to have.

Preparations for the new record were not Plant's sole reason for being glad to get away from Jennings Farm, however. Despite their Moroccan sojourn, relations between Plant and wife Maureen were souring—had been rocky, in fact, for a few years. In the past, the shock, guilt, and mourning that surrounded the death of their son Karac had seemed cause enough for their unhappiness, and both hoped that time would heal those breaches. If anything, however, they had only worsened. Time away to work up the new album, both hoped, would allow them both to figure out what they wanted to do next.

That August, their divorce would be finalized.

It's a cliché, but that does not make it any less true. At the top of a profession in which felicity and fame make for the least likely bedfellows of all, the fact that Robert Plant was not merely married when Led Zeppelin formed, but remained married throughout their career, is one that catches a lot of people by surprise. But Maureen was always more than the mother of his children and the keeper of the castle to which he would return when he was able to pull himself off the road. She was also his No. 1 cheerleader and the wellspring of his support system, a role into which she had slipped almost from the moment they met, at a Georgie Fame gig in summer 1966.

Like Plant, Maureen was born in West Bromwich. Her parents, however were Indians, first-generation migrants from the old Portuguese colony of Goa, just two of the thousands of their countrymen who had relocated to "the mother country" after India won independence from the old British Empire in 1947, amid scenes of vicious violence and ancient score settling. Because of the preponderance of industry in the region, the Black Country was one of the areas to which this influx flocked, a circumstance that inevitably ignited its own new set of flash points and prejudices. In 1964 in nearby Smethwick, the town's own Member of Parliament, Peter Griffiths, fought his candidacy on an unrelentingly racist platform, and while he lost his seat at the next election in 1966, nobody doubted that he spoke for a lot of people—including many who would never even have considered themselves to be racist. They just didn't want dark-skinned foreigners living in their midst.

Even closer to home, Wolverhampton MP Enoch Powell was fermenting his own brand of racial disharmony, speaking out against the incumbent Labour government's apparent open-door policy regarding immigration, which culminated in April 1968 with what remains one of the most infamous and inflammatory speeches ever delivered by a major British political figure, the so-called "Rivers of Blood" address to an audience in Birmingham: "As I look ahead, I am filled with foreboding. Like the Roman, I seem to see 'the River Tiber foaming with much blood.' That tragic and intractable phenomenon which we watch with horror on the other side of the Atlantic but which there is interwoven with the history and existence of the States itself [the continued Civil Rights struggle], is coming upon us here by our own volition and our own neglect. Indeed, it has all but come. In numerical terms, it will be of American proportions long before the end of the 20th century. Only resolute and urgent action will avert it even now."

The *Times* newspaper condemned Powell's words as "evil." But for people of Plant's parents' generation, he may not have spoken *the* truth, but he certainly spoke *a* truth. Like Powell, they had been raised—and, in the process, firmly inculcated—with the lingering Victorian belief of English superiority, not only over the Empire's other subjects, but over foreigners of all persuasion. Like Powell, they had largely grown up in a society where blacks simply didn't exist outside of picture books, movies, and jazz bands.

For their children, however, there was no such defense. Since the end of World War II, Britain's once defiantly exclusionary immigration laws had grown more and more lax, and in the major cities at least, it was unlikely that anybody could grow up without seeing and hearing a dozen other lands and languages represented in the hubbub of daily life.

When he first started dating Maureen, Plant expected there to be opposition from his parents. He was more surprised to encounter it from his friends, and it is an early mark of his self-belief and capacity for self-determination that he closed his ears completely to their racist quips, and indulged himself instead in the ready welcome that Maureen's own family and friends extended to him. They, unlike their white neighbors, were happy for their cultures to integrate.

Even early in the relationship, Plant was frequently invited to eat with the Wilsons; later, once it became clear that the couple were serious about one another, he actually moved in with them, while Maureen saved what she could from her wages as a shop assistant to tide them over for the future. There, he developed a taste for Indian cuisine that was far removed from the fare served up in the handful of ethnic restaurants that were beginning to pop up, and when he was offered an introduction to the family's heritage, the music and mythologies that they had brought to England with them, he proved a ready and willing student.

Far beyond the parameters of Plant's own universe, the likes of Beatle George Harrison were taking their first steps toward incorporating a flavor of Indian music into their music—a splash of sitar here, a word about Ravi Shankar there. Plant, however, was absorbing that culture in a way they never could, not treating it as a learning experience and bookishly assembling all the ingredients so that he might one day make a curry-flavored LP. Rather, he was living within it, until he came to see Maureen's family as his own, and her voice became the closest he had ever had to wise counsel.

The couple got engaged in 1968, when they discovered that Maureen was pregnant, but they would have done so anyway. And on November 9 that same year, they married. Even then, there were those around them who said it would never last, and ultimately they were proved right. But the sixteen years that those Cassandras had to wait before their prophecy came true surely took away a lot of the impact.

Once again Phil Collins was scheduled to drum on the new album, when his own schedule allowed him the time (Barriemore Barlow, the Birmingham-born drummer with Jethro Tull, was also on board). Collins would be joining them once the sessions moved back to Rockfield Studios, which would take place only after the band spent a few weeks that summer in Ibiza, taking over the Pikes Hotel and setting up a makeshift stage by the swimming pool.

But the scenery was not the only thing that had changed since the sessions that produced *Pictures at Eleven*. Those sessions, by necessity and Plant's own state of mind, had been very much a democratic process, each of the musicians contributing freely and openly to the proceedings and every idea having as much of a chance of being taken up as any other. This time around, Plant determined to exert more control: to have the final say and, more than that, to impose his own will upon the proceedings. He'd had enough of those old jibes, especially once John Paul Jones's response to *Pictures at Eleven* had proven they were not so old after all. He was *not* simply the guy who sang the songs, and each of his bandmates came away from the sessions with the awareness that the gang mentality that fired the first record had been utterly suppressed.

None of this should have surprised them. No matter how much Plant's contributions to his storied past may have been overshadowed by the public's insistence on admiring a virtuoso guitar, drum, or keyboard solo over the efforts of the singer, he knew how much he had contributed to the sound and success of Led Zeppelin. And he was certainly not so ego-free as to be content with keeping that knowledge to himself. For the first time in his life, he celebrated, he alone was responsible for the success, or otherwise, of a project.

It was a responsibility that he relished, even as he acknowledged that sometimes, he missed having someone else around—someone who didn't just share the creative load but also challenged it. As he told *Rolling Stone*'s David Fricke in a rare moment of on-the-record vulnerability, he missed the "volatile showmanship" that came so easily, so naturally, to Jimmy Page, although he was adamant that its absence in no way played down the contributions that his new bandmates, and Robbie Blunt in particular, were offering.

In fact, he acknowledged, Blunt had the most difficult task of all, as a great guitarist in his own right but one who knew the world would be watching as he stepped into the footsteps of an even greater one. Of all the accomplishments that Blunt racked up as rehearsals and sessions went on, it was the guitarist's refusal to back down from his own vision that most impressed Plant. Because that rubbed off on Plant as well, reeducating him in a way, and for all his occasional eruptions—the apparent insistence that it's "my way or no way"—he prided himself at least on giving everybody a fair crack of the whip. He told *Record* magazine's John Hutchinson, "I'm only dominant when I don't like what's going on," remembering how disputes with Jimmy Page over the direction of a song could spill out into the most atrocious name calling. "We would curse each other to everyone else, but be very polite to one another."

64

A relationship like that takes time to breed, however. "With these new people, it's extremely difficult, because my track record is a little daunting for anyone that is going to step into that situation with me."

Indeed it was. No matter how confident a player might be, no matter how convinced that his idea is right, it still requires a lot of courage to walk up to one quarter of the biggest rock band in the world and tell him, "You know that last idea of yours? It really sucks." Besides, no matter what tensions may or may not have been generated by the creative process, the finished album betrayed none of them. Even more so than its predecessor, *The Principle of Moments* was a dynamic succession of ever-shifting musical ideas and ambitions, and it was shockingly contemporary too. Or perhaps *shockingly* is the wrong word: both Yes and Genesis, to name two of Plant's peers, had embraced the technologies and temperament of the early 1980s to utterly redesign old musical pastures, keeping up with the kids with ruthless syncopation.

Plant, too, adopted a modernistic feel, with Phil Collins's own trademark drum sound an integral element of the overall picture. But he did so without any compromise of his own sound and vision, and when the album's first single, the lascivious (but oddly Dire Straits-ish) lurch of "Big Log," emerged a major Top 10 hit on both sides of the Atlantic, it was clear that Plant's stubborn insistence on pursuing his own musical direction, as opposed to ones that his "advisers" had urged him to take, was paying off.

He had a new record label. Swan Song, the house that Zeppelin built, had crumbled; lost without the Led to lead it, and with its only other major seller, Bad Company, long past their sell-by date, the company went into irreversible decline, closing their doors for good shortly after *Pictures at Eleven.* In their stead, Atlantic allowed Plant to create his own new identity, and while Es Paranza was never intended to house any artist other than Plant, its existence still permitted him to maintain his status among that select handful of superstars marked out by their own corporate identity.

Now it was time to take that identity out on the road.

In August 1983, even as his marriage finally came to an end in the divorce courts of England, Plant was in the United States, preparing for his first-ever

solo tour. Phil Collins was firmly established in the drum seat for the duration, twenty-three arenas that included many that Plant had first visited as
a member of Led Zeppelin. The fact that his solo star was vast enough to
sustain not merely a repeat visit but also a return appearance for the "show
sold out" signs only amplified all he had achieved over the past year.

While Jimmy Page skulked in the musical shadows, his only post-Zep-
pelin prolusion a moody but scarcely remarkable soundtrack to the movie
Death Wish II, and John Paul Jones returned to the session work that was
his pre-Zeppelin milieu, Plant alone seemed set to continue pushing at the
barriers that the band once railed against, by forcing his own vision deeper
into the rock 'n' roll consciousness. And if history has not responded by
hauling at least a handful of his solo recordings up to the same stratospheric
heights as his earlier repertoire, then that only sweetens the thrill of discov-
ery for new audiences.

Where, some people asked, was the new "Stairway to Heaven," the new
"Whole Lotta Love," the next "Kashmir"? But were such songs truly absent?
Or were they merely still waiting (fruitlessly, as it transpired) for received his-
tory to elevate them to the legendary pastures of their illustrious forebears?

Certainly "Other Arms" rode a danceability that at least placed it in the
same room as "Trampled Under Foot" (or the previous album's "Mystery
Title"), while the drifting "In the Mood" was firmly cast within the kind of
staccato dream state that fired "The Crunge" and "Misty Mountain Hop"
without really invoking either of them.

"Through with the Two Step" yearned over synthesized orchestration;
"Messing with the Mekon" tracked out of a fanfare as memorable as "Rock
and Roll" and a lyric as laugh-out-loud joyful, too, its title an affectionate
nod back at the grotesque, hairless green alien who menaced space ace
Dan Dare during Plant's comic-reading childhood. Indeed, all that really
separated Plant's solo works from those he recorded with Led Zeppelin was
the safety net of a band name that conferred "classic" status upon any song
they performed. No, he had not come up with a new "Custard Pie." But
Zeppelin never came up with "Stranger Here . . . Than Over There." So,
honors even.

There was another blast from the past aboard, as Plant arranged for a private jet to transport himself and the band around, albeit one that was a far cry from the luxury aircraft of old. The Viscount turboprop plane was scarcely as well-appointed as the Starship, the Boeing 720 that ferried Zeppelin around on the 1973 and 1975 US tours, and its cabins would not bear witness to so many airborne hijinks either. But still it was a nice way to travel, and as Plant relaxed into the tour, so circulating recordings depict him relaxing into his new persona: the singer and leader of a rock 'n' roll band so confident in his new material that he never even acknowledged the audience calling for his old, and so confident in his bandmates that, when Jimmy Page showed up at the Madison Square Garden show, Plant had no hesitation about inviting him to join them for the encore.

Later, critics and onlookers would seize upon that moment as a sign, or at least a suggestion, that Plant might never shrug away the ghost of his past. But the reality tramples that notion underfoot. It was Plant—not the promise of anything or anyone else—that was booked into Madison Square, Plant whose name alone sold it out, and Plant whose regular live set had already reduced the audience to paroxysms of glee. Even as Plant introduced his old ally to the audience, and the resultant roar all but raised the roof off the building, he knew that Page's appearance was simply the icing on an already luxuriously decorated cake. Just as the onstage arrival of John Paul Jones at the show in Bristol, England, later in the tour, was nothing more than a special treat for an already-loyal crowd; just as a return guest spot for Page at Hammersmith Odeon, London, was just another night on the road for Plant.

Plant's insistence that neither the past nor an audience's sense of familiarity should be allowed to intrude upon an artist's vision was not reserved for his own work. Another member of the Bonham clan, John's sister (and Jason's aunt) Deborah, was planning her own entrance into the music industry, and Plant was her sounding board for many of her concerns and questions. Beginning with: should she deploy the familial name?

Plant said no, and Deborah knew precisely what he meant. The world was a very different place back then, and the music industry especially so.

Nepotism was a power in the land, whether real or perceived, and there was already a long list of worthy talents whose potential had, effectively, been snuffed out, not because they had a famous relative, but because people assumed the famous relative was somehow responsible for this latest emergence.

No matter that Deborah was not a drummer—she was, and she remains, a stunning singer-songwriter. Led Zeppelin remained a force to be reckoned with, and their reputation even more so. Plant himself remained leery of doing anything at all that might draw attention from his then still-youthful solo career, and back in the direction of the band. He could only imagine what the media would make of young Debbie. . . .

Three decades on, Deborah laughs. "I was always calling Robert up and saying, 'Can I come round to do some demos?' and it was him who alerted me to the fact that it was not going to be an easy ride if I was going to use my own name."

She was determined, however. Although she did send out her initial demos all but anonymously, revealing her true identity only when she was offered a record deal, she is adamant. "I didn't want to deny being John's sister. I am extremely proud of it, it's what made me who I am, even back then, and to change my name [as some people suggested] felt really alien to me. I couldn't do it, and I said to myself, 'I don't really care about what I'm going to face with the Led Zeppelin crowd. Everybody's going to have an opinion, they're going to prejudge, the record company are going to sell it on that, it's going to be all over the place, and I'm going to hate all of it. But as long as I'm doing my brother proud, and my family name proud, I'm okay."

Other people could make of it whatever they wanted to.

6

If It's Really Got to Be This Way
(1965–1968)

nlike Birmingham, the town of Kidderminster, seventeen miles to the west in the far side of the Clent Hills, never made much of an impact on the national music scene. Roger Lavern, a member of Joe Meek's chart-topping Tornadoes, was a native; so was Peter Wynne, a short-lived star in the Larry Parnes stable and part of the package on Eddie Cochran's final tour—and so, the locals liked to joke, were the Rolling Stones. Not *those* Rolling Stones, though. This was a purely local, and defiantly short-haired, combo that sprang up around 1962 but changed their name the following year when a bunch of London stones rolled in.

So, no major, or future, rock 'n' roll stars. At its mid-'60s height, however, Kidderminster was no less fertile a breeding ground—and in some ways, even more so. Far enough from any spotlight that its most ambitious artists could develop at their own pace, but close enough to Brum that their fingers were always on the pulse, a town best known for its carpet-manufacturing industry was littered with welcoming venues.

The Black Horse, the Black Bull, the Lion Hotel, the Playhouse, the Florence Ballroom, the Playhouse, the Worcester Cross Youth Club—they all rose on the streets that led out from the central Bull Ring (which had nothing to do with fighting bulls, by the way), while Frank Freeman's Dance Club, on Mill Street, remains one of the best-remembered venues in the entire region, as Fairport Convention's Judy Dyble reflects: "It was a fantastic place, was Uncle Frank's Sunday Club."

Certainly Kidderminster was an integral part of every Birmingham band's local itinerary, and the rest of the Black Country's too, while the Town Hall was firmly established on the schedule of every national band of importance—often to the local bands' advantage. When Donovan arrived for a gig and found his backing band hadn't made it, he quickly coopted the Huskies to stand in for them, and the Crawling Kingsnakes earned serious local bragging rights when they opened for the Yardbirds there and Eric Clapton caught Inky Watts playing his guitar. The man whom the fans were already calling God listened, and then pronounced himself impressed. There were not many local guitarists who could boast an endorsement like that.

Robbie Blunt's Accelerators were a punchy schoolboy trio that got their start on the Kidderminster circuit; the Raiders were a reformed skiffle band that launched Jess Roden on his way; Strangers Incorporated was transplanted Londoner Stan Webb's first group, which played a residency at the Central Cinema, opening not for another artist but for a movie: Cliff Richard's *Summer Holiday*.

Big Dave and the Hangmen, fronted by the contrarily diminutive Dave Deakin, brought a taste of theatrical ghoul rock to the beat circuit; Al King's Money Jungle inadvertently introduced disaster: Performing at the Adelphi in West Bromwich one night, the band underestimated the nature of the venue's revolving stage. It spun round, and their drum kit fell off.

Shades Five grasped a moment of national fame when they appeared as the band in a cornflakes commercial; Martin Raynor and the Secrets knocked the Beatles off the No. 1 spot with their debut single "Candy to Me," at least as far as the Kidderminster charts were concerned; and the Sunsetters were a very young Kevyn Gammond's first regular gig, all cavalry trousers and V-necked jumpers, performing classic rockers, doo-wop favorites, and Duane Eddy–style instrumentals.

Robert Plant plunged into this ferment in the summer of 1965, when he enrolled at Kidderminster College of Further Education to pursue a business studies course. He was no stranger to the town, of course, but now it became a home base of sorts, even after he took a temp job in Stourbridge, whiling away the weeks before term began by stocking shelves at

Stringers department store and salting away his pay to purchase a mod-
dish Lambretta scooter and a parka coat emblazoned with a Union Jack.
Then, every night after work, it was back to Kidderminster to hang with his
friends on the ever-burgeoning mod scene. Following in the footsteps of
the audiences that the Crawling Kingsnakes were beginning to attract, the
pill-chomping mods that represented teendom's latest fashionable surge,
he even trimmed his hair. He might never have become an Ace Face (as
the kings of mod were termed), but his devotion to the lifestyle, for a short
while, was complete.

He was spending time at one of "Ma" Regan's venues, the Plaza Ballroom in Old Hill, spinning records as a prelude to shows by Little Stevie
Wonder, the Walker Brothers, the soaring Spencer Davis Group, and many
more. Some nights, too, the Crawling Kingsnakes found themselves on the
bill, playing a twenty-minute warm-up spot before the headliners appeared.
It was after one of these that Plant met John Bonham, the night the drummer declared that he was better than the hapless soul currently occupying
the drum stool. The Kingsnakes took him at his word, and for the few
weeks that Bonham remained on board, he was as good as his word as well.

Inky Watts quit in September 1965, to be replaced by one of the band's
old bassists, Maverick Oates, and with the formidable Bonzo on drums,
Kingsnakes rehearsals at the village hall in Clows Top became a barrage of
sound and energy. Gigs were drying up, though—or at least, not material-
izing as fast as Bonham would have liked. One show did pass into local
folklore: the night at the Ritz in King's Heath when Bonham decided the
fastest way to get his drum kit down the stairs to the van was to throw it. And
he was correct, as well.

But the group wasn't working enough for Bonham's tastes, or for his
budget. He quit to return to his last band, Way of Life, while the Crawling
Kingsnakes ground to a halt. (Plant would not forget them. Casting around
for a band name to credit with his 1985 contribution to the *Porky's Revenge!*
soundtrack, and now accompanied by Paul Martinez, Dave Edmunds, and
Phil Collins, Plant resurrected the Crawling Kingsnakes for a stupendous
"Philadelphia Baby.")

Like Bonham's tenure with the Crawling Kingsnakes, Plant's college days proved brief. On the "60s Memories" page of the Stourbridge.com website, fellow student Hilary Whitlock recalled, "I was at Kidderminster College when Robert Plant was there—he used to strum his guitar in the Common Room but, unfortunately, he didn't impress most people and was often told to 'shut up.' . . . He was also on the periphery of the Kidderminster 'in crowd'—we used to go to all-nighters in Birmingham. My one and only claim to fame is that I once fell off the back of his scooter (he was driving) in a Kidderminster car park."

Plant quit college after just a few months. But another job, working as a trainee chartered accountant for a firm in nearby Stourport, lasted no more than two weeks. He left when the Crawling Kingsnakes announced they were turning professional, and now that the band was no more, he needed to find another gig quickly.

The Tennessee Teens fit the bill. Guitarist John Crutchley, bassist Roger Beamer, and drummer Geoff Thompson were a three-piece whose renown and stamina had already earned them a residency at the Palette Club in Fulda, near Frankfurt in Germany—just one of the myriad British bands that followed in the footsteps of the Beatles and hightailed it across to the continent to play exhausting all-nighters for voracious local listeners. Sadly, that was as far as they were able to follow the Beatles, but back home their experience amplified their renown, and now they, too, were regulars at the Old Hill Plaza. Meaning, they were as familiar with Plant's style as he was with theirs.

Plant joined, and a short time later the Teens became Listen—around the same time as Plant's parents finally kicked him out of the house, figuring that if nothing else brought the boy to his senses, a spot of homelessness would. They were wrong. He simply moved into the bed and breakfast owned by his new bass player Roger Beamer's parents.

For all their foreign experience—which itself was not unusual at that time—back home, Listen were playing around the same live circuit as every other small band and drawing their repertoire from the same places, too: Frank Freeman's on Easter Sunday 1966, the Elbow Room, the Cedar

Club, and opening slots on Ma Regan's circuit. Plant introduced Chuck Berry and Solomon Burke (the ubiquitous "Everybody Needs Somebody to Love") to their set, while their mod credentials were slammed home right from the start, with Sam and Dave's "Hold On I'm Coming" opening the show, grabbing the audience from the outset.

Listen learned another lesson as well. Every band needs a gimmick, something that will draw people's attention to them in the first place and keep it focused thereafter. The quartet started out by rechristening themselves: bassist Beamer adopted the name "Chalky," drummer Thompson was "Jumbo," guitarist Crutchley, somewhat unimaginatively, became "Crutch," and Plant became "Plonky." For good measure, Plant announced that he had recently won a dance competition in which Cathy McGowan was one of the judges — McGowan being the fabulously coiffured hostess of television's *Ready Steady Go!* and, as such, the focal point for an entire generation of youthful attention. If Cathy said something was good, the chances were that it would be. Even if it was just Plonky's dance steps.

But there was more. When the local *Express and Star* newspaper caught wind of the rumor and sent columnist John Ogden out to meet the band, Plonky told him that Listen had already been invited to appear on *Ready Steady Go!* but turned it down because it clashed with another engagement. As tall stories go, that was a colossus, but there it was in black and white, and even that was just the start.

Eyeing up another local band, the Move — whose stage show had recently evolved to include such niceties as smoke bombs, axes, and the demolition of a television set — Listen choreographed a short fight scene into their performance, Plonky and Crutch going hammer and tongs until the bouncers stepped in to break it up. They borrowed the bigger band's sartorial style too: double-breasted suits that loaned a certain gangster chic to their look. And soon, they'd fix their aim on the Move's manager as well. But not just yet.

Other bands on the circuit, too, were paying attention. The N'Betweens, the Wolverhampton crew that would soon become Slade, even considered asking Plant to become their own singer, and that despite the presence already in their ranks of Noddy Holder—destined to become the growling, gravelly bellow of '70s UK chart fame. Slade would rack up five years of unstoppable British hits once the new decade got underway, all of them powered by Holder's distinctive holler. It seems incredible that his bandmates ever considered retiring that voice, but they did, and Robert Plant was their chosen successor.

How the history of rock would have changed had this happened. But it didn't. "We were just four young kids with a local following in the Black Country," Holder told the teenybop magazine *Petticoat* in the early 1970s. "I remember one gig at the City Hall where we played with a local group called Listen, who had as their lead vocalist a certain Robert Plant. At that time, I used to help out Robert and the band by getting my old man to lend them his window cleaning van when their transport broke down."

Writing his autobiography decades later, remembering the palace coup that considered relegating him to backing vocals, Holder continued, "There weren't many good singers around at the time who would have suited our style of music. Robert . . . was one of the names mentioned. The others didn't know him, but I did. I don't know if anyone ever actually approached [him], but he was certainly one of only two or three names in the frame."

Had Plant been asked, he'd probably have said yes. With no disrespect whatsoever to his bandmates, his eye was always focused on the next rung of the ladder; he was always searching for the next chance to improve himself. He had no choice. Among the promises he made to Maureen once they started dating seriously was the pledge to remain in the music business until his twentieth birthday. If he hadn't made it by then, he'd give up.

Plus, he had a lot of balls. On May 5, 1966, the Who appeared at Kidderminster Town Hall as a three-piece, with guitarist Pete Townshend handling lead vocals. Quickly, the word went around that Roger Daltrey had quit the band—circulating the venue without the necessary caveat that *someone* was always quitting the band, and tonight was simply Daltrey's turn. He'd be back the following day, for a show in Lisburn, Northern Ireland, and a couple of weeks later, somebody else would walk out—

drummer Keith Moon, on this occasion, to discuss forming a band with his friends Jeff Beck and Jimmy Page. They jokingly declared they would name it "Lead Zeppelin"—because that is what it would go down like.

Neither Plant nor another local frontman, Steve Gibbons, were at all familiar with the innermost workings and dynamics of the Who, however; they didn't understand that one of the things that kept the group going was the knowledge that it could all come to a halt at any moment. As Townshend discovered when the stage door opened at the end of the show. He recalled a few years later what followed, in an interview with *Musician* magazine: "Robert Plant talks about the fact that when he first saw us, I was the singer. He came to see us and offered himself for the job, as did Steve Gibbons when he came to see us. Obviously, none of them thought I was any good."

Politely, Townshend declined the offers, and so Listen gigged on, their ambitions still soaring, and occasionally snatching a golden ring of sorts.

On October 20, 1966, Listen were booked to open for Cream at the Youth Club in Willenhall St. Giles. The N'Betweens and the Factotums, a Manchester band that had already come to the attention of Rolling Stones manager Andrew Loog Oldham, were also on the bill, and history now stares open-mouthed at the menu. Even Live Aid, twenty years later, could scarcely compete with a bill that placed Robert Plant, Eric Clapton, Jack Bruce, Ginger Baker, Noddy Holder, Jimmy Lea, Dave Hill, and Don Powell all on the same stage.

Which doesn't alter the fact that most people present really only wanted to see Cream.

The supergroup trio of Eric Clapton, Jack Bruce, and Ginger Baker had only launched a few months earlier; they were touring now on the back of a debut single, "Wrapping Paper," that all three admitted had little to do with what the band was all about. A low-key tour of even lower-key venues was their opportunity to explain what they meant by that.

Noddy Holder: "We were all on the same bill as the Cream that night, who apart from Clapton were unknown. Robert [Plant] used to like to move about the stage a lot even in those days before he joined Led Zeppelin. Unfortunately, Ginger Baker had a huge drum kit which was spread all over the stage—drums everywhere—I remember Robert very timidly going up to Ginger and asking him if he would mind moving some of his kit off the stage."

Baker refused, and he doubtless cracked a smile when Plant and Crutchley went into their fight routine and disappeared over the edge of the tightly packed stage. When Plant reappeared, he had sustained a broken ankle.

By now Listen had a manager, Mike Dolan. Owner of a local tailoring concern, in an age when, for many bands, a manager simply meant somebody who had the money to keep them on the road, music-business experience not essential, Dolan did succeed in landing the band an agency deal. Their horizons expanded accordingly. No longer were they confined to the Black Country gig circuit. Packed into a van they got from Ma Regan, Listen played venues all over the UK, deep into the South West, far into the North East, and all points in between. Their average fee of £15 a night, to be spread between four band members and their driver, Eddie, wasn't spectacular, particularly once fuel and food entered the equation, but it wasn't bad for the time, and the band was happy enough. Even happier after Dolan financed a trip to a local recording studio, where Listen banged out a three-song demo, which Dolan duly mailed around the record labels—and was rewarded with a three-single deal with CBS.

Again in keeping with the mood of the times, the powers that be cared only for making the best record possible. The feelings of the musicians whose names may or may not have been on that record were utterly immaterial. Playing the demo, producer Danny Kessler decided that the only truly remarkable thing about Listen was their singer. Therefore, Plant alone was required in the studio; his bandmates would be replaced with session men; and again, no matter how mistreated Crutch, Jumbo, and Chalky may have felt, no way had they been personally singled out for the ignominy.

Even the Love Affair, "Everlasting Love" hitmakers a couple of years later, were left at home while frontman Steve Ellis alone voiced the song that would make them stars. Other top acts of the day, Herman's Hermits included, essentially existed as two separate bands: there were the four guys who accompanied singer Peter Noone on stage and promo photographs,

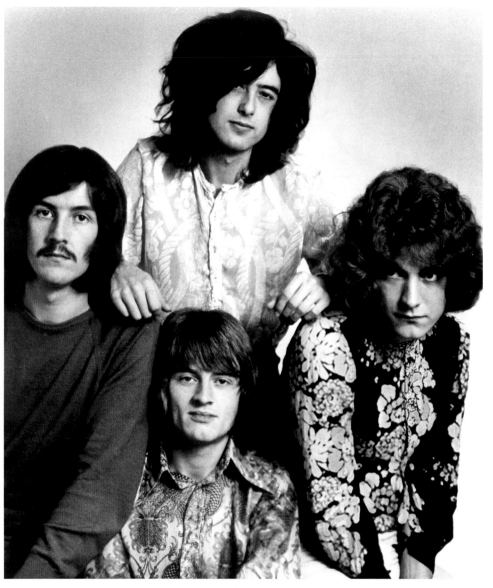

The classic Led Zeppelin look, 1968. *Clockwise from left:* John Bonham, Jimmy Page, Robert Plant, and John Paul Jones. (Photofest)

Plant singing with Zeppelin in the '70s, and baring the chest that launched a thousand flashbulbs. (Photofest)

Jimmy Page reaches for the heavens, 1973. (Photofest)

Bonzo, the wild man of rock. (Photofest)

John Paul Jones, characteristically serene. (Photofest)

Bo Diddley in the 1960s — the meanest, peachy-keen-est guitar-toting gunslinger there ever was. Seeing him changed Plant's outlook on music. (Photofest)

Jeff Beck, one of Led Zeppe-lin's earliest supporters. (Epic Records/Photofest)

Atlantic Records founder
and Zeppelin's greatest
cheerleader, the immortal
Ahmet Ertegun.
(Photofest)

(*Left to right*) John Paul Jones, Peter Grant, Robert Plant, and Jimmy Page pick up Zeppelin's award
for Outstanding Contribution to British Music at the May 1977 Ivor Novello Awards in London.
(Trinity Mirror/Mirrorpix/Alamy)

Plant and Page at their combined peak,
in 1973. (Photofest)

Plant with Zeppelin in
the great outdoors.
(Photofest)

September 1970: *Melody Maker*'s Best Male and Female Vocalists of the Year—Robert Plant and Sandy Denny—share a hug. (Trinity Mirror/Mirrorpix/Alamy)

With manager Peter Grant (*top left*) and Atlantic Records' Jerry Wexler (*top right*), Zeppelin reap their first precious metal awards, circa 1969. (Photofest)

Plant sporting a notorious T-shirt at Zeppelin's penultimate US concert—July 23, 1977, at the Alameda County Coliseum in Oakland, California. (Photofest)

and there was the coterie of session men, unknown names like Jimmy Page and John Paul Jones, who played on the actual records. You could make a tidy living from session work in those days, and a lot of players did. And they didn't care whose name was on the label.

No record seems to exist of who accompanied Robert Plant on his first-ever vinyl sojourn, although he did recall singers Lesley Duncan and Kiki Dee being among the backing chorus, and drummer Clem Cattini was certainly there as well. None of which served to deaden the growing sense of nervousness that was suddenly consuming the young singer. His entire career, he suddenly realized, had so far been devoted to convincing people that he had something to offer. Now, walking into the studio, seeing the musicians, singers, and engineers who had been gathered in his name, he knew that it was time to deliver. "To squawk my way through these things was incredibly tense," he told *Tracks* magazine in 2004.

Not that it mattered how he felt. Listen's debut single was a Young Rascals song called "You Better Run," and all concerned made a decent stab at it. Unfortunately, on the other side of London at more or less the exact same time, the N'Betweens were doing an equally good job of the same song themselves, for release as their first single. And when their respective labels, CBS and Columbia, got wind of the coincidence, they did the only thing they could. They scheduled the two singles for release on the same day, then sat back to await a Black Country civil war.

The N'Betweens won, at least according to Noddy Holder. "It actually went to number one in the midlands, because we had a name there and our fans knew the song from our live show." And possibly because it was the superior version, the combination of the full N'Betweens line-up and maverick American producer Kim Fowley was always going to sound more alive than a nervous Plonky in a room full of strangers, singing to an arrangement he'd only just been played. Listen's single scraped the local Top 50 for a week and then disappeared.

As did Listen. Manager Dolan had spent a considerable sum of money on them, not least of all in his attempts to win the Battle of the Covers, and the band was both deep in debt and out of breath. Only Plant had the wherewithal to carry on; moving out of the bed and breakfast and into the spare room at Maureen's parents' house, he also had the CBS deal to fall back on, as it became apparent that A&R man Danny Kessler had only wanted the singer in the first place. He had no interest in Plant the blues-man, Plant the soul singer, or Plant the mod either. As 1966 turned into 1967, and the youth of the day started turning onto the psychedelic sounds of the London and San Francisco undergrounds, Britain's record industry knew precisely what they needed to hear next: good, old fashioned, big-voiced balladeers.

Tom Jones was already soaring; Scott Walker of the Walker Brothers was preparing to do likewise. Even the extraordinarily unlikely name of Engelbert Humperdinck was girding his loins for stardom, not only climb-ing to No. 1 with the impassioned bellow of "Release Me," but also becom-ing the first person since 1962 to prevent a new Beatles single, "Strawberry Fields Forever," from topping the chart.

So yeah. The kids might pretend they liked all this far-out hippy music. But when it came to buying records, they wanted something with class and gravitas. Something like "La Musica è Finita," a recent Italian chart topper that would most logically have been retitled "The Music Is Finished" for an English-language release, but instead became "Our Song," a strings-and-syrup-laden production over which Plant draped his most impassioned (and surprisingly pleasing) vocal. Plant's personal choice for his sophomore single, a cover of "Incense" by the Anglos, was thrown unconsidered (and unrecorded) to one side.

By the standards of the time, and the ilk to which it conformed, "Our Song" really isn't a bad record—or a bad performance. But the *Express & Star* review condemned it as "a waste of a fine soul singer," and Plant is alleged to have claimed it took him ninety takes, and at least one bout of tears, before he delivered a vocal that met publisher Eddie Kassner and producer Kessler's satisfaction. And after all that, "Our Song" sold less than a thousand copies, and disappeared even faster than "You Better Run."

For all his studied disdain for this new musical direction, however, and despite his own suspicion that maybe the labels were wrong about the way the musical wind was blowing, Plant did indeed see some sense to Kessler's insistence that he was born a balladeer. There was, after all, very little call for rock 'n' roll styled soloists at that time; from Cliff Richard to Barry Ryan, from Scott Walker to P. J. Proby, and onto the Joneses and Humperdincks, the image of the successful solo singer was that of a besuited gentleman, trendy but respectable, aching and breaking his heart across lovelorn tear-jerker after soul-baring confessional.

Even if we employ great lashings of hindsight and look at the solo singers who emerged in the early 1970s at the helm of the glam rock explosion, we find David Bowie, David Essex, and even the primal stomp of Gary Glitter wrapping their late '60s tonsils around the majestic swell of big ballad pop.

Farewell, then, Robert A. Plant. Hello, Robert "The E Is Silent" Lee, cabaret hopeful extraordinaire. Next stop, the Tony Billingham Big Band.

It didn't last. Plant would cut one final single for CBS, "Long Time Coming," which was a very short time going, and he played a handful of live shows with the Big Band, taking the stage in his suit and bouffant and really trying to squeeze himself into the respectable confines of a jazzy dance band.

Even his parents applauded his efforts; in fact, it was Plant Sr. who made the introductions in the first place, after being commissioned to do some work on Billingham's home. But neither audiences nor Plant's new-found bandmates ever took to the rocking square peg in their well-oiled round hole, and by spring 1967, even before his final CBS single was released, Plant was letting his hair grow down and out once more and putting together a new band.

One of Maureen's cousins, Vernon Pereira, came in on guitar; organist Chris Brown introduced both keyboards and a band manager, his father; and Robert Plant and the Band of Joy set sail on the lysergic seas of the Summer of Love. For Plant had been right and the record labels wrong. The freaks and hippies were taking over, dividing the pop charts between their sounds and the oldsters but making statements that traveled far beyond the "farewell my lovelies" of the Engelbert set.

Pink Floyd, Jimi Hendrix, the Move, Cream—and Traffic, spawned from the self-same Black Country clubs that Plant frequented, bringing psychedelic stardom to Chris Wood and Steve Winwood—these bands were the vanguard now, while across the seas a similar wave was building: Jefferson Airplane, Buffalo Springfield, the Grateful Dead, Moby Grape, Love. And Plant fell for it big time. "All that music from the West Coast just went bang!" he told *Melody Maker* three years later, "and there was nothing else there for me after that. Three years before I had been shuddering listening to Sonny Boy Williamson. Now I was sobbing to Arthur Lee."

Kidderminster College student Abdul Benson, keyboard player with another local band, Custard Tree, pieced together a psychedelic light show for the band, the first in the town. Every rehearsal found them getting to grips with a host of favorite covers, delving into albums that all their audience seemed to know by artists who might never visit the Black Country in person, and piecing together a set that doubled as the American West Coast's greatest hits. Moby Grape, Love, and the Airplane were firm Plant favorites, and when the band wasn't gigging, he'd be back home on Trinity Road with Maureen, listening to DJ John Peel's *Perfumed Garden* hissing over the waters from pirate Radio London, and educating a devoted late-night listenership in the best of the psychedelic underground.

Soon Peel himself was appearing in Kidderminster, playing Sunday-night DJ shows at Frank Freeman's, and often accompanied by some artist or other whom he had taken under his wing: Tyrannosaurus Rex on Easter Sunday 1968; Captain Beefheart on May 19, an evening immortalized by a snatch of conversation between the DJ and the Captain. Peel was asked what the venue was called.

"Frank Freeman's Dance Club," answered Peel.

"What a groovy name!" said Beefheart.

"No, it's not groovy at all," replied Peel. "It's a dance club run by a man named Frank Freeman."

Plant was there every night he could be, or sending friends along if he was gigging elsewhere, with instructions to report back on every record Peel played.

Meanwhile, the Band of Joy was working regularly, graduating from opening slots behind Denny Laine's Electric String Band to headlining appearances of their own, the band coming out onstage in kaftans and beads, bangles and flowers—archetypal hippies playing the music that all believed would one day change the world.

But Plant was also warring with the band's manager (the keyboard player's dad), and Band of Joy was clearly not long for the world. The group sacked its singer, much to his utter bemusement, and the only people who thought of Rob Plant as a rock star were the guys on the construction team that he now found himself working with, laying tarmac on West Bromwich High Street. They rechristened him "The Pop Singer."

He was not going to give up, though. Plant formed a new Band of Joy even as the old one continued on through its death throes, brought Listen's old manager Mike Dolan in to handle their affairs, and immediately found himself involved in a stunt that would make everybody in the region sit up and play attention. Or so they thought.

Tootling around in his old Ford Popular one day, Plant was hauled over by the police on a charge of dangerous driving. A court date was set, August 10 at Wednesbury Court, and Dolan thought it would be a great idea for Plant to arrive at the court not as a contrite motorist come to take his medicine but as the focal point of a massive Legalize Pot rally.

The wheels were set in motion immediately, the pair of them speculating upon how many hundreds of like-minded hairies they could rely upon to follow Plant to the halls of justice. Upon the signs they would carry and the slogans they would chant. Upon the shock and awe that would register on the faces of the straights who sat in judgment on a generation, in court and on the high street.

Then the great day dawned . . . and seven people showed up. Including, mused a brief passage in the *Express & Star*, "two girls in mini skirts," a nurse named Dorette, and Maureen's younger sister Shirley. And just to hammer in one final ignominious nail, any thoughts Plant and Dolan might have entertained of the judiciary cracking down hard on the dope-smoking cancer in their midst were shattered when Plant was cleared of the motoring charge as well.

Home for Plant now was a crumbling house on Hill Road in the small town of Lye, near Stourbridge. There, he and a small crowd of other waifs and strays, many of them impoverished students from the college down the road, lived in a state of communal disrepair, every room given over to whichever pleasures its occupant deemed most suitable, while the basement was converted to a rehearsal studio for the Band of Joy. Wherein a not-yet-permanent lineup of musicians would experiment both musically and visually, transforming the old Band of Joy imagery into full-blown tribal performance art by painting their faces and unleashing wild choreography.

"It frightened everybody to death," Plant told *Melody Maker*. "This big, fat bass player would come running on, wearing a kaftan and bells, and dive straight off the stage and into the audience. I howled so much that I couldn't do anything at all." Not even object as that bassist left, to be replaced by the original group's Paul Lockey.

Chris Brown, presumably free of his managerial parent, was likewise lured back; so was Bonzo Bonham. But the real coup was when Plant recruited Kevyn Gammond, once of the Sunsetters, but more recently playing with Shakedown Sound, and gigging with reggae star Jimmy Cliff too. As much as Plant's vocals and Bonham's already-characteristic bombardment, Gammond's guitar would become a Band of Joy trademark, while his local renown exceeded that of any of his bandmates.

Jimmy Cliff was still a few years away from chart success at the time; brought to the UK in mid-1966 by Island Records' Chris Blackwell, his greatest renown was among the West Indian community—one of whose prime focal points was the Birmingham suburb of Handsworth. Gammond and Shakedown Sound drummer Sean Jenkins were both recruited to his band on the strength of an audition in summer 1966, but it turned out that Cliff had already seen them play, at a Shakedown Sound show in Birmingham, and author John Combe declares, "Kevyn's rasping, chopping guitar style worked well" with Cliff's own music.

Somewhat mischievously, Chris Townson, drummer with the London band John's Children, recalled Cliff's stage act. The two bands gigged together at the Bus Pavilion in Paris in May 1967. "His act used to start with him coming onto a totally darkened stage, the only light would be an ultraviolet one stuck up on the ceiling. And he used to dress completely in black, apart from these white plimsolls, so all you could see would be these plimsolls come hopping across the stage. We [John's Children] always used to sit up the front and kill ourselves laughing at it; we wanted to run on and introduce the 'Fabulous Dancing Plimsolls,' but we'd be laughing so much that we couldn't move by the time they appeared."

Plant first encountered Cliff, Gammond, and Co. when the original Band of Joy opened for them at the Black Horse that same month, May 1967 — and again at the Adelphi in West Bromwich a couple of months later. Where his enthusiasm for a fresh lineup of the band, and what Gammond recalls as his "dreams of utopia," were enough to convince the guitarist to quit Jimmy Cliff in October 1967 and throw in with this new band as soon as they returned from a short Scottish tour.

The new-look Band of Joy launched into a spell of vivid visibility. Locally, they were regulars at the Chateau Impney in Droitwich and the Black Horse in Kidderminster.

Christmas saw Band of Joy play the end-of-term dance at Kidderminster College, opening for Plant's old friends Tony Billingham's Dance Band, although neither act seemed to impress the students too much, at least if the local paper's "On The Inside" column's review was anything to judge by. As John Combe recollected, "Nobody wanted to know" about Billingham's set, while Band of Joy "were hardly the kind of group you wanted to dance to with their West Coast 'progressive rock.'"

They visited London, playing the legendary Middle Earth in Covent Garden on January 26, 1968, and experiencing for themselves one of the centers of the city's psychedelic scene, and back in Kidderminster they became regulars at Frank Freeman's Dance Club, where the nightly diet of soul and blue-beat deejaying kept Plant entertained even when he wasn't gigging.

In late February 1968, Band of Joy auditioned as the backup band for Tim Rose, the American folkie whose song "Morning Dew" was in the repertoire of seemingly every blues band in the country, and who had also popularized "Hey Joe," the song that gave Jimi Hendrix his first hit and that likewise was ubiquitous around the UK live scene. A countrywide tour followed, and an even more prestigious London show; on February 23, 1968, the Marquee shook, first to Rose's Band of Joy–fueled set, and then to the heavy blues majesty of Aynsley Dunbar's Retaliation. Another of those nights for future historians to conjure with, two of the era's greatest drummers playing together in the same tiny room. "Live performances were at once magical and disastrous," Plant reflected later, in the liner notes for *Sixty Six to Timbuktu*. "Always edgy and far out." The group would have been far better suited to the streets of Haight-Ashbury, he insisted, "than the Top Rank Ballroom in Sunderland."

"Hey Joe" was also one of the songs that Band of Joy took into the studio when Mike Dolan booked them a session at London's Regent Sound Studios to cut a demo tape. It was joined by another of their live staples, Buffalo Springfield's "For What It's Worth," and a couple of the band's own compositions, "Memory Lane" and "Adriatic Seaview." Both of which were so unremarkable that when Plant returned to the demo for his *Sixty Six to Timbuktu* anthology in 2003, he completely ignored their existence.

So did CBS, to whom Plant was still nominally contracted, and the remainder of the music business was likewise nonplussed. There was just one ray of sunshine. Dolan wrangled the band a residency at the Speakeasy, one of the industry's prime late-night watering holes, knowing that if Band of Joy were ever to be "discovered," that was where it was likely to happen.

And so it transpired. One evening as the band cooled down in the dressing room following their set, the door opened and in strode Alexis Korner, one of that select handful of British bluesmen who could truly claim to have midwifed the national scene. He'd never broken through himself; rather, he existed in the shadows, a name that everybody seemed to know and admire but who was neither destined for nor especially interested in stardom. Tonight, all he wanted to do was say hello, to let the band know how much he enjoyed their performance, and he told them to return the favor the next time he played in Birmingham. They said they would, and off he went.

That was the extent of Band of Joy's big-city exposure. They went back to Birmingham, no better off than when they left, and when Tim Rose came calling once again, asking if he could borrow Bonham for his next set of dates, the band knew it could only speed downhill from there. John Trickett, drummer with the Walsall-based band the Answer, replaced him on a "when available" basis, but clearly the joy had leaked out of the band.

The final straw came on the road. Throughout the band's career, booker Barry Dickens at the Malcolm Rose Agency thought nothing of scheduling shows at completely opposite ends of the country—Exeter one night, somewhere in Scotland the next. The band thought nothing of fulfilling them either. At least until the night Gammond quit, midway through that very same journey, simply getting out of the van as it passed through Kidderminster and going home.

Gammond went onto a new band, Mad Dog, which ultimately morphed into Bronco, a virtual Shakedown Sound reunion with Jess Roden and Johnny Pasternak plus the Accelerators' Robbie Blunt. The Band of Joy, meanwhile, played out their scheduled Scottish show without him, replaced him with Mickey Strode for a handful more gigs, and then folded.

Again, Plant returned to civilian life. He picked up another job in the construction industry, Maureen was pregnant, and his twentieth birthday was just three months away. His time was almost up.

7

Promised Land
(1984–1985)

Three months is a long time when you're nineteen and counting down to zero on what's left of your ambition. It's a lot less time when you're thirty-five and counting down the last days of what now passes for a regular life before boarding the musical treadmill once again.

Not that Plant was complaining. Financially he had long since passed the point where he needed to work to maintain his lifestyle, and creatively he knew there remained a lot more juice in the tank. But still, when he and the band came off in the road in February 1984, following a massively oversubscribed Japanese tour, it was with the knowledge that the next three months, at least, were his. His to waste, his to fritter, his to do whatever he wanted with. It was only the outside world that had any kind of problem with what happened next, as ex-wife Maureen's younger sister Shirley, hitherto married to Plant's farm manager John Bryant, moved out of one house on the Jennings Farm estate and into another one. With Plant.

In some ways, the apparent shift of Plant's affections from one sister to another was a case of wish fulfillment for a lot of people — particularly those who reported lasciviously on Plant's sexual appetite when Zeppelin were on the road and wondered how he kept it in check when he was home with the family. As Paul Rees, author of the biography *Robert Plant: A Life*, delicately puts it, "Led Zeppelin insiders had been gossiping about Plant and the Wilson sisters for years." Plant's own inner circle, meanwhile, simply accepted the couple's love as the inevitable consequence of a closeness that had been developing for so long, particularly as Plant's marriage to Maureen slowly collapsed.

Like Maureen, Shirley had known Plant since their teens; the affection between them was as deep-seated as any twenty-year friendship can be. Shirley and her husband lived on the farm; the two couples were always in one another's orbit, and when Plant needed to talk as he and Maureen drew apart, it was natural he would turn to the only other person who knew her as well as he did. Maureen herself seemed to accept the situation, eventually moving back to Jennings Farm with the children, while Shirley's husband continued working there for a time as well.

In fact, as field days for spiteful tattletales go, the torrid tangle of Robert Plant's love life was really something of a nonstarter. Although you do have to love the comment made by an anonymous Zeppelin roadie, again in the Paul Rees biography: "When you've seen Robert shagging his way through 16,000 women, there's nothing very shocking about another, whoever it is."

In fact, for many people, and Plant's fan club can be included here, the biggest surprise he had in store that year had nothing to do with his domestic arrangements. It was his decision that May to enter the studio with Tim Palmer, an engineer whose only prior experience of any major note was among the studio team responsible for Kajagoogoo's "Too Shy." At a time, it should be added, before bassist Nick Beggs became an icon of the modern prog rock scene and when singer Limahl was best regarded for an almost painfully fashionable haircut. Stints in the studio with electro-maven John Foxx; Dire Straits frontman Mark Knopfler, as he worked up the soundtrack to the movie *Local Hero*; and most recently, gender-bending dance sensation Dead or Alive lurked elsewhere on Palmer's resume, and he was as shocked as anyone when the call came in from Plant.

But Plant knew what he was doing. Among the albums bending his ears that spring was the latest by Depeche Mode, popularly dismissed by the rock cognoscenti as a bunch of synthesized sillies who wouldn't know a rock guitar if you wired one into their brains. But move beyond the self-conscious daftness of Depeche's pop-television appearances and the deceptive confections they put out as singles, and behind all that was a band whose grasp on modern technology, whose ear for sounds and eye for ef-fects, pushed them to the forefront of sonic possibilities, at least within the framework of modern music.

Some Great Reward, Depeche's latest album, arrived bristling with a metallic attack that nobody had ever applied to mere pop in the past—and that is "metal" in a literary sense. Half of the album appeared to have been recorded without resort to even unconventional musical instruments, just sheets of iron being pounded with hammers. Plant was impressed.

Even his choice of studio, Marcus Studios in Bayswater, West London, spoke toward his outlook. Small and intimate, it was a far cry from the historically steeped environments in which Plant customarily functioned. The Smiths, all but unknown at that time, were among the studio's im-mediate clientele; Tubeway Army, Fashion, and Classix Nouveaux ranked among its most storied.

There were fewer surprises among the lineup he selected to accom-pany him on this latest adventure. Richie Hayward, once of Little Feat, was planted on the unsettled drum stool, and a teenaged backing singer, Toni Halliday, joined the gang too. But the meat and potatoes of a functioning rock band seemed less of interest to Plant than the possibilities of the new technology, as Hayward was presented with an electronic kit, and his own ears seemed attuned only to the fresh keyboard sounds that Palmer and Woodroffe were conspiring to create. Without anybody saying as much, it was becoming increasingly clear that neither Blunt nor Martinez would be around much longer, even after the sessions moved back to the familiar pastures of Rockfield.

Shaken 'n' Stirred, Robert Plant's third solo album, would not ultimate-ly see release for another year, by which time cynical ears could complain that some of its more cutting-edge notions had already been dated by the ever-increasing pace of studio technology. It is a sad but true fact that much of the music made during the 1980s by artists poised, or reaching, for the outer limits of what was possible was ultimately granted a far more finite life expectancy than records (or increasingly, CDs) recorded using the tried-and-tested tools of old.

But Plant remained unrepentant. It was vital, he believed, to escape the typical trappings of what passed for "rock 'n' roll." He wanted to capture the mood of the moment, and the wild adventure of surfing technology wherever it might take him. Whether or not his traditional core audience would appreciate that adventure was to remain undecided for now, however. In the meantime, Plant had another project to undertake, and one that, if he was perhaps totally honest with himself, said far more about his personal musical tastes than any number of electro beats and rhythms.

"The reason Ahmet [Ertegun] asked him to reinvent the Honeydrippers was to try and persuade him to go back to basics," Peter Grant alleged. "Everybody at Atlantic felt he was trying too hard to remain competitive with everything else that was going on in the charts, and while that was good for short-term success, hit singles, and MTV, it was damaging his long term credibility."

Plant was in Japan when Ertegun first suggested he turn his hand to an album of oldies: '50s American covers bashed out with the most kick-ass rock 'n' roll band he could muster. Plant was intrigued, perhaps all the more so as he knew that had he floated the same idea back in 1981, he would probably have been howled out of the room. But the Honeydrippers tour was a cherished memory now, and the possibility of reconvening the band name, if not the musicians, was certainly tempting. Particularly as pre-production of the new studio album marched on, and Plant realized it would probably take as long as the actual recording had.

Not one of the original Honeydrippers would ultimately be involved, not even Robbie Blunt. Instead, Plant flew to New York where Jimmy Page, Jeff Beck, Chic's Nile Rodgers, Paul Shaffer, and a crack local rhythm section of Wayne Pedziwiatr and Dave Weckl awaited him at Atlantic's own studio. Ahmet Ertegun was producer, and that was a large part of why Plant agreed to do it. For all the years that he and Ertegun had worked together, Plant had never experienced the man's studio expertise. This was his chance.

The first decision was that they were not aiming for a full album, but rather a mini-album, bigger than an EP, smaller than an LP. Five songs were settled on, including Plant's mother's favorite, "Sea of Love." Ray Charles's "I Got a Woman," Ben E. King's "Young Boy Blues," Roy Brown's "Rockin' at Midnight," and Wynonie Harris's "I Got a Thrill" completed the menu, a decade's worth of American rockers that were bashed out in barely more time than it took to play them, and rushed out in not much longer. Raw and raucous, frantic and febrile, any one of the songs could have been kicked out at any time in the past thirty years and would not have sounded at all out of place.

Back in the day, Led Zeppelin had frequently relaxed during sound-check or rehearsal by blasting through a handful or two of favorite old-ies—songs that they'd grown up with, that were musical mother's milk to them all. Chuck Berry, Gene Vincent, Johnny Kidd and the Pirates, Cliff Richard and the Shadows. Bootlegs of these moments of carefree un-self-consciousness rank among the most precious, and revealing, of all Led Zeppelin recordings, because they *are* un-self-conscious, four musicians simply playing for themselves, laughing at their mistakes, helping one another past forgotten chords and lyrics, just throwing themselves back to a simpler, easier, time.

These latest sessions were not *that* relaxed. The performances needed to be honest, but they couldn't be slapdash, and so a few takes of each song would be hammered down, and then the best ones pulled out for the final disc. But still they remained as brash as they needed to be.

The Honeydrippers Volume One, wryly titled in the firm knowledge there would never be a volume two, was in the stores by November 1984, spun off a Top 5 single in "Sea of Love," and maybe, just maybe, reac-quainted old fans with the Robert Plant they thought they might be losing. The still-unheard *Shaken 'n' Stirred* would probably have dispatched such fans screaming to the hills. In fact, maybe it did anyway.

The first reviews of *Shaken* were enthusiastic, though, and the passage of time did not dent the sheer shock with which the needle hit plastic for the first time. The opening "Hip to Hoo" faded in on dissonant shadows and the sound of a party in a far distant room before melding into a percussive thump that echoed around Plant's impulsive vocal; "Trouble Your Money," with its foreboding bass line and finger-popping rhythm, could have been a Bryan Ferry masterpiece, and was sharp and current as Christmas.

Writing in *Creem* three years later, Chuck Eddy still described *Shaken 'n' Stirred* as Plant's best LP yet, the repository of "some of the most structurally outlandish commercially successful white rock this decade. The second side had nods to the Human Beinz and the Police, plus a creepy hit single . . . ; the first side was mainly abstract soundscapes with bizarro changes, stutters, skids, and added-and-subtracted-tracks."

By the time he reached "Too Loud," Eddy was seeking comparisons as far afield as Afrika Bambaataa "and certain Mark Stewart and the Maffia obscurities"—names that themselves would have been hopelessly obscure to the people who normally bought a Robert Plant album. But he did so for a reason. Mostly, Eddy decreed, *Shaken 'n' Stirred* was the sound of Plant "making some kind of music that doesn't have a name yet."

As if to compensate, circling musical psychologists zeroed in on lyrical fragments to try and haul something recognizable from there. Chuck Eddy suggested that "creepy" hit single ("Little by Little") was possibly about the death of Zeppelin; others posited one final eulogy for either John Bonham or son Karac. The cavernous "Pink and Black" may have been the final resolution of a reformed sexual gadfly (and would have made a great Robert Palmer single); the album as a whole, some even suggested, was so splintered and contradictory that it could only have been a reflection of Plant's own mental state.

This was a colossally presumptuous charge to lay at either artist or album's doorstep. Perhaps the recent transitions of Plant's love life did strike some people as unconventional; maybe they did add credence to a decade-old legend that the song "What Is and What Should Never Be" was about an already-thriving relationship with his sister-in-law. But that was scarcely Plant's concern, or any kind of scar on his happiness either—he and Shirley would remain together for close to the next decade and have a child together, Jesse Lee, in 1991.

Perhaps, too, the contradictory nature of his last two releases, one primal rock 'n' roll, the other startling sonic trickery, suggested some kind of conflict within his own musical intentions. But more than likely it didn't, and Plant's explanation for *The Honeydrippers Volume One*, that it was a piece of fun arrived at after laying a wager with Ahmet Ertegun in a Tokyo hot tub one night, really should be taken at face value. What could not be denied was that by following his own musical instincts and apparently trusting his audience to either follow or abandon him, Plant had finally succeeded in convincing them to take the latter course.

It is utterly absurd to describe *Shaken 'n' Stirred* as a failure, as many chroniclers have. The album itself reached No. 20 in the US; "Little by Little" topped *Billboard*'s Mainstream Rock Track chart. But total sales were less than half of either of the album's predecessors, while a thirty-date arena tour set to run through summer 1985 became Plant's first not to sell out weeks in advance—or even sell out at all. In many cities, venues were still offering plenty of good seats on the night of the show, and while reviews of the evening's entertainment tended toward the ecstatic, tickets didn't move any faster as a consequence.

This was a shame, because it was a great show. On a stage decorated by inflatable Cadillacs, and with Honeydrippers fans catered for by a short set of that band's material too, Plant was ring-mastering a performance that was at least the equal of any other on the road that season. *Almost* any other, at least. There was one event on the horizon with which nobody on the road that summer could reasonably hope to compete, and the only consolation for any of them was that most of them were taking part in it.

Live Aid was the culmination of seven months' desperate work by Bob Geldof, once best known as the garrulous frontman for midstream Irish new wavers the Boomtown Rats, but now cruising towards canonization as the Blessed Bob, Patron Saint of the Ethiopian Famine. Watching a TV report on that disaster late in 1984, Geldof was moved to call together the cream of current British popdom to perform a fundraising single: "Do They Know It's Christmas?"

It promptly became the fastest and biggest-selling single in British history, and was followed in America by the similarly inspired, similarly all-star "We Are the World." What followed, however, made the logistical tangle of making those singles happen look like booking a one-man band: two stadiums, in London and Philadelphia, simultaneously hosting the vastest one-day rock concerts of all time, and rounding up the great and good from every generation in sight. Bob Dylan, Paul McCartney, Bryan Ferry, Mick Jagger, David Bowie, Paul Young, Madonna, the Thompson Twins—superstar followed superstar onto the bill, and that was the easy part. Because next, Geldof started to alchemize the impossible.

He convinced Black Sabbath to re-form with Ozzy Osbourne for the first time since a gruesomely acrimonious split at the end of the 1970s. He arranged for Phil Collins to appear onstage on two continents in the same afternoon; he got the Who back onstage, four years after their Farewell tour; he reunited Crosby, Stills, Nash & Young . . . and barely had he asked Robert Plant if he'd perform than Jimmy Page and John Paul Jones were on board as well.

With Phil Collins and Chic's Tony Thompson sharing drum duties, and Paul Martinez playing bass to allow Jones to concentrate on keyboards, it would be unfair to describe Live Aid as a true Led Zeppelin reunion. But the core trio seemed to treat it as such, and with time to perform just three songs, there were few surprises as to what they'd be: "Rock and Roll," "Whole Lotta Love," and "Stairway to Heaven."

And it was . . . *awful* is far too strong a word, although that is Robert Plant's chosen adjective. He told *Details'* Danny Fields, "Live Aid was awful, I mean for *us*. We were awful." Coming straight after three successive shows with his own band, with Zeppelin's own typically grueling rehearsals on top, "when I came to sing that night I had nothing left at all."

He likened the ensuing performance to "some kind of aimless dog trying to bite its tail." Page's guitar was out of tune, the guitar leads weren't long enough; everything, Plant swore, conspired to reduce the show to "one of the worst performances I've ever done in my life. . . . It was a most peculiar sensation. The idea of doing that every night is probably one of the least attractive things I could think of.

"Being in Cleveland the day afterwards with my own band was much more fun," he concluded. Even if there were rows of empty seats staring back at him.

Plant himself was astonished, not to mention surprised, by just how powerful his reaction to the reunion felt. He'd played with both Page and Jones since the split—whether as guests at his own shows or, in Page's case, in the studio as the Honeydrippers. And there the sole emotions were happiness, being reminded of the good times they'd shared, and a fuzzy sense of nostalgia as he looked around and saw that old familiar face alongside him. The difference was, there, they *were* guests. It was his show, his songs, his audience, his band—and the ghosts were simply passing through, a special treat for the crowd.

Live Aid was different. Live Aid, or Zeppelin's fifteen minutes of it, had nothing to do with Robert Plant, solo star, and everything to do with reawakening the past. It was as if—and this only hit him as he walked out onto the Philadelphia stage—someone had marched up to him on the street one day and told him, "Here's the band, here's the crowd. Now give them absolutely everything that Led Zeppelin ever meant, that it ever stood for, that they ever dreamed it could be. And you have a quarter of an hour, starting *now*."

He froze, and he has continued freezing ever since. No matter what entreaties have been made for Led Zeppelin to allow their performance that afternoon to be reshown, either in televised memories of the Live Aid afternoon or as part of the official DVD package, the answer has always come back the same.

No.

Some memories are too painful to be given a second viewing. And Plant was not only thinking about their Live Aid set when he arrived at that conclusion. He was thinking about Led Zeppelin themselves as well. No matter what trials and tribulations his solo career might lead him through as the future scrolled by, no matter how many other aspects of his past he finally felt comfortable enough to revisit, one always remained strictly out of bounds. Led Zeppelin—the Led Zeppelin that deep down, he cherished so preciously—existed in a time and a place that could never be revisited. So for another twenty-two years, he refused to try.

It's just a shame that so few people could actually understand why he felt that way, even among those who had taken the same ride alongside him. Which was why, whenever he pored through his past for future inspiration, he always returned to a time before he'd even met them.

8

Killing the Blues
(1968–1969)

For all of Norrie Paramor's nomenclatural trickery, there never was a distinct Birmingham sound, even early on. Unlike Liverpool, where most of the new talent either recorded songs written by the Beatles or were handled by their manager Brian Epstein, the Birmingham scene never came wholly under the sway of any single influence. At least in musical terms. But one man could be said to have dominated the city's musical aspirations, to the point where he sometimes felt synonymous with the scene: a former merchant seaman turned outrageous publicity hound named Tony Secunda.

Through the 1960s, as manager of first the Moody Blues (as they topped the chart with "Go Now") and then the Move (with a string of hits beginning in early 1967), Brummie bands both, Secunda was the Black Country's link to the London music industry. Especially since his taste for wild promotional stunts, and his ability to pull them off whatever the cost, ensured that neither he nor his charges were ever far from the headlines.

True, his activities could occasionally backfire, and do so with spectacular results. Secunda's relationship with the Move ended especially acrimoniously, after he circulated promotional postcards for the band suggesting that the then–Prime Minister was having an affair with his personal secretary. Which, it turned out, he was, but Secunda had no proof. Royalties for the band's latest single were confiscated in perpetuity, the Move moved away, and Secunda turned his attentions elsewhere in the city.

Before that happened, however (and even after, for Secunda's career only continued its meteoric rise, to embrace Procol Harum, T Rex, Steeleye Span, Motörhead, and even Paul McCartney's Wings), Secunda's name and reputation hung over the Birmingham scene like a second sky. And an ear that was permanently pressed to the ground soon got wind of the Band of Joy.

Interviewed for his autobiography in the early 1990s (a project that was tragically derailed by his death in 1995), Secunda recalled first seeing Plant somewhere around 1966: "Because it was impossible not to see him. Every show he was at, he'd be the one at the front pestering the band to let him join them onstage, whether they knew who he was or not."

In fact, that was one of the qualities that turned Secunda away from seeking a formal introduction. "He was like a big bouncy puppy dog—no direction, no discipline, and no loyalty either. He was a bit like Rod Stewart in that respect—no matter what he had, he always wanted more, and word got around. He was a great singer, but he'd only be your singer until something else came along."

But Trevor Burton, the Move bassist whose opinion Secunda always listened to, played him the Band of Joy demo, and something about it tweaked his attention. "It was the singing. I knew he was a great singer, and if there'd be any market for cover bands at that time, they would have been great. So Denny [business partner Cordell] and I called them down to London for a meeting, and to see what else they could offer."

Plant and Kevyn Gammond alone made the journey, hitchhiking to London where they were booked into the Madison Hotel, a none-too-salubrious step-up from a fleapit located close to Secunda's office.

The following day at the Marquee Studios, the pair was sat down at a table and told to write a song. Cordell helped them demo it, and that was it. The pair hitched back to the midlands, and they never heard from Secunda again. Their new demo, he would recall, was "as bad as their old demo. There was nothing there for us, even though we still liked Robert's voice. So I started putting the word around that there was this terrific singer cooling his heels in the midlands, and if any band needed a vocalist, they should go take a look at him."

One of the people he mentioned this to was Jimmy Page.

Meanwhile, back home, Plant was reacquainting himself with Alexis Korner, the veteran bluesman who said hi to Band of Joy at the Speakeasy. Korner was playing the Cannon Hill Arts Center in a duo with drummer Steve Miller, and as they ran through their set, Plant in the audience started accompanying them on his omnipresent harp.

"Which took a lot of cheek," Korner said years later, "because if Steve and I had wanted a harp player, we'd have brought our own along. Anyway, this kid asked if he could do a number with us onstage. I told him no, but said he should stop by the dressing room during the interval, and we talked then and I said okay, we'll do some eight bars at the end of the set."

Korner and Miller were impressed. "Okay, we said, maybe we do need a harp player, so I invited him back to London with us, told him he could crash on my couch, and we did some gigs as a trio and some recordings ["Operator" and "Steal Away"], and a couple of years later, once he had Zeppelin going, I recorded 'Whole Lotta Love' with my own band CCS, which did well. But it was always very casual. I think we talked about doing an album together, but there were always ideas going around, and he wanted to get home to his girlfriend, so that was it."

At a loose end again, Plant found a new band to sing with. John Trickett's band, the Answer, were playing a gig at Dudley Zoo, and after he and Maureen caught their set, he started hanging around with them more. At first it was just friendship; although he still had those three months left before the guillotine descended upon his rock 'n' roll dreams, Plant had already started to acquaint himself with life away from the stage. Until the evening when Tommy Burton, the Answer's regular singer, went down with a dose of food poisoning . . . and quickly found himself out of a job.

Plant seamlessly replaced him, first for the one show, and then forever; the luckless Burton's departure was confirmed when his bandmates announced they were changing the band's name, the musical equivalent of changing the locks when you kick someone out of the house. They became Obstweedle, a peculiar name for what keyboard player Billy Bonham (no relation)'s father insisted was a rather peculiar band. It was he who came up with the name:

"obs" as a contraction of "obscure," "tweedle" as a whimsical reference to Lewis Carroll and *Alice in Wonderland*, as author and children's book alike enjoyed a quite unexpected renaissance at the hands of sundry psychedelic acts. A band called Boeing Duveen had set Carroll's "Jabberwocky" to music for a startling single; Jefferson Airplane's "White Rabbit," of course, was Alice through and through; and when Plant introduced that song to the new band's repertoire, even the dullest onlooker asking what "obstweedle" was supposed to mean must surely have seen the light.

Rehearsing at the Bloxwich pub that was also operated by Bonham's parents, the Three Men in a Boat, Obstweedle played their first show in those same surroundings, on March 13, 1968. Like Band of Joy, their repertoire was largely covers, primarily songs that Plant liked to sing. Moby Grape, Buffalo Springfield, the Airplane of course. And around the local circuit they went, a twice-weekly residency at the pub they called home, and then anyplace else that would book them.

Compared to the circuit that Band of Joy had been playing, it was something of a step back, and Plant was never especially serious about the band's chances of advancement. In fact, he would later condemn them as flattering to deceive, for compensating with bombast and visuals for all that they lacked in terms of genuine musical content. But it kept him busy, it was fun at the time, and it brought him to the West Midlands College of Education in Walsall, the night that Jimmy Page drove up there to see for himself the singer that people kept telling him about.

Tony Secunda was not Robert Plant's only cheerleader, it seemed. Terry Reid, a singer in Mickie Most's stable, was also a fan, having played some shows earlier in the year with Band of Joy opening for him. When he turned down the opportunity to join the band that Page was then putting together, he dropped Plant's name as someone else he should check out.

Page's dream, two years earlier, of forming a band called Lead Zeppelin had never been going to get off the ground. Neither Keith Moon nor John Entwistle, who also thought about joining, were ever likely to leave the Who, and Jeff Beck was still in the Yardbirds at the time. Then, when he did leave that band, it was Page who replaced him.

But now the Yardbirds were no more. After five years, four guitarists, and a fistful of legends, the most blueswailin' birds of them all had combusted, shattered by the rigors of touring behind an album that they really didn't believe in (*Little Games*) and disillusioned by their own utter apathy toward a follow-up.

Their last few years had been hectic, so much so that Page sometimes wondered why he'd ever volunteered to join. He'd been making a comfortable living as a session musician until then, playing on so many artists' records that it could make your ears ache just counting them. When the Yardbirds originally asked him to come on board, following the departure of guitarist Eric Clapton, he refused, and suggested they invite his friend Jeff Beck instead.

They did, and Beck accepted, and that was when Page started to wonder if his initial response had maybe been a little too precipitous. The sight of Beck rejoicing in the sheer musical anarchy of the Yardbirds certainly gave Page pause for thought, and when bassist Paul Samwell-Smith quit the band in July 1966, Page stepped into the breach.

The fact that he had never really played bass in the past didn't bother him, and the band weren't in any position to say no. Their next show, at the London Marquee, was just days away, and there was a flood of gigs looming behind it. Even if the Yardbirds did intend seeking out that promised replacement, they would never have time to do so. Instead, rhythm guitarist Chris Dreja switched to bass, and suddenly the Yardbirds had two lead guitarists, a frontline of such scintillating magnificence that there was no way it could survive. The new-look Yardbirds cut one single together, then Beck quit and Page was on his own. No way could he leave them now.

A change of management saw the Yardbirds brought into pop impresario Mickie Most's empire, and informed in no uncertain terms that Most was in the business of making hits, and the poppier the better.

At first, the Yardbirds thought he was kidding. For the past three years they'd ranked among the most adventurous and experimental rock bands in the land, at least among those who were also having hits. But then they heard what Most had wrung out of Jeff Beck, the bubblegum perfection of "Hi Ho Silver Lining." So they did what they were told, and Most was granted his wish. Although his work with the Yardbirds—the *Little Games* album and a clutch of decidedly un-Yardbirds-like singles—never recaptured the band's glory days, the band remained a fair attraction in the United States. But now it was all over. The Yardbirds' final recording session in New York on June 2, 1968, was a disaster, even saw them falter when presented with Page's "My Baby," a song that would soon be developing into the classic "Tangerine." Three days later, when the group played their last-ever American show, in Alabama, the musicians already knew that the clutch of British dates that awaited them upon their return home would be the end.

The Yardbirds played what was intended to be their last-ever concert on July 8, 1968, at Luton Technical College. Somehow, however, it seemed that news of the group's final demise had not quite taken root in management's mind. Even as the band was preparing to deliver their final performance, Most's right-hand man Peter Grant was arranging a Scandinavian tour for September, with further dates in Japan, Australia, and the USA just awaiting his final confirmation.

Keith Relf and Jim McCarty shrugged. Their own project, Together, was already underway; the day before the Luton show, in fact, they linked up with Nicky Hopkins, Tony Meehan, folk guitarist Jon Mark, and producer Paul Samwell-Smith to begin work on the new group's debut single. As far as they were concerned, there was no going back.

Jimmy Page and Chris Dreja were less dismissive. Neither had given much thought to precisely what they intended doing next, beyond the vague possibility of trying to start up a new band together. Advising Grant only to revise the Scandinavian contract somehow, to make it apparent that the Yardbirds themselves would not be touring (Grant opted to rename the band the New Yardbirds), they began casting around for suitable members, beginning with a singer to succeed Keith Relf.

Page's first choice was Terry Reid, whose solo career under Mickie Most's auspices had never achieved the breakthrough it deserved. Critically, Reid was regarded as among the greatest vocalists around, and the two albums he'd cut with the producer contained some of the most far-sighted music of Most's entire career, But the public simply wasn't biting . . . yet.

Reid remained convinced that he was on the right track, though, and he turned Page's invitation down. But when he echoed Tony Secunda and recommended Robert Plant, Page, Dreja, and Peter Grant agreed it was time to head north. There, within the distinctly unglamorous surroundings of a Birmingham teacher-training college, on July 20, 1968, Page caught sight for the first time of Robert Plant, a singer who was so good that Page was convinced there had to be something very wrong with him as a person. Nobody this great could still be laboring in the obscurity of a band called Obstweedle.

Page decided to take a chance, however, and, no sooner had Plant accepted the awestricken trio's offer than he was pushing forth one of his own friends to make up the numbers: John Bonham, now touring the country for £40 a night in Tim Rose's group. Again, Page had already been turned down by the drummer he first dreamed of playing with, Procol Harum's BJ Wilson. Maybe he should give Bonham a listen.

Just days after his own first meeting with Page, Plant was accompanying him to another show, this time to see John Bonham playing behind Tim Rose. Again Page was impressed, a lot more so than Bonham was when he heard Page's plans. They were all up in the air, after all, based on assumption and ambition, whereas Bonham had a steady gig and a two-year-old son, Jason, to think about. Only when Peter Grant weighed in, offering Bonham the princely salary of £35 a week, did the drummer agree to give it a go, and so the pair reported for the new band's first rehearsal in the basement beneath a friendly London record store.

"We were dealing from the same pack of cards," Plant said of Page in 2006 in *Rolling Stone*. "You can smell when people . . . had their doors opened a little wider than most, and you could feel that was the deal with Jimmy. His ability to absorb things and the way he carried himself was far more cerebral than anything I'd come across before, and I was so very impressed."

Talking with journalist Matt Snow of *Mojo* in 2007, Plant described the Band of Joy as "the real schooling for Bonzo and myself," in that it taught them how to take what others might regard as conventional pop music, and break it down, transform it into something new. A direction in which Page, with the Yardbirds, had also been journeying, although the pair did not realize that. "All we knew of the Yardbirds was the occasional single recorded by Mickie Most. Their profile by then was more American than English, so we didn't have very much idea of this mystery guitarist. But when we started playing with him, we knew it was a crucial combination."

Page already knew what he wanted from the band. Cream, the leviathan that effectively blueprinted the blues as a dense, deafening roar, were on the way out—they would announce their breakup early the following year. The Jeff Beck Group, revolving around an axis of Beck, singer Rod Stewart and bassist Ron Wood, were blazing, but they were equally unstable, torn between their guitarist's sharp-tempered restlessness and the ubiquitous Mickie Most's insistence that they ought to be making pop singles.

If a group would rise up in the footprints of them both, but do so without any of the flaws that were eating away at them, with everybody pulling for the same common cause, Page—and Grant, installed as the band's manager—believed they would clean up.

In early August, the New Yardbirds—Page, Dreja, Plant, and Bonham— undertook their first rehearsal, running through a clutch of old Yardbirds songs, beginning with the highly appropriate "The Train Kept A-Rollin'." But though the afternoon went well and the band was sounding good, Chris Dreja knew it wasn't for him. His heart just wasn't in it; he simply didn't have the energy to be starting a new band all over again. "I wanted to be independent, and not have to rely on loonies." He wasn't sure how he expected the others to react to the news; the Scandinavian tour, after all, was just six weeks away. But when he told Page of his decision, it turned out that he needn't have worried. Page already had a replacement lined up.

Like Page, John Paul Jones made his living, and had amassed a massive reputation, on the session circuit. He and Page regularly ran into one another in that world, and the guitarist was still in shock as he delivered the news to Dreja, as he told the *San Antonio Light* in 1970: "John Paul Jones is unquestionably an incredible arranger and musician—he didn't need me for a job."

If Page was astounded by Jones's enthusiasm for a new, unknown band, however, he readily understood his reasons. Like Page in the years before he joined the Yardbirds, Jones had spent his entire career playing what other people told him to. It was time to begin expressing himself, "and he thought we might be able to do it together. He had a proper musical training, and he had quite brilliant ideas. I jumped at the chance of getting him."

Page did not, of course, get everything his own way. Casting around for other musicians, he invited pianist Nicky Hopkins, another longstanding veteran of the UK sessions scene. Hopkins turned him down flat. "I was tempted, but only inasmuch as it was work. It sounds odd to say it, but I couldn't see a future in it. John [Paul Jones] would still play keyboards in the studio, the whole band was writing, John and Jimmy were both great at arranging. Really, what would be left for me to do?"

Grant wrangled the group a short lease on a rehearsal room in central London, beneath a record store on Gerard Street in Soho, while Plant moved into Page's house in the village of Pangbourne, surrounded by all the luxuries that a decade in session work had afforded him. It was Plant's first true taste of the lifestyle that, in just a few short years, rock 'n' roll music had made possible, one that would have been unimaginable to his parents' generation. Antiques bedecked the rooms, a Bentley purred in the driveway; even the neighbors were cut from the most refined cloth. And the band they had created was sounding better every day. The New Yardbirds were complete, and there wasn't a single "old" Yardbird in sight. Even before his once-fateful twentieth birthday dawned, Plant was able to turn to his bride-to-be and tell her, "I think we should give it a few more years."

Not that witnesses to their first shows, a half-dozen through Denmark and Sweden, seemed to care about that. Although the group was absolutely unknown and untried, they nevertheless left nobody in any doubt as to their awesome potential. Photographer Jorgen Angel, a seventeen-year-old student from Copenhagen, caught the band's opening night—September 14, 1968—and spoke for many in the club when he recalled:

As for these "New Yardbirds," I didn't expect much. Not long before the concert actually began, there were still a lot of talking on whether they were going to play under the name of "The Yardbirds" or under the name of "The New Yardbirds," and how people would react. Because in the club magazine, they were billed as "The Yardbirds," with a photo of the Yardbirds, not of Bonham, Plant, Page, and John Paul Jones.

Plus, in these days, when you saw a band turning up with the word new in its name, you knew that something was murky, that it wasn't the same group anymore. Can you imagine a group called "The New Beatles"? Of course not, you would be disappointed even before hearing a single note. So before these New Yardbirds even went on stage, I remember I was annoyed. I wanted "the real thing." But as soon as they began to play, I was hooked!

In keeping with their name, the group's repertoire was firmly grounded in a variation on the Yardbirds' final set, although that in itself offered plenty of clues as to the new group's future. The showcase "Dazed and Confused" was already in place, albeit under the alternate title of "I'm Confused," while the band members' shared love of blues introduced "Babe I'm Gonna Leave You" and "How Many More Times" to the brew.

Casting around further, Page seized upon the Stax churner "The Hunter," a delirious standout in the live repertoire of that most glorious of all London blues bands, Paul Rodgers and Paul Kossoff's Free (the two bands, Free and the Yardbirds, shared the same publicist, the veteran Bill Harry). Every one of these numbers would be included on the band's debut album, a disc that would be recorded with as much haste as the quartet could muster—as fast, in fact, as the band made the decision to change their name. Maybe (with just a minor change in the spelling) the Led Zeppelin could take flight after all?

The New Yardbirds' final Scandinavian date was September 23; Led Zeppelin's maiden UK tour was to kick off at the Surrey University on October 15. That, then, was the window during which the band would record their debut album, moving into Olympic Studios to bang down the live set they'd just tweaked to perfection.

"I Can't Quit You Baby," "How Many More Times," "Dazed and Confused," the newly composed "Communication Breakdown," the acoustic instrumental "Black Mountain Side"—within no more than thirty-six hours (and according to Page, as few as fifteen), *Led Zeppelin I* was complete. Peter Grant did the rest, convincing Ahmet Ertegun of Atlantic Records that he could not afford to pass up the band—and proving his own faith by setting up Led Zeppelin's first American tour before they'd even played more than handful of shows in Britain.

With *Led Zeppelin I* set for release in January 1969, Zeppelin would commence their assault on the US concert circuit by opening for the Vanilla Fudge in Denver on December 26, 1968, before launching into a cross-country tour of venues handpicked by Grant from his experiences road-managing the Jeff Beck Group—five nights at the Whiskey in LA, four at the Fillmore West in San Francisco, three at the Boston Tea Party. The Beck tours had introduced him to the cities that were interested in the kind of music that both bands played; now he was out to consolidate that interest and transform it into devotion.

In Britain, on the other hand, Led Zeppelin were still fulfilling the kinds of engagements that Grant had been landing for the Yardbirds—the Marquee, various universities, the Bristol Boxing Club, the Bath Pavilion, and deep into the provinces.

Already the band's stock was rising. Journalist Mick Farren, frontman at that time with the Deviants, recalled opening for the newcomers at the Roundhouse in London, and again a few weeks later "somewhere in the west country. We'd . . . met Plant a number of times previously when we'd worked with his earlier group, Band of Joy, and *they'd* been opening for *us*." Now, however, "the entire music industry was watching to see whether LZ was actually going to take off, ad promoters were hedging their bets and printing the words 'ex-Yardbirds' on the posters and press announcements almost as large as the name of the band."

Audiences were not necessarily convinced. The Deviants had already roused the locals into a state of near riot even before Led Zeppelin came on, much to Bonham's amusement. "You must have been fucking terrible," he told them as they staggered into the dressing room.

He spoke too soon. The headliners were just a song and a half into their own set, with a phalanx of police stationed between them and the crowd, when the near riot became a full one. "[The audience] couldn't mount a frontal assault on the stage, so they hurled missiles," Farren recalled. "This was more than enough for Led Zeppelin, who beat a hasty retreat.

"Now it was our turn to do the laughing. 'You must have been fucking terrible.'"

Recovering their poise, the band journeyed on, and on December 13, they arrived at the Bridge Country Club in Canterbury. Which is where Jeff Beck caught his own first in-concert glimpse of the burgeoning juggernaut that was Led Zeppelin.

It was not a representative show, or so Page told his distinguished visitor later. "Things went slightly wrong," Beck laughed, including the unscheduled explosion of Page's amplifier. Beck recalled, "I went 'What's up with that, Jim?' and then I realized it was my amp, because my roadie had moonlighted and rented Jimmy my equipment. And he'd changed the impedance on the back, so it sounded like a pile of shit." Nevertheless, after weeks of hearing the grapevine (or at least, Peter Grant) extolling the virtues of Led Zeppelin, Beck finally understood what the fuss was all about.

"I could see the potential. It was just amazing, blew the house down, blew everybody away." Everything about the group was tailored for success, at least when he compared them with his ragtag little band. "[They] had a better-looking lead singer . . . he had golden curly locks and a bare chest, and the girls fell in love with him. They also had Bonzo on drums, creating all sorts of pandemonium."

It was "a much better package than I had," and Beck freely admitted, "I was blind jealous, [although] maybe jealousy is the wrong word, because it's a negative emotion. But envy and frustration all rolled into one, because . . . I couldn't [even] find a drummer or a singer who wanted to experiment and do outrageous stuff. I wanted to break barriers and you need people around you to help you do that. And money! I couldn't even spring for a session, let alone keep them all on retainer. So obviously they did better."

Led Zeppelin I was issued on schedule, in January 1969, and immediately set about drawing listeners in one of two directions. Either it was, as *Rolling Stone*'s John Mendelsohn pointed out, no more than an inferior twin of the Jeff Beck Group's *Truth*, offering "little that . . . [they] didn't say as well or better three months ago," or, as the bible of the British underground *Oz* enthused, it was one of those rare LPs that so defy "immediate classification or description, simply because [they are] so obviously a turning point in rock."

Both opinions are valid. The patent lifting of a version of "You Shook Me" was only the first of the debts that *Led Zeppelin I* owed to *Truth*. Elsewhere, "Black Mountain Side" echoed the acoustic interlude offered by "Greensleeves," while the very sound of the two albums posited heavy blues extremes toward which no other act of the time dared to journey. Zeppelin even borrowed Beck's typographer for the occasion: Royal College of Art student George Hardie worked with photographer Stephen Goldblatt on the *Truth* sleeve, and was rewarded with an introduction to Peter Grant. He went on to design the sleeve to *Led Zeppelin I*.

For all these similarities, coincidences, and borrowings, however, Beck is honest in his assessment of the two records. "The thing with *Truth* was, it was never really developed. We had a sound, and it turned out to be a colossally influential one, but we weren't interested in just making the same record again and again. Which means I've had to sit back here for the past thirty years, watching people perfect it, and when Led Zeppelin started doing huge concerts, I was sitting in my garage listening to the radio, and going, 'What's going on? I started this shit, and look at me!'"

Ultimately, what Led Zeppelin had that the Jeff Beck Group didn't was vision. Even before he ever put his finger on a life beyond the Yardbirds, Jimmy Page knew that he would be in control of his destiny. "The one thing I was sure of was that I was going to produce the band myself, because I knew about the studio." He told journalist Nick Kent, "I'd been an apprentice for years, and I'd discovered things that someone like Mickie [Most] didn't have a clue even existed."

Without even appearing to question the right, Led Zeppelin took absolute control of everything they did. *Everything.* Although Peter Grant still operated out of Most's RAK Music Management offices on Oxford Street, and RAK financed the physical recording of *Led Zeppelin I*, it was clear from the outset that there was no room for Mickie Most in the new setup. And why, Most admitted later, should there be? Displaying every last ounce of the arrogance and self-confidence that both friends and enemies so admired him for, and a shameless ability to revise history, he threw his own opinion on Led Zeppelin into the same camp as the band's detractors.

Yes, they were a great band; yes, they had some good ideas. But whatever Led Zeppelin might have achieved so far, he'd already been there, done that, and bought the souvenir T-shirt. "*Truth* was a forerunner to Led Zeppelin," he declared. "A great album—which I made."

Unfortunately, neither he nor the Beck Group were capable of topping it. *Cosa Nostra Beck-Ola*, the group's second album, was an unfocused mess. Zeppelin, on the other hand, were going from strength to strength, juggernauting across the United States and not only taking everywhere by storm (because that's a cliché that every band can lay claim to at one time or another) but actually writing their own history as they journeyed.

At the Fillmore East on January 31, Zeppelin's performance was so intense, and the audience reaction so hysterical, that the headlining Iron Butterfly delayed their own onstage arrival by forty-five minutes in the hope that the crowd would calm down. They hoped in vain, and Led Zeppelin never went out as a support group again.

Their next UK tour in March 1969, a return visit to Scandinavia that same month, and another US outing, kicking off at the New York University Jazz festival on April 18, would see them headlining every venue they played. By the time their second album, the matter-of-factly titled *Led Zeppelin II*, was unveiled in October, there wasn't a venue in the Western world that they couldn't have filled. And that song would remain the same for the next ten years.

9

Little by Little
(1985–1988)

Coming off the road at the end of the *Shaken 'n' Stirred* tour, himself shaken by the realization that it was not an outing he would be proud to remember, Plant's own thoughts could not help but fold back to the early days of Zeppelin, not for the sake of the band itself, but for the sense of adventure, excitement, and novelty that permeated everything the musicians said and did together.

There was no vast master plan when Led Zeppelin was born, no preordained belief that they were destined for the stars. Just four musicians bonding in a fashion that none of them had experienced before, knowing that even in the pits of the most fiery disagreement, it was not ego or selfishness that were screaming bloody murder but a fervent belief in what was right for the band. Nothing else—not the audience, not the record company, not any grandiose vision of fame—mattered. Not one of them, after all, had truly experienced those things in the past; not one of them really expected it.

Yes, Peter Grant was his bullish self, insisting to all who came near that his boys had the best band in the world. But that was what he was paid to do. It was what managers did. They looked after the band, and they looked after all the things that related to the band. And for all the differences that he and Plant would encounter over the years, and even the less-than-happy conclusion to their working relationship once Zeppelin crashed, Plant missed that unswerving sense of belief, missed having somebody who was so single-mindedly devoted to the music and its makers that nothing could deflect him from dragging them both to the top of the hill.

Whereas who did Plant have? His band had effectively crumbled away without him even needing to call up and formally dismiss them. They parted at the end of the tour with barely even a "See you next time" to one another, all just happy to have gotten it out of the way. He said farewell, too, to Benji LeFevre, his right-hand man for almost fifteen years. If he had to begin again—and the more he thought about the last tour and album, the more he believed that he did—it would be from a completely new direction.

The 1980s were a funny old decade, not only for Robert Plant but for almost every musician who marched into them from a position of power in the years before. Almost without exception, the superstars of the '70s, and those of the '60s who'd clung onto power, met the new era head-on and triumphant: David Bowie with *Let's Dance*, the biggest album of his entire career; Yes with *90125*, home to their biggest hit single; the Rolling Stones with *Tattoo You*, which transformed an ages-old outtake into the anthemic "Start Me Up"; Paul McCartney with *McCartney II*—and so on and so forth. When Robert Plant launched his solo career and his numbers barely hiccupped from where he'd left off with Zeppelin, he was simply marching to a rhythm that people thought would last forever.

But then things started to change, and it doesn't matter who or what history chooses to blame, be it bad business, lousy albums, cruddy videos, whatever. Suddenly, people stopped caring so much. Maybe the stars lost touch with their people; maybe people lost interest in the stars. Being a rock god in an age gone by was no longer enough, though, and when the time came to follow those monster-selling albums, anticipation was eroded by apathy and yawns, with Live Aid ironically confirming the worst.

While (comparative) young guns like U2, Dire Straits, Simple Minds, Duran Duran, and Run DMC turned in performances that all agreed were so stellar, only Queen, of the old guard, seemed to be at their best, with Bryan Ferry possibly easing in a close second. But Zeppelin, Sabbath, McCartney, Dylan, Jagger, Bowie, the Who, and Elton John all rolled out so underwhelmingly—disappointing, even perfunctory, as though they believed that merely turning up for the concert and playing a few old favorites was all they needed to do. And why? Because they either forgot or overlooked the one thing that all true stars need to remember. They were not simply competing with the rest of the pack to turn in a show that would ring through the ages. They were competing with their own selves as well, with the past that had placed them where they were today. And not one of them could hold a candle to the things they did before.

That was the realization that Robert Plant came to as he looked back on a summer that he wished had never started. Always susceptible to a bout of self-excoriation, never content to rest on laurels that he suspected might well be snatched away tomorrow, he was well aware that the music he'd made in the past was still all that people wanted to hear from him; that if he went out on tour tomorrow and announced each show would be determined by requests from the audience, he'd be lucky if a single song from his last three albums even merited a half-hearted mention.

But what was the answer?

Beyond the confines of Jennings Farm, if one thing did come out of Live Aid that could be considered worthwhile, it is that it reopened the avenues of communication between Plant and his bandmates. It was an open secret in the music industry that Page had always been hopeful that the trio could work together again, that Jones had never ruled it out and that it was Plant who was the obstacle. And why? Because Plant wanted to prove, to himself as much as to anybody else, that he wasn't just the guy who sang the songs, he was an equal member of the team that wrote and arranged them as well. And the only way to do that was by doing it again. In the aftermath of Live Aid, in January 1986, he reconvened with Page and Jones to discuss the ramifications of flying together again.

But long before their discussions hit stalemate, he knew that his heart wasn't in it. Not because they didn't get on or because he didn't think they could work together, but because he doubted they could ever attain the same standards again. The band's final album, maybe even their last two, had both disappointed compared to what had passed before them. Did they really want to continue on that same downward slope, just for the sake of applause and cash? Or did they want to prove themselves all over again by trying something fresh?

His bandmates' responses have never been revealed. But Led Zeppelin did not reform in 1986. With Tony Thompson reprising his Live Aid role, the quartet got together in a small village hall and just started batting ideas around. Some of them even sounded promising. But no matter how keen everybody was to do it, the timing was all wrong.

In 1984, Page had finally put together a new band, teaming with former Free and Bad Company frontman Paul Rodgers in a project they called the Firm. A hit debut album duly followed, and a second album, *Mean Business*, was imminent. "And I think he was a bit confused about what he was doing," Plant told *Rolling Stone* in 1988.

Socially, too, there were difficulties, as Page took to staying at his lodgings, disdaining any opportunity to socialize with his bandmates. Even after Plant and Jones discovered a local club, within easy walking distance of headquarters, and open till a most acceptable 2 a.m., Page kept himself to himself. "Which is hardly the way to get everything back together again," Plant continued. But if anything finally drove a stake through the project's heart, certainly as far as Plant was concerned, it was the car crash that left Tony Thompson hospitalized just a week into the proceedings. He wasn't seriously hurt, but he would not be playing drums for a while. And Plant, who needed no reminders whatsoever of the hostile forces that so often seemed to stalk Led Zeppelin, was not in the mood to confront them again. Although the band had one more rehearsal, with a roadie sitting in on the drums, Plant had had enough. He headed home.

Despite everything, Plant and Page would reunite onstage during 1986. That October saw the sudden death of guitarist Johnny Pasternak, the switchblade-touting founder of the Crawling Kingsnakes and a veteran of the Shakedown Sound. A hastily arranged tribute concert saw a host of local musicians gather in his memory, and included an impromptu set featuring Plant and Page.

≈

Back in 1977, Robert Crash was the distinctively shorn blond bassist for the Maniacs, one of the most exciting London live bands in the seething punk ferment. From there, with a growing fascination in electronics, he led the Psychotic Tanks through a deliciously growled and threatening take on Elvis's "Let's Have a Party," one of the first releases on the infant 4AD label, before moving to the other side of the desk to produce the Eurythmics' sophomore album, *Sweet Dreams (Are Made of This)*. Now he was being introduced to Robert Plant by their mutual friend Dave Stewart, as the singer spent the summer experimenting with a host of different potential sidekicks: Bruce Woolley of Camera Club and Buggles fame ("Somewhere at the bottom of a drawer back home, there is a very strange-sounding cassette," laughs Plant), guitarist Robin George, and Stewart himself.

Crash was in the studio with Robert Plant, writing the first songs destined for what would become Plant's next album: "Why" and "Dance on My Own." Both delivered a template that would take Plant further from his audience's comfort zone than anything he had done in the past: stark dance anthems led by electronics, unerringly aimed toward darkened corners in sweat-soaked, badly lit nightclubs—and destined to be delivered by a new band cast unerringly around their grasp of current technology.

Guitarist Phil Johnstone and drummer Chris Blackwell were recruited from The Rest Is History, a band Plant discovered when his music publisher sent him one of their songs, the souped-up hyperpop of "Heaven Knows," and the singer decided to record it. Guitarist Doug Boyle and bassist Phil Scragg were likewise unknowns. But together in Marcus Studios, they alchemized an album that made even *Shaken 'n' Stirred* appear a masterpiece in restraint.

Tim Palmer was back as producer, reveling in Plant's open-mindedness, gleefully conspiring with Plant and Johnstone as they assembled a barrage of samplers, synthesizers, drum machines, and more. Indeed, at one point Palmer found himself suggesting they *add* guitars to the brew, so far had Plant leaned in the opposite direction. But Plant would not be dissuaded.

The vision in his head, which his bandmates were expected to flawlessly translate, was of the spirit of old-style blues and rockers, revived and imbibed by the latest sonic innovations. If Howling Wolf had had access to a sequencer, what would "Smokestack Lightning" have become? If Sonny

Boy had a synth, where would "Good Morning Little Schoolgirl" have gone? The new songs, for the most part, were not styled as the blues, but that was a part of the plan as well. Writer Chuck Eddy had suggested that *Shaken 'n' Stirred* was a new, unnamed music. Now Plant wanted to discover where it might lead.

There would be tensions as the sessions unfolded. Particularly after Jimmy Page was invited along to add solos to "Heaven Knows" and "Tall Cool One." Which, in turn, was before he was informed that the latter would feature a brace of Zeppelin samples. "The Wanton Song" and "Custard Pie" both flash through the ether, with Plant laughingly pointing the finger of blame at the New York hip-hop trio the Beastie Boys. Their "She's Crafty" had sampled "The Ocean," and it felt like a good idea at the time. It still does, in fact.

Plant would swiftly return the favor, cowriting a new song, "The Only One," for Page's solo debut album, *Outrider*, and dropping by the studio to sing it as well. But it was scarcely a golden moment in either man's career, and it certainly pales to deathly white in comparison with all that was wrought by "Tall Cool One," a song that stands as the epitome of all that Plant dreamed the new album should be: a title he borrowed from the Wailers, a Seattle garage band of the early 1960s; quotes from Gene Vincent and rockabilly hero Charlie Feathers; and the entire thing, he explained, "tipping my hat to the original song," even as he drifted miles out of its orbit.

He was, he declared to *Creem's* Chuck Eddy in 1988, a technobilly, "trying to do something that's not been done before, even at the risk of not making that extra buck. There's so much I want to get in there on my records—it's hard to get in everything that I'd like to." He raved about Let's Active and the Swans—bands just commencing their maniacal sonic journeys at the time, but already destined to make some of the most influential music of the age—and announced, "I want to cut through radio with a hot knife, this idea where they say, 'We're only gonna play stuff guaranteed on being a hit.' I wanna stretch it out some. People like Tom Verlaine and Hüsker Dü are making quite important music now, and people aren't hearing it because it never gets played."

No less than punk rock a decade before, but with less vocal opposition from the musicians themselves, Plant was flying the flag for new music. Perhaps he was not so far out on the edge as his interviews suggested he thought he was (although the primitive rockabilly distortion of "Billy's Revenge" still feels dramatic and edgy today). But more than any other artist of his stature, he was at least giving it a go, and trusting his reputation and fame to open doors through which the next generation could pour.

That, too, was something he'd done before, when the colossal success of Led Zeppelin paved the way for an entire generation of likeminded imaginations. It worked then, and it worked again this time. *Now and Zen*, as the new album would be punningly titled, was destined to dominate American radio in a manner that the solo Plant never had. With almost every track spinning into rotation, with the gorgeous "Ship of Fools" becoming *the* slow dance of the year, and with sales that pushed it to triple platinum and the Top 10 in both the US and UK, *Now and Zen* reestablished its maker as a leading force at a time and in a climate where he might well have continued redundant, while earning him reviews that were all the more laudatory because of that.

Its nine tracks, said *Rolling Stone*, "don't simply sound contemporary; they point to new ways to transmute roots-rock verities of swing and harmony amid the technological conventions of late-Eighties pop." It humanized what many people still regarded as the icicle inhumanity of so much electronic music, and was "so rich in conceptual invention" that you almost missed the fact that Plant's vocals were as good as any he had ever unleashed. "Better, in some ways, than ever."

Later, observers attempting to explain the album's success would point to any number of contributory factors, including the presence of Jimmy Page on those two songs. In reality, however, that was simply a name on the door, and ultimately of no more value to Plant than his contributions were to the success (or otherwise) of *Outrider*—which scarcely made the Top 30. Page's presence had nothing to do with the overall sound, mood, and confidence of the album, nor the innovations that it posited—the sonic subversion of all that had grown tired and derivative about "rock" in the

'80s by seizing upon the genre's most subversive offspring and bringing them face to face with their parent.

Inevitably Plant ignited a tour in the album's wake; gratifyingly, it proved one of the most successful he had ever undertaken. With another young unknown, Charlie Jones of the Bath band Violent Blue, replacing Phil Scragg on bass (and soon becoming Plant's son-in-law; he was dating and would eventually marry daughter Carmen), Plant unveiled the new lineup with a pair of semi-secret pre-Christmas shows, one in Folkestone, Kent, and the other close to home in Stourbridge. At both he astonished audiences, not only with the ready transition of the new material from disc to stage, but also by finally breaking his self-imposed embargo on performing Zeppelin oldies. He had no need to hide them anymore.

"Misty Mountain Hop," "Rock and Roll," and the band's trademark reassemblage of "Traveling Riverside Blues," immortalized on their second album as the juvenile favorite "The Lemon Song," were all included in the show, while Plant's newly installed manager, Bill Curbishley (overseer of both the Who in their pomp and another midlands mob, Judas Priest, at their peak) looked on with something approaching satisfaction and relief. Like so many other people circulating around Plant through the '80s, Curbishley knew that a nod to a past that everyone wanted to relive would put butts on seats wherever they touched down. He was the first person ever to convince Plant of that, but only after Plant had finally convinced himself that the butts would come regardless.

The full tour got underway in spring 1988 around the UK before hitting the US for the summer season. And Plant appeared to be having the time of his life, "wriggling around like some aging big girl's blouse," as he put it, but "what else am I going to do?" That, he said, was what he was good at, and even as he pushed the age of forty, he pulled it off with an assurance that too many of his peers had replaced years ago with bad parody and self-conscious posturing. Compared to Plant's last tour around the US, *Now and Zen* was vivid daylight to the dark and stormy night of *Shaken 'n' Stirred*. Which made it all the more remarkable, *not* that Zeppelin-shaped lightning should strike yet again, but that Plant would permit it to.

Atlantic Records was celebrating its fortieth birthday with a star-studded concert at Madison Square Garden. Asked what he would most like as a gift to mark the occasion, Ahmet Ertegun—who, with jazz promoter Herb Abramson, started the label in 1947—had just one wish. He wanted to see Led Zeppelin back together again. The Coasters, Wilson Pickett, Phil Collins, Crosby, Stills & Nash, Roberta Flack, Yes, and the Bee Gees had all agreed to perform, a cross section that summed up at least three of the label's four-decade history, and Plant's own band was already booked in for a set. He could manage a few more songs with some old friends . . . couldn't he?

Plant agreed. "Top-secret rehearsals," duly reported in a raft of newspapers, preceded the show, Page, Plant, and Jones joined by Jason Bonham for the occasion (he and Page were already working together on *Outrider* and the tour that would accompany it).

No less than at Live Aid, Zeppelin's performance would be short: five songs in thirty minutes at the end of an eleven-hour day, taking the stage at 1 a.m. to the drama-soaked rhythms of "Kashmir" and moving on through "Heartbreaker," "Whole Lotta Love," and "Misty Mountain Hop" before wrapping with a "Stairway to Heaven" that was so rapturously received that many people didn't even notice that Plant forgot the lyrics to a song he'd again not wanted to perform in the first place.

He didn't even give it much of an intro, just a grinning "Good evening" and then an understated "Okay." And watching the performance as it was simulcast round the country, it wasn't that far off the mark to say he even looked bored as he sang. Later, few people described the performance as anything more than lackluster, four musicians whose heads and attention seemed anyplace but together, as if Ertegun received the birthday present he had asked for but the batteries weren't included.

Either that or the internal political dynamics that once fired the Zeppelin's engines had finally been turned upside down.

10

Let the Boogie Woogie Flow
(1969)

L ed Zeppelin was a democracy. All four members decided on the group's direction; all (at the discretion of Peter Grant, of course) decided on its ambition. But there was one place where democracy was cast aside: in the studio.

As the most experienced musicians in the band, Page and Jones naturally assumed control of the recording process; they did so without even thinking about it. Any questions that their bandmates might have asked—"How do we do this" or "How did you do that"—one or the other would know the answer. If a procedure or process needed to be explained, it would be Page or Jones who did the explaining. A decade apiece spent working in every major studio in Britain had taught both of them all they needed to know, with Page automatically assuming the role of overall producer and Jones the unquestioned authority on arrangements. "I knew exactly what I wanted to do with the band," Page admitted. "I knew precisely what I was after, and how to get it."

Plus, he controlled the purse strings too, with Plant and Bonham still on a weekly wage and therefore forever aware that one word from Peter Grant could see either or both of them cut adrift. And already, both had too much to lose. Zeppelin received an unprecedented $200,000 advance from Atlantic Records—unprecedented, that is, for an unknown band—and both Plant and Bonham were promptly handed £3,000 apiece, to do with what they would. They bought matching gold Jaguars. For Plant, this went some way toward compensating him for missing his own wedding reception, as Zeppelin's gig at the London Roundhouse pulled him away from the festivities, and for missing his first Christmas as a married man too. Zeppelin were off to America.

They flew into Los Angeles and booked into the Chateau Marmont in the company of Richard Cole, a roadie whom both Grant and Page knew from the final Yardbirds tour. It was he, more than their bandmates, who would be responsible for easing the new boys, Plant and Bonham, into the rhythm of life in America, acquainting them not only with the high life with which every touring rock band of the era was to become *au fait*, but also with the less salubrious aspects. Why they shouldn't consider going out to a gig in that particular part of town. Why they could visit this record store here, but should probably avoid that one there.

Growing up in England, Plant had long since grown accustomed to being harangued on the streets for having long hair, to the point where he no longer thought anything of it. It was Cole's responsibility to inform him that Americans often let their fists do the talking if they saw something they didn't like. Their fists or worse.

Likewise the police. The old-fashioned British Bobby was already a thing of the past at home, as rumors flew of the police's penchant for planting drugs on hapless hippies. American cops, however, didn't have an especially warm and fuzzy reputation to shake off in the first place, and they could bang you up for a lot less than a few grams of suspicion.

Politically, America was at war with itself, as the conflict in Vietnam continued dividing society down every line it could, while poverty, race, and injustice all spewed their own bitter pills into the pot. The ensuing seismic splits shattered American society like so many dropped vases. But there was one thing that everybody seemed to agree on. Rock 'n' roll, and the people who made it, was the scapegoat for almost all of the country's ills. And for all Peter Grant's bluster as he promoted the band around the USA, Led Zeppelin were not yet big enough that fame could offer them any protection whatsoever.

They would make friends, however, whose own reputation would serve them well. Bill Graham, the bearlike owner of the Fillmore in San Francisco, was one, his instant admiration for the group establishing him as the most prominent of the myriad cheerleaders they gathered on that first tour. He was by no means the only one, though, as word of their performances spread among promoters, audiences, and even other musicians, who suddenly found themselves dreading the call to take the stage in the wake of a Zep support slot and try to follow the barrage they laid down.

Compared with what the group would go on to accomplish onstage, those early shows were little more than competent blasts of the blues, interspersed with virtuoso elements that could bore as many people as they delighted (as many people took the drum solos enacted by bands throughout the first half of the '70s as opportunities to head to the bar for a refill as actually sat and enjoyed them). And John Bonham's displays were no exception. Guitar solos, too, could grow boring after a time, and some of Page's did.

It was Plant, then, who captivated. Even before he ever set foot on a stage, he demanded attention with his very appearance. Now, honed by six years of stalking the tiniest stages in front of audiences whose only requirement, as they stood with their arms folded, staring fully at the stage, was to be *impressed*, he had become impressive.

He was shameless. Moves that he borrowed from every performer he'd ever admired—Elvis and Jagger, Daltrey and Relf—were regurgitated as though he had only just created them, and it was a mark of the aplomb with which he played the part that many onlookers actually agreed with the impression. They had never seen a frontman like him. Then he'd open his mouth to sing, and every other revelation was suddenly merely an appetizer.

Singers still sang in the '60s. Even those vocalists whose lungs would become an object of wonder in later years—Roger Daltrey again, Deep Purple's Ian Gillan, Black Sabbath's Ozzy Osbourne—did so in the aftermath of Plant. Of contemporary rock 'n' roll stars, only Arthur Brown, whose Crazy World scored the monster hit "Fire" in 1968 and did nothing else of commercial note thereafter, had truly harnessed the passion of the unbridled scream—not only while he was actually screaming, but elsewhere in his tone as well.

Track back in time, and sidestep genres as well, and James Brown and Little Richard had been doing a similar thing for years, taking notes and holding them long after mere mortals might have run out of breath. So neither Brown nor Plant were doing anything new. But genres were important now, as radio streamlined its Top 40 past into more specialized niches of individual taste and record stores started segregating sounds by their marketing. In the world of white rock 'n' roll, which would soon become heavy rock, and then heavy metal, Robert Plant was unique. A man, as writer Nick Kent put it, "who preened and screamed out blood-curdling notes that seemed capable of sending [a] venue's . . . architecture crashing down around us all in a heap of rubble like Joshua's trumpet destroying the wall of Jericho."

Peter Grant's job, and Richard Cole's too, was to convince the world that the rest of the band shared that quality. Not as musicians, not as a band, but as an entity. That Led Zeppelin was more than a band, they were hard news as well.

They started small, encouraging the musicians to make themselves seen and heard. They worked on Plant mostly, with Bonham by his side; the less outward-going Jones and Page were worked less, unless there was something extra-special going on.

Friendships should be cultivated, photos should be taken. A shot of Plant at the Whiskey with Janis Joplin or Grace Slick had far more value than a picture of the band onstage or hanging out together in front of a local landmark. In one photo, they were isolated, just another bunch of hairies. In the other, they were hobnobbing with the already-anointed royalty of rock. Gilt by association.

"What we did with Zeppelin," Grant explained years later, "was no different to what the Colonel did with Elvis, or what [Tony] Defries would do with Bowie. We created a myth. Right from the beginning, when I was first talking to Jimmy, that was the idea." They had watched past superstars rise and fall, and Cream and the Beck Group were just the most recent. They'd watched, and learned from their greatest mistake, which was the insistence that the stars did not want to be stars, that the fame that rose up to consume them was merely a by-product of their talent.

Led Zeppelin did not want that; they did not want to be known purely as a great band and then forgotten until the next tour rolled around. They wanted to *epitomize* a great band, to become the blueprint for every great band that came after them and a role model for all who followed them too. And it was no coincidence that Grant would reference Tony Defries, because the two had worked together briefly in the employ of Mickie Most—Grant as the legendary producer's Mr. Fix-It, Defries as part of his legal team. They did not, at that time, discuss the future, because at that time there was no future to discuss. Grant had yet to branch into management, Defries had not even heard of David Bowie. But side by side regardless, the two men would erect monoliths set to bestride the 1970s, and they did so by making myths.

Until David Bowie came along in 1972, and Elvis aside, nobody had ever heard of a rock star employing a personal bodyguard. Bowie had one, a foreboding man-mountain named Stuart. Why? Because it would make people wonder why he required one.

Grant watched, and soon Zeppelin had their own private heavies—a mass of muscle that ultimately resolved itself, in 1977, in the form of John Bindon, a hard-man actor whose greatest gangster roles were drawn from his own past history as a gangster in real life. With exquisite serendipity, Defries had known Bindon back when they were teens.

Defries employed a gaggle of Warholian actors to act as Bowie's promotional team, knowing that their natural gift for gossip would ensure that his name and his antics were always on the grapevine—and also that if his own antics did not measure up to their standards, they were more than capable of inventing some and spreading those tales instead. Grant engaged his own little coterie to serve the same function for Zeppelin: journalists who could be relied upon to make certain a story both spread and stick, road crew and assistants to deliver first-hand accounts, groupies who would be proud to document their dealings in superhuman stud-farm detail, and so on. It all cost money; of course it did. But Grant knew that if all his ducks were in place, Led Zeppelin would be making money. And a lot of it.

"It came down to keeping your ear to the ground," Grant continued. "You'd hear such and such a band did this or that thing to a girl, or a venue, or a hotel suite, and before they got their story out to the public, or while it was still floating around as an unattributed rumor, we'd start the whisper that it was Zeppelin who did it. As long as it was outrageous, and as long as it sounded good."

The Mudshark incident, for example: a willing groupie squirming bound and naked on the bed while her hosts, the Vanilla Fudge, fished for mudsharks from their window at Seattle's Edgewater Inn. Or for red snappers. Or even for octopus and squid. And then introduced her to the curious fish. In very intimate ways.

Or maybe the girl was in the bathtub. And maybe it wasn't Vanilla Fudge, but members of their support band, Led Zeppelin. Maybe the Fudge's Mark Stein filmed the whole thing. Maybe he didn't.

There's a clutch of supposed eye-witness accounts, and not one of them agrees with the other. Frank Zappa even set the whole saga to music, and his version makes it clear that the Fudge were the dudes who did the deed. But it was Zeppelin's legend that took the credit, and Zeppelin that reinforced it four years later when the band returned to that same hotel and were banned from ever staying there again after leaving their rooms strewn with dead, stinking fish, presumably to replace the furniture they'd thrown into the bay outside.

And as late as 2012, in a poem condemning the sexual depravity with which recent news sensations had revealed the show-biz '70s to be rife, poet Heathcote Williams condemned Led Zeppelin for amusing themselves by "[tying] a red-haired teenage groupie to a bed" and doing unmentionable things to her with a red snapper.

Forty-three years on from the night in question, the story still had the capacity to shock and awe. Now, *that* is myth-making at its finest.

None of which is to suggest that, even as first-time visitors to the United States, the occasionally homesick youngsters were a bunch of shrinking violets. Indeed, according to the groupie grapevine, shrinkage was the last thing that Robert Plant ever worried about—and that despite him not even playing ball with the crown princesses of American groupiedom the night the legendary Plaster Casters came to call.

Their modus operandi was simple. To preserve, in plaster of Paris, a life-size, life-*like* representation of the sexual organs of visiting rock stars. A lot of rockers had succumbed to their blandishments, too, and even admired the castings of their contemporaries.

Not Robert Plant. Back in England, interviewed by the *International Times*, Plant confessed:

> These two girls came into the room with a wooden case, suitably inscribed and all very ceremonious. All of a sudden, one of them starts to take her clothes off. She's rather large, no doubt about it, and there she is, standing naked as the day she was born.
>
> Then she covered herself with soap, cream doughnuts and whiskey, all rubbed in together, head to toe, and she's this moving mountain of soapy flesh. At first, she dug it. But her friend, who come along for the ride, began trying to disappear under the bed. Eventually, she got into the shower, grabbed her clothes and split.

Nevertheless, anybody puzzling over Plant's rechristening with the nickname "Percy" (and maybe doubting the later insistence that it was derived from his unwillingness to ever open his purse) needs look no further than a movie of the same name, released in the UK in 1971, detailing the none-too-unpleasant travails of a young man who underwent a penis transplant and found himself blessed with unslakeable lust.

Plant, at least, looked back on this first tour with just a hint of self-reproach. "I must have been pretty insecure to want to run around, pushing my chest out, pursing my lips and throwing my hair back like some West Midlands giraffe," he told *Q* magazine in 1988. And insecurity can often lead to people either taking the credit for, or actually, physically, undertaking, actions and behavior that they might not want to tell their wives about.

But the fact remains, or so Grant confirmed:

> Led Zeppelin were no worse behaved on tour than any other band at the time, and really didn't do much that other groups

would have considered out of the ordinary. I saw, or heard about, far worse things going on when Jimmy and I toured with the Yardbirds, and the same with Jeff Beck. Bad Company, the Pretty Things . . . if a girl, or girls, were up for it, there's not many boys who'd turn them away.

Plus, you have to remember that Percy, Bonzo and Jonesy were all married men, and Jimmy might as well have been, because Charlotte [girlfriend Charlotte Martin] was always around. I'm not saying they didn't misbehave. Just that a lot of the things people think they did . . . they didn't.

Not so much Hammer of the Gods, then, as much as Floppy Rubber Mallet Such as Clowns Sometimes Have?

"Maybe. But even they can leave a bruise if they catch you correctly."

If tales of Zeppelin's superhuman debauchery may have been exaggerated by people whose job description included embroidering half truths into rock legend—and if a recitation of their purported misdeeds is interesting more because of who they were than what they actually did—those pertaining to the Zeppelin organization's capacity for violence are somewhat less open to interpretation.

As an ex-wrestler himself, Grant was renowned for his ability to cow even the most recalcitrant promoter, and he purposefully staffed the band's entourage with like-minded souls. John Bonham, too, had a ferocious appetite for destruction, coupled with a bottomless capacity for alcohol and a sense of fun that *began* at most people's outer limits. When animal rights organizations rose to condemn Zeppelin after reports that a flock of geese had been assembled at a New York City hotel reception and then chased out onto the street where several were killed by the traffic, it was Bonham who had done the chasing. When some London record executives were found mummified in sticky tape and deposited in the middle of Oxford Street, it was Bonham who had wielded the tape gun.

But perhaps the story that best sums up Bonham was another recounted by Peter Grant: "We were at a party, and somebody came out with the

[joke] about 'What do you call a man who hangs with musicians . . . a drummer.' Bonzo walked over, towering above this guy, and asked, 'And what do you call a man who hangs with drummers?' Then he just picked the guy up and swung him over the balcony, about twenty floors above the ground." Grant laughed. "I never did hear the punchline, but I'm so glad the guy didn't say 'Let me go.' Bonzo probably would have."

For all the acclaim that awaited the live show, *Led Zeppelin I* did not receive an easy ride at the hands of the critics. Many regarded it as a pale imitation of the Beck album, released almost a full year earlier; others got their kicks from reading through the writing credits, then finding earlier versions of the songs that Led Zeppelin claimed were their own. Disputes and lawsuits dating from the band's first few records were still being sorted out years, even decades, later, and some of them proved as difficult to unravel as any attempt to actually pigeonhole the album.

Blues consumed much of the disc. But folk, too, played its part in the record, and so did something approaching conventional pop, as "Communication Breakdown" rose out of its staccato-riff intro to become an apocalypse in under three minutes. All of which either thrilled or repulsed the critics who heard it, with many in the latter category even switching off the stereo long before they reached the album's climax: two songs (although the credits listed just one) that remain the single, shining example on that first LP of all that Led Zeppelin would go onto create.

Albert King's "The Hunter" was a recent addition to the bluesman's own catalog; he cut it for the first time in 1967, but it immediately moved into Ike and Tina Turner's repertoire, and also into that of the then-fledgling Free. Zeppelin took it too, jamming their own interpretation of Howling Wolf's "How Many More [Years] Times" one night in the studio, and then slipping seamlessly into a few lines of "The Hunter" and sliding sweetly into overdrive.

There is no showboating, no grandstanding. No single instrument outplays any other, no ingredient is less focused than another. No matter which player you choose to focus your ears upon, he is unleashing his greatest performance ever. For some, it is Plant's so-intuitive vocal, locating his true voice for the first time on the record. For others, it is the gymnastics turned by both Page and Jones. And for others, it is Bonham's drums that raise "The Hunter" to glory, chasing the melody with such deliberate strength that the song still ranked among his very finest outings even during the band's last days. And *that* was the spirit that they took onstage with them.

By Led Zeppelin's own standards, they played good gigs and they played bad ones, nights when the equipment didn't work correctly, or the venue's acoustics seemed ranged against their sound, or maybe someone's mind was elsewhere and a few cues were dropped or solos flew south. By their audience's standards, however, enshrined as Zeppelin had been by the miasmic meanderings of so many of the era's best bands—and even Vanilla Fudge, for all their bombast, were capable of some staggeringly inane slabs of noodle—they represented the return of rock to something approaching its earth-shattering, sense-crushing origin. At a time when the Who were dragging *Tommy* round the country, subverting their natural might and majesty for a collection of passages that only flared intermittently; with the Beatles broken and the Stones off the road; with the Dead drawing doodles and the Doors fast descending into more paunch than punch, Led Zeppelin arose from nowhere to slam a heavyweight fist into the belly of bland complacency. And if the critics didn't get it . . . then who cares? When was the last time a critic paid for music anyway?

Back home, the *International Times* did understand, referring to the band as "the Archetypal rock supergroup," and—even more importantly—one in which all four members were equal partners, both on stage and in the media. There was no single stand-out musician, no one player to whom the public made a singular bee-line. Ten Years After (Alvin Lee), Fleetwood Mac (Peter Green), and the Nice (Keith Emerson) all represented examples of that particular snakepit. Led Zeppelin would face no such crisis.

Work on Led Zeppelin's second album began in Los Angeles in April 1969 and continued on over the remainder of the year, a far cry from the speed with which *Led Zeppelin I* was hammered down, but an unavoidable consequence of their workload. Off the road in the States, they were touring the UK; breaking from that circuit, they were back in the States. New material was still flowing, though, as Plant resurrected his old "Lemon Song" showstopper for an even more lasciviously pleading, dripping, slice of salacity; as "Heartbreaker" and "Thank You" swaggered into view; as the broad and so exquisitely landscaped "What Is and What Should Never Be" chased light and dark, quiescence and chaos, across the musical spectrum.

True, the freshness of ideas was certainly flagging by the time they came to add John Bonham's "Moby Dick" drum solo to the running order, a workout that might indeed have been physically and technically brilliant but really is a drag to listen to more than once. But balancing that was another new song that, more than any other in sight, would guarantee *Led Zeppelin II*'s immortality—at the same time as not simply blueprinting the entire future history of Heavy Metal but also dispensing with any need for it to even have a history. "Whole Lotta Love" said it all in five minutes.

Across the first album, Plant had been constrained from taking any songwriting credits by his two-year-old contract with CBS. Freed from that now, his lyrical nous was spread across the disc, including several songs with very fixed eyes on his life outside the band: "Thank You," written for Maureen; "Ramble On," with its blatant dedication to his beloved *Lord of the Rings*, name-checks for "the darkest depths of Mordor," and "Gollum, and the evil one." And "Whole Lotta Love," infused not only by his pen but, when the band performed it live, by his love of so much other music, a showcase for stolen moments that ranged from "Boogie Mama" to Joni Mitchell's "Woodstock."

And while the critics again grumbled that the song was already remaining the same and *Led Zeppelin II* was mere lumpen idiocy playing to rock's lowest common denominators, audiences positively went wild for it. Released in October 1969, it chased the Beatles' latest up the chart and then knocked it off the top. A little more than a year later, Alexis Korner's take on "Whole Lotta Love" was beginning a decade-long life as the theme to British TV's *Top of the Pops*, the single-most influential music show of the age—and that despite Zeppelin never even releasing a single in Britain and thus removing themselves from the show's catchment area. And across both the US and Europe, news that Led Zeppelin were flying overhead saw concert halls placed under hysterical siege.

Led Zeppelin I had subverted the blues, but largely remained within their parameters. Most listeners imagined that *Led Zeppelin II* would continue plying that same boisterous journey. Instead, the band had skewed off on a new route entirely, and produced a second record that in no way echoed their first. Which is a very clever trick if you can pull it off properly. And one that Robert Plant would not prove at all averse to repeating, twenty years on down the road.

11

The Last Time I Saw Her
(1988–1994)

Off the road for a short time and then back to the US at the end of 1988, Plant whisked the band back into rehearsals in the new year, with a new album paramount on his mind. Anybody expecting a prompt follow-up to the textures and passions of its predecessor, however, was in for a major surprise. Early sessions at Plant's newly purchased home in Monmouth painted his intentions in vivid neon: a complete reversal of *Now and Zen*, a record that sounded as basic and heavy as he could possibly get away with.

Even his choice of studios spoke of his ideal, as he returned to Olympic in the London suburb of Barnes, the very same surroundings in which *Led Zeppelin I* took shape back in 1968. It was as if he were acknowledging the problems of the Madison Square reunion by—again—going back to the source of the legend in the first place and rebuilding it in his own image.

His scheme appeared to be working, too. On November 21, 1989, with the sessions done and dusted, Plant arranged for what the record books record as the third Led Zeppelin reunion, although this one was to take place far from the spotlights of the world. Daughter Carmen was celebrating her twenty-first birthday with just a couple of hundred friends, at the Hen & Chickens pub in Oldbury. Of course she wanted a live band to play, and of course her father was happy to oblige. Accompanied by his old friends John and Jimmy, with Chris Blackwell and Phil Johnstone dropping by as well, Dad serenaded his firstborn with a selection of the songs that she had grown up alongside: "Rock and Roll," "Misty Mountain Hop," and "Trampled Under Foot." There may even have been a couple more. But nobody was keeping score. It was a private party, for goodness' sake.

Manic Nirvana, Robert Plant's fifth solo album, reached the racks in March, 1990, a shock to the system for anybody expecting Plant to have continued pursuing the paths of *Now and Zen*. The opening "Hurting Kind (I've Got My Eyes On You)" set the stage, with slashing guitars punctuating lyrics that bled '50s insurrection and verses that defied any kind of convention—almost random snatches of speech and melody that resolved themselves only when they hit the seven-word chorus—while Plant's vocals wailed like a siren. "Big Love" reinforced the attack, choppy rhythms and scattershot riffs that the occasional ear compared to mid-period Zeppelin, musical unmusicality that could have found a happy home among the shorter shots on *Physical Graffiti*, but updated in a manner that gave the entire disc an edgy air.

There was no easy listening here, no sense that Plant was settling back into anything approaching his fifth decade on earth. "Nirvana" churned on hardcore-guitar assault, manic indeed even after the big drums echoed the '80s through the mix. "Tie Dye on the Highway" swirled on an angry, gothic axe attack, vicious and relentless, a loping loop that paused for mere seconds before the crackled wax thunder of "Your Ma Said You Cried in Your Sleep Last Night" reeled back to an undiscovered primal rock 'n' roll vibe, "Heartbreak Hotel" meets "Summertime Blues" in the radioactive bayou night.

"Liars Dance" sailed resplendent over heartwarmingly mournful acoustic guitar, if only to ensure that "Watching You" could pound paranoia from the battlements.

And from the same sessions (but reserved for a B-side), "Oompah" felt like a Disney soundtrack, with a subtitle that was pure Monty Python—"Watery Bint" is a line from their *Holy Grail* movie, tormenting the Arthurian legend of the Lady of the Lake, as a serf confronts the King on his claims that he is rightful ruler of the land because a watery bint lobbed a scimitar at him. Dialogue at the end of the song, incidentally, was lifted from Wolves hero Steve Bull's comments on Wolves' club-call line.

From start to finish, front to back, *Manic Nirvana* was pure testosterone, an ear pressed to the wall of a garage-band rehearsal, then painstakingly realigned so that every sound hung in exquisite isolation.

It may have been too much. It certainly sat in dissonant awkwardness alongside the rest of the year's offerings, with even the most common comparison, to Neil Young's furious *Ragged Glory*, little more than a limp nod toward a certain common ground. Young's album, for all its deliberate noise making, retained a warmth rootsiness amid its innovation. *Manic Nirvana*, by comparison, was the sound of breaking glass, a CD that demanded you play it loudly and wreck the house while doing so.

The ensuing tour was less abrasive, the new material scaling its extremes back to become more of a whole with the older songs, although it says much for the general critical response that far more print was expended on rumors that Plant was seeing rather a lot of Alannah Myles, the support act on the current tour, than on the events of the tour itself. Back at Jennings Farm, however, Shirley awaited his return, and nine months after Plant got home from the tour, in January 1991, the couple celebrated the birth of their own first child, Jesse Lee. And this time, for the first time in Plant's life, he intended to be there to watch his son grow up.

There was no return to the studio to crank out a successor to *Manic Nirvana*, no restless urge to get back on the stage. For two years, Robert Plant was a superstar no more, sitting back while the music scene revolved through its next set of convolutions, and not really caring one iota for it. In the past, through the '80s, as he sought to establish his solo chops, he had listened to the radio and new music ceaselessly, driven to compete with whatever new material he heard, and generally succeeding too. But that task was complete now. He had proven himself to his own satisfaction, and had bucked the trend of the failing old farts that so many of his peers had tumbled headlong into. Now it was time to relax, and that meant listening to music for fun, to remember what he loved as opposed to what he should be learning, and to bury himself in books—old favorites, new interests.

Only once did he interrupt his seclusion. On October 27, 1991, his old friend and mentor Frank Freeman, host of the Dance Club in Kidderminster, collapsed and died. Plant had remained loyal to Freeman's long after his fame moved beyond Kidderminster's reach; every Christmas that he could make it, he and his family were guests at the Dance Club's festive party. When he heard about the tribute concert that was being arranged in Freeman's memory the following spring, Plant not only agreed to perform, he also interrupted rehearsals for the somewhat higher-profile Freddie Mercury Tribute Concert to do so.

Plant performed two numbers at the Mercury show, at Wembley on April 20, 1992, Queen's "Innuendo" and "Crazy Little Thing Called Love," plus a couple of crowd-pleasing Zeppelin snatches, "Kashmir" and the intro to "Thank You." Then it was home again to continue pondering—though he scarcely said a word to anybody about it—a new album, *Fate of Nations*. One that he intended would restate every one of the core values he held most dear.

"Right after the *Manic Nirvana* album, I knew what I was going to do," he told *Interview*. "Go back into my past. I wanted to know what I really loved to listen to, what I could really associate with." He was tired, he said, of "drinking from the cup of the contemporary sonic order," because he had suddenly realized, "I didn't need to."

He did not abandon the musicians he'd been working with. Charlie Jones, Doug Boyle, Phil Johnstone, and Chris Blackwell would all take part in the sessions, although their contributions would necessarily be competing with those of an array of other players—among them a new producer, Chris Hughes, whose own roots included a spell playing drums for Adam and the Ants. Later, sundry members of the old band spoke out about those sessions, the sense of uncertainty and unease that permeated recordings that clearly were not intended to engender a mood of security.

Perhaps thoughtlessly, although with commendable honesty, Plant made no secret of the fact that he had two or three players in mind for every instrument, and particularly during the first set of sessions, at the RAK Studios in London, his regular musicians could scarcely avoid the sight of the newcomers hanging out. Later, too, as the sessions moved to the residential Sawmills Studio in Cornwall, Plant thought nothing of calling somebody else in, *not* because he didn't think the players around him could do what he wanted, but because he knew that somebody else could do it better. And swirling in and around them, just as their contributions to the record would swirl in and around the expected instrumentation, was a wealth of unexpected guests: classical violinist Nigel Kennedy; hurdy-gurdy maestro Nigel Eaton, string arranger Lynton Naiff, Jethro Tull multi-instrumentalist Maartin Allcock, guitar legend Richard Thompson, Celtic siren Marie Brennan, and a trio of Indian musicians—Nawazish Ali Khan, Gurbev Singh, and Sursie Singh—adding violin, dilruba, sarod, and sarangi to the stew.

Yet this portrait of its esotericism is but the opening fanfare to what even Plant's career-encompassing *Nine Lives* box set would describe as "quite simply the best album Plant had made with any band . . . as unexpected as it was unprecedented . . . epic, adventurous and deeply challenging." This was no casting back to the folkier pastures of *Led Zeppelin III*, the 1970 album that so furiously recanted the band's burgeoning reputation as heavy metal pioneers. No reimagining of the proto–World Music landscapes that whipped "Kashmir" into shape. It was so much more fulfilled than either.

The opening "Calling to You" saddled Western rock riff and Eastern energies alike, while staccato drums nailed down a rhythm that would have been ponderous were it not all so exciting. "Come into My Life," with Richard Thompson's guitar so instantly recognizable, molded itself into the imagination even before Marie Brennan's spectral backing vocals slipped into earshot. "If I Were a Carpenter," the Tim Hardin composition that Plant had adopted as a showcase back in the Band of Joy days, rode sensitive strings and a softly picked mandolin, and "Great Spirit" slithered across the floor, a funky second cousin to Patti Smith's "Ghost Dance," mourning man's destruction of the planet and calling upon its natural spirit to arise and repair the damage.

Plant sang with heartbreaking passion of his lost son Karac in "I Believe," and the gossips had a field day with the assumption that he'd written a song for Alannah Myles too, "29 Palms." And then there was "Network News," a savage assault on the Western world's so-recently concluded Desert Storm assault upon Iraq and the manner in which it was portrayed by the media.

"I was disgusted with all the propaganda surrounding the Gulf War," Plant chided. "The constant flood of details and death was so obscene, and taking in all this carnage was just too much." "Network News" put that rage into focus—and beyond that, the album's very title spoke to the brittle balance that is international politicking. But it was the feel of the album, the constant questing for something more than rock and noise and energy, that truly encapsulated Plant's feelings and his hopes for the future.

It was a stellar album, then, albeit one destined to receive far greater plaudits later in time than it would upon release. Commercially overshadowed by even *Shaken 'n' Stirred*, its downfall was only exacerbated when Plant went out on tour and found himself *opening* for Lenny Kravitz, an American performer who had established himself as the latest absurdly judged "future of rock," essentially by basing his entire act upon the genre's most sainted past.

The two artists were conjoined for only a handful of dates around Europe that summer, and Kravitz's own star was destined to soon fade. But for anybody with a soupçon of history in their veins, it was a reversal of fortunes that could never been imagined, albeit one that should have been expected, which was, even in the short history of rock 'n' roll, an inevitable consequence of the passing of time.

In the '80s, old prog fans had gazed in horror upon bills that placed Marillion, who wouldn't have existed without the giants of the past, ahead of Peter Hammill, one of the mightiest of those giants. In the '60s, it was the Rolling Stones headlining over Bo Diddley that sent the purists white with rage. A new generation is always going to trump those who came before, because otherwise what purpose does it serve? If the old guard remains forever on the throne, then all future growth will wither and die.

In 1993, Robert Plant was as about relevant to the average teenager as Frankie Valli would have been to a mid-'70s Zeppelin fan, or Dinah Shore to Plant when he was fifteen. So what if they'd made some good records in the past? A forty-five-year-old man is never going to speak to the fascinations of a teenager, not when there's other teens-or-thereabouts making music that does. It was now the turn of Nirvana, Suede and Saint Etienne, Pearl Jam and Pavement, Nine Inch Nails. And good luck to the lot of them.

All of that said, the early 1990s were somewhat less harsh with respect to another of Plant's generation. True to Jimmy Page's word, the Firm had acknowledged their infirmities after that second album, but the guitarist had not yet tired of the supergroup format, as he teamed up with one-time Deep Purple/Whitesnake frontman David Coverdale to create the no-nonsense double billing of Coverdale-Page.

It was, by either man's standards, a grisly enterprise. Coverdale, whose vocal abilities rarely strayed far from an anguished shriek, and whose lyrical talents seldom found their way outside his pants, certainly imbibed their album with a modicum of bite. You couldn't argue with its chart success, either, an American Top Tenner at the same time as *Fate of Nations* barely nibbled the toes of the Top 40. But it all seemed very desperate, routine clichés piled upon half-baked hooks, as though both musicians simply phoned in their parts from a call box someplace sunny. And when Page seemingly acknowledged that he'd only done the Coverdale thing because the singer he most wanted to work with was busy, then maybe that singer pricked his ears up as well.

Plant's next American tour did sell out at most of its halts, but only because the halts themselves were smaller than any he'd played since the Honeydrippers back in 1981: theaters and converted movie houses mostly, two-to-three thousand people a pop—sometimes more in the most loyal markets, but nothing like anything he'd grown accustomed to playing.

But in a lot of ways, it worked. *Fate of Nations* was not an album for arenas. It demanded an intimate setting, an audience that could see what was going on with their own eyes, and whose proximity washed up to the stage to the players. Last time out, in 1990, Plant had played the Seattle Center Coliseum, an echoing concrete barn that might have been designed as an Olympic-sized swimming pool for all the ambience it possessed. This time around, it was two nights at the Paramount, a beautifully preserved 1920s movie house that now staged both concerts and theatrical presentations.

Plant tailored the live set for the surroundings, but also for the loyalty of the fans that filled the venue. Just two songs into the set, "Ramble On" rambled out of the Zeppelin songbook. Later, and elsewhere on the tour too, three or four of a seemingly bottomless bagful of Zeppelin classics would be hauled into view. "Thank You," "Going to California," "What Is and What Should Never Be," "Babe I'm Gonna Leave You," "Whole Lotta Love," "Nobody's Fault but Mine," "Living Loving Maid," "Immigrant Song," "Custard Pie," "Trampled Under Foot," "You Shook Me"—every night, a set that lasted around seventy minutes would pause in its perusal of the latest album and the best of the rest that preceded it to deliver an opening rumble that every soul in the venue knew.

Now the reviews bounced back, and as word spread of the tour's nightly triumphs, so MTV approached Plant to record a show for what had long ago established itself among the channel's most popular programs ever, the very sensibly titled *MTV Unplugged*. The format was simple. Take a band, any band, and strip away their electric instruments. *Unplugged* was an acoustic showcase, a chance to allow a song to breathe without the accoutrements of amplification and effects. And it worked fabulously.

Squeeze were the first band to headline the show back in 1989, but it was Paul McCartney's appearance in 1991 that truly established it, not only as a broadcast, but also as a recording of his performance spun out as his own *Unplugged* album. Since that time, Mariah Carey had topped the US chart with a single drawn from her *Unplugged*, and Eric Clapton grabbed six Grammys when he released a CD of his broadcast. Neil Young and Bob Dylan both took the *Unplugged* route, and Nirvana's airing in late 1993 stands as many viewers' final memory of frontman Kurt Cobain before his suicide the following April. At least for now, *Unplugged* was more than a showcase for the artists who appeared. For many, it was the most valuable television exposure they could get.

Of course Plant agreed, and initially he saw the show as the ideal introduction to his next scheduled project: an album built around a collection of North African loops and drones that the French producer Martin

Meissonnier, husband of the Tunisian singer Amina, had collected from the University of Tunis and was now assembling for him. But manager Bill Curbishley had his eye on richer prizes. His client base had recently expanded to include Jimmy Page as well. Maybe the pair of them could do something together?

On November 20, 1993, as Plant prepared for the first of two nights at Boston's Orpheum Theater, Page flew into town and watched the gig, then after the show the pair sat down to talk. Plant was open to a collaboration but remained adamant that he wanted to work with Meissonnier's drones, as Page told *Rolling Stone*'s David Fricke later on. "He had these loops and it was, 'Let's see if Jimmy can come up with anything. Or is he about to get in the limousine with David Coverdale?'"

Page surprised him. "I'm fine with a challenge."

He was, but Plant remained uncertain. He had recently been working with Tucson-based, Berlin-born guitarist Rainer Ptáček, recording a clutch of what Plant described as "eerie and very open" songs at RAK Studios in London. Now the pair were seriously considering taking their collaboration to the next level. Plant asked for more time to think about the Page project, first as his tour continued on through South America and then once he got home to Wales again. (The Ptáček project never got off the ground. In 1996, the guitarist was diagnosed with the brain tumor that would kill him the following November. Before that happened, Plant and Giant Sand's Howie Gelb schemed a tribute album, *The Inner Flame*, to raise funds for Ptáček's continuing treatment; Page and Plant contributed one song, "Rude World," to it.)

It was April 1994 before Plant gave his assent, after he and Page got up to play at a tribute to Alexis Korner, who'd died the previous New Year's Day. It was the first time they had shared a stage since Jason Bonham's wedding party, almost four years ago to the day, but whereas John Paul Jones had again completed the quartet on that occasion, this time it was to be just the pair of them.

They came up with a name for the project as well. It was to be called *UnLedded.*

The venture was never intended as a Led Zeppelin "reunion" in any shape or form. Rather, it was an opportunity for two former members of the band to revisit their past in the guise of their own current fascinations— which, with Plant sticking to his guns, meant either reworking or recreating any old songs they wanted to play, to conform with the North African disciplines he was determined to mine. In fact, one of the first pieces they completed to their satisfaction was a completely new song, constructed directly around one of Meissonnier's loops, titled "Yallah."

Plant was, he insisted in a 2007 *Mojo* interview, a very different person from the one Page had worked with all those years before. "The whole idea of being able to brandish the Arab link was so important to me and really crucial. If you don't modify it or present it in hushed tones, but mix it the way we are, a couple of questionable characters of ill repute, then you make a totally different form." In another interview, with *Show*, he admitted, "I don't want to bring too much attention to the past, beyond the fact we're old fuckers who can still do it and have a history."

The choice of accompanying musicians reinforced his determination that no matter how the show might be billed, it remained *his* edition of *Unplugged*. Rehearsing with Charlie Jones and drummer Michael Lee, recruited to the set-up for the *Fate of Nations* tour, Plant added arranger Ed Shearmur and Egyptian percussionist Hossam Ramzy, whom he'd first heard on the soundtrack to Scorsese's *The Last Temptation of Christ*. Ramzy in turn was placed in charge of building a band of his own countrymen, in whose hands "Kashmir" became the first experimental guinea pig—and, in places, barely recognizable, as the Egyptians slipped into their homeland's own blues, baladi, and then bade Plant and Page blend their intentions the best they could.

The result was eerie, alien, ecstatic. They were on their way.

In many ways, the rehearsals for this latest collaboration harked back to another, a little over twenty years before, when Plant and Page—again infused by the quest for new sounds and experimentation—decamped for a few weeks to India, to record with the Bombay Symphony Orchestra. Two songs reworked from the then-recently released *Led Zeppelin IV* and its predecessor, *Led Zeppelin III*, were attempted, "Four Sticks" and "Friends." And while that enterprise was ultimately deemed a failure and consigned to the archive, its spirit—and indeed those same two songs—was an instant touchstone for this new outing.

So was a second trip the pair took in 1972, this time to Morocco, where with tape recorder in hand, they listened to and captured the sound of the country's master musicians. It was a trek that the Rolling Stones had undertaken back in 1968, which Brian Jones preserved on what became the *Brian Jones Presents the Pipes of Pan at Joujouka* album. Plant and Page had no such grandiose ideas at that time. But now, as they talked and schemed their latest project, the emotions they experienced and the music they heard on that adventure came screaming back into focus.

Other instruments eased in. Porl Thompson, guitarist across the Cure's late '80s output, and hurdy-gurdy man Nigel Eaton joined the sessions. When "The Battle of Evermore" was suggested as a possibility, Plant leapt at the opportunity to transport the song from the mists of English myth to the burnished lands of djinn and marid. Najma Akhtar, an English-born Indian singer, joined the team, and in August 1994, Plant and Page moved on to Marrakech, Morocco, where they would shoot a series of filmed interludes to be run during the MTV broadcast, with the Gnaoua master musicians as their accompaniment. Other footage was filmed in a slate quarry close to Plant's home in Snowdonia, and then it was time for the concert itself, spread over three consecutive nights at the end of the month, with the London Metropolitan Orchestra added to the soundscape.

Not every reinvention was successful, although few fans can agree which ones. But "Gallows Pole," a song that was old even before the American collector Francis Child reeled it in for his esteemed anthology of ballads in the late nineteenth century, swung as carefree as any song about a hanging ought to do, while "When the Levee Breaks"—remembering the great flood that drowned much of Mississippi in 1927—swept away the years. Across the board, the opportunity to reinvent so many old favorites with new eyes and ears, and develop old notions into fresh compositions, was clearly one that both Plant and Page relished. Indeed, so vast was the acclaim, and so successful the album that appeared in time for Christmas (so aptly titled *No Quarter*) that when the offers came in for more of the same, both Plant and Page agreed.

They would remain on the road for more than a year, and in the process bring the ears of a whole new generation to what remains the original band's finest album.

12

Let's Have a Party
(1970–1971)

As Page and Plant pieced together the repertoire for their 1990s re-union with the whole of Led Zeppelin's career at their fingertips, one album resurfaced again and again in their thoughts. Their fourth LP might, at the end of the day, have commanded the most revisions, as the set list settled into at least a vague simulacrum of *Led Zeppelin's Greatest Hits*. But it was their third that provided both the most fascinating challenges, and the most rewarding reinterpretations.

"Immigrant Song," "Gallows Pole," "Tangerine," "Friends," "Hey Hey (What Can I Do)" (the non-album B-side to the "Immigrant Song" 45), "Celebration Day," and a seldom-less-than-sense-shattering "Since I've Been Loving You" all peeled from the grooves of *Led Zeppelin III* as the tour progressed, some to become a constant presence in the repertoire, others to merely thrill the fortunates present on the night they were performed. Hearing the so-distinctive cry that ignites "Immigrant Song" rising over the crowds at the 1996 Glastonbury festival remains a precious memory for all who were there, no matter that it quickly resolved itself into a performance instead of "The Wanton Song." For a few moments, the Vikings took the Summerlands.

Led Zeppelin III remains the band's most divisive album, at least among their first half dozen. To the group members themselves, it was the acid test for all of the ambition that shaped Led Zeppelin in the first place. To their audience, and many of their critics, it was a brazen abrogation of all that they had promised.

Two albums to date had established the group among the most monstrous sounds around, with the occasional dip into calmer waters regarded as mere moments of contrast before the next heavy hitter crashed into earshot. *Led Zeppelin III* was to be *all* contrast. It was an album that would allow Plant to exercise his folkloric passions, and place his love of fantasy into soundscapes a little more appropriate than "Ramble On"; one that would permit Page to give vent to his folk music past, and remind people that not every session he played on in the '60s was a rocking R&B song or play-by-numbers pop.

In the early 1960s, Plant was a huge Joan Baez fan, and he repaid her for a string of much-loved albums by revisiting her interpretation of "Babe, I'm Gonna Leave You" on *Led Zeppelin I*. Later in the decade, he was a part of the team that soundtracked Donovan's rise to glory, often linking with John Paul Jones across the five albums that encapsulate the sheer magnificence of Donovan at his peak. *Sunshine Superman, Mellow Yellow, Hurdy Gurdy Man, A Gift from a Flower to a Garden*, and *Barabajagal* (the last powered also by two cuts recorded with the Jeff Beck Group) ache with echoes of traditional Celtic folk and lore, exquisitely redrafted through the fascinations of the Summer of Love. Donovan himself admits, "I wrote my best songs in response to events around me. There was an entire generation looking for a spiritual path and my music responded to that. It worked like a soundtrack to that search."

In many ways, the search had been called off, as the idealism of the '60s shattered into the bitter factionalism of the decade thereafter. But Page could still conjure the sounds that accompanied it, and Plant—whose own lyrical ambitions far exceeded the "baby yeah ooh" simplicity of the average rock 'n' roll chestbeater—still ached for a psychic return to the innocent passions of that era. Particularly once his next royalty check afforded him the luxury of buying Jennings Farm, the retreat in the hills of his Tolkien-tossed youth, where every sunrise broke like a new song over the horizon.

It was certainly a distant cry from the urban machinations that now propelled the Zeppelin. That first American tour with the Fudge was the last time they'd play second fiddle to anyone. Established now as headliners in their own right, and with Peter Grant's insistence that they were the biggest band in the world finding less and less opposition every time he said it, Zeppelin itself became the madness that Plant needed to escape from.

Barely two years had passed since he walked the streets of Birmingham, London, Stourbridge, *wherever*, in complete and absolute anonymity. Now, even the glimpse of him in the window of a hotel or a dressing room drove crowds of waiting onlookers—and wherever Zeppelin went, there were *always* waiting onlookers—to paroxysms of excitement. And no matter how wild the dreams he had once entertained—of fame and fortune and instant recognition—the reality outstripped them a thousandfold.

He had never had problems making friends. Now he had hundreds and thousands of them, and most he had never even seen before. He'd never had difficulty meetings girls, either, but now they queued up to meet him. A successful West Coast lawyer today, "Lisa" was backstage for the band in Seattle in 1970, and she laughs as she remembers, "I'd have done *anything* to meet Robert"—before adding that she knew plenty of girls who had. "Done *anything*," that is.

Which is the other thing to remember when considering the library full of stories pertaining to Led Zeppelin's on-the-road debauchery: just how few of them actually mention the band members by name. It's simply "Led Zeppelin did this, Led Zeppelin did that." Reminding us that it's not necessarily the musicians who have the wildest fun. It's the roadies and lighting guys, security men and concessions sellers, anyone and everyone within the orbit of the central star. Not that the band members go without, unless of course that's what they prefer. But it's their employees who know all the perks of the job, and "What's in it for me if I get you backstage?" is a pick-up line that has rarely been known to fail.

Get backstage, of course, and there was no longer any need for pick-up lines at all. Particularly when the fan was confronted with what Pamela Des Barres, perhaps the best-known groupie of them all, described as "Robert Plant . . . tossing his gorgeous lion's mane into the faces of enslaved syco-phants. He walked like royalty, his shoulders thrown back, declaring his mighty status." The moment Led Zeppelin reached Los Angeles, she wrote in her memoir *I'm with the Band*, "the groupie section went into the high-est gear imaginable. You could hear garter belts sliding up young thighs all over Hollywood."

They didn't even need to be fans. The *NME*'s Charles Shaar Murray encountered one such young lady when he joined the band in that city, in time to see a gaggle of girls escorted *away* from the dressing rooms by Plant himself. "Plant has no patience with groupies these days," Murray wrote, while one of the luckless ladies consoled herself by declaring, "I don't even *like* Led Zeppelin. I'm only staying here because my friends have a room. I think Zep are really tacky." All of which was fabulous fun while the madness was in full motion. But when the tour was over and the last girl sent home, home itself was the sanctuary where normality reigned. Time to read, time to think, time to sleep. And time to write, which is why, even before Plant met up with Jimmy Page to begin considering their options for album No. 3, he was already sketching ideas out, and leafing through favorite books and records too, pinpointing the urges that now drove his muse.

Which were . . .

A return to basics, similar to those that fired America's the Band and, closer to home, Steve Winwood's Traffic. Also, discovering a form of roots music that was uniquely your own but offered a shared fascination for other people too. Concurrent with Led Zeppelin's own rise to glory, the British underground had been beset by a folk revival that owed little to the nascent strummings of early Baez, Dylan, et al. It was one that was fired, instead, by an awareness, if not the disciplines, of rock 'n' roll, emerging from a potpourri that fermented around the same folk clubs Plant had once fre-quented so religiously and taken off from there.

Top of the pile, in terms of esotericism, was the Incredible String Band, a sometimes-duo of Robin Williamson and Mike Heron that tormented ears with a glorious succession of increasingly eccentric folk-infused vi-sions, each one delivered beneath an ever-more-dramatic title: *The Hang-man's Beautiful Daughter*, *5,000 Spirits or the Layers of the Onion*, *Wee Tam and the Big Huge*. It would be some time before Plant truly opened up about his admiration for the Incredibles, how they took the soul of folk music so far from the fields that everyone seemed to know and into the realm of true mythology, *Beowulf, Taliesin*, and *Mabinogion*. But the music he heard in his head as he and Page schemed *Led Zeppelin III* was certainly firmly in their thrall.

Plant was spending time, too, both musically and physically, in the company of Fairport Convention. Dave Pegg, their newly acquired bassist, was his old friend from the Black Country circuit days, and a one-time bandmate of John Bonham's, too, in the Way of Life. Four albums old by the time Pegg joined them, Fairport were *the* undisputed giants of the British folk-rock scene, the Zeppelin of their own musical domain. And as Plant listened to their latest album, Peggy's debut *Full House*, and in particular lost himself in the LP's most epic moment, "Sloth," the sense of light and dark, of depth and perception, but most of all the drama of cause and effect—all became beacons he instinctively recognized as a part of his own songwriting vision. A vision that nothing he had written before came close to fulfilling.

Early in the new year of 1970, Plant closed up Jennings Farm and, with his family in tow, headed west to a cottage that he'd visited in his childhood, high up in the Dyfi Valley overlooking Machynlleth. An eighteenth-century stone dwelling that he'd been able to rent for the next month, it was called Bron-Yr-Aur, Welsh for "golden hill," after the nearby mountain Cadair Idris. It was a Spartan spot: no running water in the taps or toilet (there was a chemical setup, with an adjoining cesspit), no electricity, and little warmth beyond a couple of gas heaters. But he arranged with the landlord of a nearby pub to use his facilities whenever they were required, and in any case, the isolation guaranteed one thing. There would be no interruptions from fans, friends, or the music business.

There, the Plant clan would meet up with Page, Page's girlfriend Charlotte, and a couple of trusted roadies, Clive and Sandy; and while the families explored the surrounding countryside, Plant and Page investigated its moods and melancholy, the myths that swirled in the morning mists, the legends that had so inspired the young Plant to read—and would now inspire him to write. "[It] was a fantastic place in the middle of nowhere,"

Plant enthused to *Uncut* in 2005, "with no facilities at all. . . . It was a fantastic test of what we could do in that environment. Because by that time we'd become obsessed with change, and the great thing was that we were also able to create a pastoral side of Led Zep."

Page, he continued, had been listening to a lot of Bert Jansch and Davey Graham recently, British folk guitarists whose personal and distinct musical approaches had done so much to encourage the folk genre's earliest interests in experimentalism. Plant looked back to a teenaged fascination with John Fahey, an American guitarist taking similar strides on the other side of the ocean. Taken together, they created a common ground many miles away from the musical unity he and Page had already forged, while the absence of electricity ensured, as Page later laughed in a 1977 Trouser Press interview, there would be no "crashing away at 100-watt Marshall stacks. It was acoustic guitar time."

The pair wandered the countryside, guitars in hand. "That's the Way," Plant later revealed, was written as the pair of them sat by a brook one day, Plant strumming the chords, Page embellishing them. Other songs fell as easily into place, not only those that would consume the album, but others that would be held back for another day: "Over the Hills and Far Away" and "Down by the Seaside." They were in Wales for just a month, and the bulk of the new album was written.

They were not, however, finished with self-deprivation. To actually record the final record, they opted not for a well-appointed modern studio in the heart of a major city but rather the village of Headley in Hampshire. There they rented the Grange, a dilapidated mansion house whose history, since it was built as a workhouse in 1795, included its partial destruction by a rampaging mob and a stint in crumbling dereliction.

An unhappy history indeed. In its original guise, it had been a virtual prison for those local unfortunates who could not even subsist in the outside world and were forced to turn to cruel charity for support. If you've read *Oliver Twist*, you've seen the workings of the workhouse: the prison-like conditions, the awful food and living areas. England was changing fast through the first years of the nineteenth century as the Industrial Revolution introduced a whole new layer of oppression into society, and the work-house was its vilest manifestation.

The structure needed to be destroyed. In 1830, Southern England was wracked by unrest and uprisings, as the people finally tired of falling wages, rising prices, and the insouciant greed of their self-styled "betters." The so-called Swing Riots would be the last truly popular insurrection in British history until the Poll Tax riots of 150 years later, and the historians J. L. and Barbara Hammond proclaimed, "[Had] these riots . . . succeeded, the day when the Headley workhouse was thrown down would be remembered . . . as the day of the taking of the Bastille."

Instead, the uprising was crushed. But not before the rioters descended upon both Headley and the neighboring Selbourne workhouse in November 1830, enraged by a local economy that saw them pay more in tithes to the church than they earned for themselves. Escorting the inmates to safety, the rioters embarked upon an orgy of destruction, smashing the furnishings, burning the fixtures, and effectively rendering both buildings uninhabitable—even by the subhuman standards to which workhouse occupants were accustomed. Later, nine local men were charged with leading the assaults, and all nine were sentenced to transportation to Australia. But the workhouse lay in ruins for many years more, until it was purchased in 1870 by the builder Thomas Kemp, and the modern Grange arose from the rubble.

Still, Headley Grange was scarcely Downton Abbey. Even the lawns on which Led Zeppelin parked the Rolling Stones' mobile studio were overgrown and weed strewn, while the echoing, icy caverns that passed as the interior of the house still echoed with the emptiness of the building's sordid past. One night, according to Richard Cole, the inhabitants were forced to tear down one of the building's bannisters to use as firewood to banish the cold.

They could not, however, banish the spirits of the poor and insane folk who had died there. Strange noises in the night that remained inexplicable even after you considered the current occupants of the building—four rock 'n' rollers plus their roadies and crew. The sound of movement in rooms that they knew were emptied; lights and shadows in the periphery of vision.

"It was very Charles Dickens," Page told *Guitar World* in January 2002. "Dank and spooky. The room I chose to live in was at the very top of the building, and the sheets were always sort of wet."

Page liked the place, even when he saw things that bothered him. "I remember going up the main stairway on the way to my room one night and seeing a gray shape at the top. I double-checked to see if it was just a play of light, and it wasn't. So I turned around pretty fast, because I didn't really want to have an encounter with something like that. But I wasn't surprised to find spirits there, because the place had a miserable past."

Robert Plant was less enthralled. "It freaked [him] out," Page continued, and when Led Zeppelin returned to Headley Grange to cut their next album, neither Plant nor Bonham would stay there. There was a nearby hotel that was more to their tastes.

Still, the music that they made at Headley Grange would represent, in their own minds if not a shocked audience's, the most cohesive and self-sufficient that Led Zeppelin had ever constructed. There was no pandering, even subconsciously, to their audience's expectations; the complaint with which many first-time listeners emerged, that there was no new "Whole Lotta Love" on there, could be followed by equally valid complaints that there was no "Communication Breakdown," "Ramble On," "How Many More Times," "The Lemon Song," or "Heartbreaker" either.

Only "Since I've Been Loving You," an epic eight-minute blues that oozed passion and longing from every quarter, truly glanced in the direction of pastures they'd visited previously, a second cousin, perhaps, to the first album's "Babe I'm Gonna Leave You." But a fully grown one, conveyed in a voice that not only knew the words to the song, it understood what they meant as well. Even within the realm of the British blues, wherein it seemed that every classic number had been done to death by every singer there was, Plant's execution of "Since I've Been Loving You" was possessed of an authenticity and a depth of emotion that few, if any, other artists had captured. Which made it all the more remarkable that it was a brand new composition, one of the first songs written for the new album, and one of the first to be recorded too.

One take was all that it required, and the result was so perfect that even the sound of a squeaky bass drum pedal was allowed to remain on the tape—much to Page's annoyance twenty years later, when he revisited the recording for Led Zeppelin's first box set ("It sounds louder and louder every time I hear it!"). And with that in the can, the rest of the record fell effortlessly into place.

The first opportunity that audiences got to hear the new material arrived in late June, when Led Zeppelin headlined the 1970 Bath Festival. Not all of the album was on display—"Immigrant Song," the so-stirring epic of Viking valor that would open the finished LP, had itself only just been written, in the aftermath of an Icelandic gig earlier in the month. Another song, a mutated version of Bukka White's "Shake 'Em On Down," was still untitled, and would remain so until the very day of the festival, until the band watched Roy Harper perform his afternoon set and promptly christened the orphan for him: "Hats Off to (Roy) Harper."

Then it was back to the US, with the album now complete and a tour that simply picked up where the last had left off, in terms of both size and audience response. And in September, Zeppelin's stay at the Continental Hyatt House hotel in Los Angeles was allegedly the catalyst for that establishment's unofficial rechristening as the Riot House, as band and crew alike took the concept of redecoration to brand-new levels. One night, Plant laughed, he was even forced to ask the front desk to supply him with a new room. "The clerk protested until I asked him how he'd like to reside in a room with wall-to-wall hamburger patties, cola-drenched bedsheets, French-fried plastered walls, mustard-smeared mirrors, a sixteen-piece telephone, and gutted cushions where the furniture used to be. I got a new room immediately."

The gang mentality persisted, of course—the suddenness with which all four could erect an entire world of their own around themselves, safe in the knowledge that no one could penetrate it. Many a journalist ran into that, sitting down to interview one member of the group while the other three sat around and watched, making comments beneath their breaths, laughing at questions before they were asked, and encouraging the interviewee to become as uncooperative as they. The *New Musical Express*'s Nick Kent even suffered the ignominy of the entire band walking out of one encounter after he brought up the subject of Zeppelin's sometimes-misleading songwriting credits.

But the band relished companionship too, particularly that of other musicians. John Entwistle of the Who spoke merrily of his band's on-the-road meets with Zeppelin, and Fairport's Dave Pegg as well. Indeed, it was during that same stay in Hollywood that his band and Zeppelin enjoyed their best-known encounter, when Plant led his bandmates down to the Troubadour, where Fairport were enjoying a residency. Of course their arrival ignited a late-night jam session, with songs that took Plant and Bonham both back to Birmingham, "Morning Dew" and "Hey Joe." And then everybody got drunk.

Life, then, was settling into something approaching a routine. The band would tour, and leave the cities they visited with a wealth of anec-dotes about what may or may not have happened there. And then they would go home and try to go about their normal lives, knowing that even the most insignificant outing would become fuel for someone's gossip, or memoirs, somewhere down the road.

Even Plant, still circulating the same geography as he had grown up with, and therefore a familiar figure to almost everyone he passed, was (and remains) astonished to discover that his most mundane trip to the pub, or most casual greeting to someone he recognized, could become the center-piece of anecdotes that are still being told today. When really, all he did was say hello ("but it was the way in which he said it") or stop by the local gun shop to pick up something for the farm. He was trying to live a normal life in between chapters that were absolutely abnormal, by doing the same things that everyone else did—never imagining that by being normal, he struck everyone else as weird. Shouldn't he be arriving at the pub in a fleet of helicopters? Couldn't he have sent the butler out to buy a loaf and a pint of milk? What's he trying to prove?

That he's still a *regular guy*?

13

Tie Dye on the Highway
(1995–1998)

Twenty-five years later, Plant was still trying to prove that he was a regular guy. And it was still difficult. Regular guys don't get inducted into the Rock and Roll Hall of Fame.

On January 12, 1995, Robert Plant, Jimmy Page, and John Paul Jones, the three surviving members of Led Zeppelin, arrived in New York City for the annual bean feast that passed as the induction ceremony.

It was a richly deserved honor, of course, albeit one that it is easy to regard with cynicism. As so many past nominees (and non-nominees too) have remarked, rock 'n' roll is about a lot of things, but being fossilized in a self-congratulatory museum is scarcely one that its founding fathers foresaw. But ever since the first rock bands became eligible for the honor (itself conferred after a minimum of twenty-five years' active service), Led Zeppelin had been a shoo-in for this year's award, shared with Neil Young, Janis Joplin, the Allman Brothers, Frank Zappa, Al Green, and Martha & the Vandellas.

What gave the event a little extra fission was the presence of John Paul Jones. Loudly excluded from the *Unplugged* performance, and from the *UnLedded* tour that was set to follow, no way did his necessary presence that night portend an evening of relaxed bonhomie and backslapping. It was an open secret, at least among those folk who claim to have an ear for such details, that he was not at all happy about his omission from the unfolding project—that he publicly described his old bandmates as "discourteous," with their own silence on the subject adding insult to injury.

Apparently, the first he heard about the upcoming event was less than a month before the MTV program was broadcast, by which time *UnLedded* had been underway for six months—although it is ironic that, for at least one Zeppelin fan, Jones's most recent activities had demonstrated just how far *he* had moved since the old days. He was on the road with avant-garde performer Diamanda Galas, "and one night . . . there was somebody in the audience [who] called out for 'Kashmir,' or something. And Diamanda just fixed them with a glare, shot something back at them, a 'Fuck you' or something, and you could see the whole crowd just parting around this poor guy, leaving him standing on his own in the middle of the floor."

The other pair's supporters have pointed out that both Plant and Jason Bonham joined Page on his *Outrider* album, and nobody questioned Jones's absence from that. Which is true. But *Outrider*, unlike *No Quarter*, was not predicated around the reinvention of music within which Jones was an integral component. Nor was it titled for a Led Zeppelin song that most people associate solely with Jones; like Page's marathon "Dazed and Confused" and John Bonham's "Moby Dick," "No Quarter" was reserved for Jones's solo turn. Indeed, when a journalist asked him outright what he thought about "No Quarter," he replied, "I always reckoned it was one of my better tunes."

Compared with what some people were expecting, then, although probably not people who knew him very well, Jones's acceptance speech at the Hall of Fame was a masterpiece of understatement. He simply said he was glad that this bandmates had finally found his phone number.

Neither was there any sign of discord as the trio, accompanied by Jason Bonham, Michael Lee, Steven Tyler, Joe Perry, and Neil Young, launched into a performance that was more of a jam than an actual set, rounding up "The Train Kept A-Rollin'"; a first-ever live performance of "For Your Life"; "Bring It On Home"; a blues medley that incorporated "The Prison Blues," "Gambler's Blues," and "Baby Please Don't Go"; and an epic "When the Levee Breaks," which acknowledged Young's presence with a dive into a song that Plant had performed in his own early days, Buffalo Springfield's "For What It's Worth." Then it was back to business, and the Page and Plant world tour: a full band augmented in every city by a different local orchestra, rehearsed the day before each gig by Ed Shearmur.

It was, on the surface, a relaxed outing, particularly when compared with the madness that engulfed the pair the last times they toured together. But old differences were never far from the surface, not least of all Page's reluctance—and more often outright refusal—to mix with the rest of the tour party. Unspoken but apparent too was Page's unhappiness with the compromises he'd made in order for the tour to even happen—including, as it transpired, both the absence of John Paul Jones from the band and that of "Stairway to Heaven" from the live show.

Ignited in the US, the tour moved onto Europe and a clutch of festivals, including the annual Glastonbury bash, and then further afield: a second string of American dates, South America, Japan, and Australia. There might have been more, too, but Plant was growing restless. Too many of the old band's demons had returned to haunt his relationship with Page, with the guitarist's eye for the bottle only exacerbating their differences.

Neither were darker shadows ever far away. On November 21, 1995, just months after attending Page-Plant's second night at London's Wembley Arena, Led Zeppelin's old manager Peter Grant was felled by a massive heart attack, and so the three surviving band members were united once again, this time by Grant's funeral at Hellingly Cemetery. His misgivings growing deeper, and more widely shared every day, Plant made it clear that the final show on the current schedule—in Melbourne, Australia, on March 1, 1996—would be the last.

For all the differences and dissatisfaction, the music itself seldom suffered. Just as he had on his *Fate of Nations* tour, Plant set about resurrecting songs that even the original Zeppelin rarely performed live. Traditional concert chest-beaters like "Since I've Been Loving You," "Kashmir," and "Dazed and Confused" of course played their part in the set. But in a show whose prime intent was to reevaluate rather than rehash Zeppelin's career, that also left room for "In the Evening," "Four Sticks," "Friends," and even "Hey Hey What Can I Do," a song that had only ever been aired on a 1970 B-side. There was even a nod toward Porl Thompson's past, a deliciously chilling dance through the Cure's eerie paean to arachnophobia, "Lullaby," while those final dates in Australia saw the band indulge themselves in a televisual treat that rivals even Plant's appearance on *Tiswas*.

The Money or the Gun was a surreal music show whose features, bizarre as it may seem, included its weekly guests being forced to perform "Stairway to Heaven" in their own inimitable fashion. An album of the greatest renditions, sensibly titled *Stairway to Heaven*, was released in 1992, including distinctive and occasionally excruciating versions by such Aussie TV staples as Kate Ceberano and the Ministry of Fun, "Love Is in the Air" hit maker John Paul Young, a B-52s tribute act called the Rock Lobsters, and veteran comedian/singer/artist Rolf Harris, who rendered the song in the spirit of his own "Tie Me Kangaroo Down, Sport" and was promptly rewarded with a UK Top 10 hit.

For Page and Plant to have honored the show with their own version of a song they had written would, of course, have been futile—and in light of the fact that Plant had refused to perform it anyplace else, impossible. So host Andrew Denton offered them an even bigger challenge. Pay tribute to Rolf Harris instead. He bade them play Harris's "Sun Arise" ("My favorite!" laughed Plant), and no matter that the song had already received a rock treatment once before, when Alice Cooper covered it on 1971's *Love It to Death*, still Page and Plant turned in an absolutely unexpected, and utterly priceless, rendition.

Plant returned home after that, accompanied by singer Najma Akhtar, the latest woman in his life. He stewed around the house for a time, decompressing from a year on the road, but inactivity was never a state he could tolerate for long. Soon he was heading off to China for a vacation that took him along the historic Silk Road and onto the Great Wall, then back to England for a spot more recharging of the batteries.

He went to the pub and played soccer with his friends, and busied himself in the fashion of the gentleman farmer he sometimes wished he had become. He resumed his twice-monthly worship at Molineux, the stately but slowly decaying home of his beloved Wolverhampton Wanderers, and watched in a state of disbelief as the club's new chairman, Sir Jack Hayward, began pumping unprecedented sums into the team in a bid to elevate them to the uppermost echelons of the English game.

For a decade since the side diced with extinction in the bleak mid-1980s, Wolves had been knocking on the door. Two promotions in successive seasons took them up to the league's second tier; Steve Bull, a suitably bullish young forward who would spend his entire playing career with Wolves, was knocking in goals for fun, and in 1989 he became one of the first lower-league players ever selected to play for England's national side. Now Wolves were almost there. Twice in the mid-1990s, they were so close to promotion to the top division that their fans could almost taste it, and Plant was as shattered by their failure to take that one final step as anyone else in the crowd. But he continued going to the games.

Plant did not turn his back on music throughout that year away from the bright lights, although very few people were aware of the fact. His local tennis club, Bewdley, was appealing for funds, part of its annual charity drive, and Plant agreed to do what he could to help out.

Choosing a guitarist was easy. Kevyn Gammond, his guitarist back in the Band of Joy, now counted among Plant's neighbors. He also headed up a music course at Kidderminster College, from whence he introduced a drummer: one of his fellow tutors, Andy Edwards. They rehearsed a handful of favorite covers, songs that resonated with all of them, then turned out in front of the two or three hundred souls who had come out to support their tennis club.

Nobody recorded the show, nobody reviewed it. It was off the radar in a tiny place that many folk might have considered was off the map as well. And once it was over, Plant went home.

It was the death of his mother that proved the catalyst for him to start moving again. Of course they had long outgrown the period of estrangement that saw him kicked out of the house as an unruly teen—outlived, too, the sense of disappointment that wracked his parents as they watched him embark upon a life that was a far cry from any they may have mapped out for him. Indeed, there had been times since then when his parents felt like the only truly reliable constants in his entire existence, and losing his mother, as with other past anchors, seemed to force him to begin making fresh changes in his own life.

Breaking with Akhtar was one, but reuniting once again with Jimmy Page was another, a musical decision focused as much on his need for familiarity and comfort as on his continued urge to keep pushing his music forward. Back during the earliest days of the *UnLedded* project, the pair had discussed the possibility of recording a new album together. At that time, an exhausting tour schedule forced the possibility from Plant's mind. Now he was ready.

There would be no extra flourishes this time, no armies of outsiders to blur the lines around the two stars' contributions. Only two further players were recruited to the project, the rhythm section of Charlie Jones and Michael Lee; while their choice of producer, Steve Albini, echoed their determination to take their partnership back to basics, the greatest indication of all that this was not to be Led, or even UnLed revisited.

Still a schoolboy when the old band broke up, Albini's reputation was built upon some of the most uncompromising records of the '80s and '90s, brutal slabs of hardcore punk carved out with such disdain for mainstream tastes that when Nirvana elected him producer of their third album, the follow-up to one of the biggest-selling records of the decade, most observers accused them of plotting commercial suicide before they'd even entered the studio. Of course it did not turn out like that, and *In Utero* was at least as vital as *Nevermind* before it. But still Albini's name was enough to turn the average industry executive pale, and the notion of his sonic terrorism clashing with the giants of classic-rock legend felt unimaginable to even both sides' most fervent admirers.

Which made the finished record all the more remarkable when it was released in April 1998. Recorded at Abbey Road in no more than seven weeks, the four musicians playing live for the most part, hunkered down in one room together, *Walking into Clarksdale* was titled in tribute to the Mississippi town that haunted so many British bluesmen's dreams, and one listened in vain for more than the occasional spectral echo of past Zeppelin heights. Despite boasting no less than twelve brand-new songs composed by Page, Plant, and Lee, it felt like a Robert Plant solo set in all but name, awash in the same ear for a stark modern edge that he applied to his own work and almost painstakingly shy of stepping into what might have felt like recognizable territory.

It is a mood with which Plant seemed to agree, at the same time as acknowledging the album's deficits when, a little over a decade later, he revisited the best track on the original record, the keening "Please Read the Letter," during his collaboration with Alison Krauss—and proceeded to produce a far more satisfying rendering of the song than he and Page ever managed. Which is not to say *Walking into Clarksdale* was a disappointment. Combining the eclecticism of the *UnLedded* live show with the contemporary stylings that Albini brought to bear, *Walking into Clarksdale* could even be seen as an attempt to bring the Zeppelin sound into the mid-1990s, and as such, it succeeded.

The question it did not answer, for reasons that should be obvious, was whether the Zeppelin sound actually needed to be brought there—or whether its original form was timeless enough that any move to modernize it would ultimately wind up sounding hollow and, incredibly, dated. Complaints that could never be leveled at the original act. Played back today, *Walking into Clarksdale* scarcely demands a second listen; it might easily be ranked among the weakest of all Robert Plant's recordings. (Although it was still better than Coverdale Page.)

Perhaps surprisingly, but also inevitably, the band toured in the aftermath of the album, opening with a mini-tour around Eastern Europe in the weeks before its release, then the US and Europe through the end of 1998. And once again, had Plant only had the appetite, more dates and indeed more albums could have followed. But he was growing bored again, not only with the routine, but also with audiences that were so easily sated by the handful of oldies they knew to expect. On his own tours, even those he embarked upon after he lifted his embargo on the oldies, Zeppelin songs were paced and placed in a manner that merely framed the new material. This time around, no less than before, they were the be-all and end-all of the audience's expectations. The new material barely stood a chance.

14

Trouble Your Money
(1971–1973)

T he new material barely stood a chance. Although *Led Zeppelin III* was an instant No. 1, both at home and abroad—and though the band effortlessly topped the annual *Melody Maker* readers poll, the first group that wasn't the Beatles to take the best band in the world category—the album's lifespan was that of a mayfly compared with the mammoth that preceded it.

In and out of the charts in just weeks, not months, and with sales that were but 20 percent of those racked up by *Led Zeppelin II*, the album's cover attracted more attention than its contents, a (literally) revolution-ary wheel that spun within a pocket on the front flap of the jacket, as if to give the listener something different to do while he waited for the crashing metal chord that would finally wake the record up. And which never came.

Fascinating, too, were the inscriptions on the vinyl around the label, hitherto the playground only of arcane details of cataloging information, matrix numbers and pressing codes. That's all that was there on their first two albums, anyway. But this time around, all changed. "Do what thou wilt" read the note on side one; "So mote it be," declared that on side two, the first excerpted from the Thelemic laws devised by Aleister Crow-ley ("Do what thou wilt shall be the whole of the law. Love is the law, love under will"), the second from the rituals of the Freemasons, a fourteenth-century addendum commonly (if not altogether accurately) aligned with the Christian "amen."

Both spoke, in the eyes of those who scour their idols' output in search of hidden mysteries, to Jimmy Page's fascination with the occult in general and Crowley in particular—the self-styled "wickedest man in England," whose death in 1947 had allowed a fascinating, if occasionally ridiculous, philosopher/magician to become the epicenter of a new generation's own understanding (or lack thereof) of magic and ritual.

Page's interest in the subject was naturally another tool in the ongoing campaign to mythologize Led Zeppelin. Whereas his bandmates purchased homes in the wilds of the English countryside, Page bought Boleskine House, Crowley's former home, up in the Scottish highlands. While Plant and Bonham at least played at being "gentlemen farmers," Page opened an occult bookshop and publishing house, Equinox on Church Street, Kensington, and published a facsimile edition of Crowley's 1904 *The Book of the Goetia of Solomon the King*, outlining the correct means of summoning seventy-two demons.

Journalist Mick Houghton is one of the writers who tried to pin down Page on this subject, in a 1976 interview with *Sounds*. But Page was not playing ball:

> I'm not trying to interest anyone in Aleister Crowley any more than I am in Charles Dickens. All it was was that at a particular time he was expounding self-liberation which is so important. He was like an eye into the world, into the forthcoming situation.
>
> My studies have been quite intensive, but I don't particularly want to go into it because it's a personal thing and isn't in relation to anything I do as a musician, apart from that I've employed his system in my own day to day life.

Not that his audience were buying that. As bookstores go, Equinox was heavy duty, exactly what you'd expect from a shop that was also named for one of Crowley's works. It was *the* best occult stockist in the country, and that belief was reinforced by its clientele. On the one hand, there ranged

Robert Plant and his wife, Maureen, during filming of *The Song Remains the Same* in 1973. (Warner Bros./Photofest)

Plant with Maureen and his daughter, Carmen, backstage at Knebworth in August 1979. (Tracksimages.com/Alamy)

Plant in the '80s. Not ready to become a museum piece just yet. (Atlantic Recording Corp./Photofest)

Paul Martinez onstage with the Adverts, October 1979. Martinez became Plant's bassist and bandmate through the first half of the 1980s. (Dave Thompson)

Robert Plant—all that a well-dressed early '90s rock star should be. (Photofest)

Plant strips down on a warm night in Washington State—May 27, 1995, in the city of George at the Gorge Amphitheater. (Dana Nalbandian/Shutterstock.com)

Plant and son Logan take in a Wolverhampton Wanderers soccer game in 2006. (David Bagnall/Alamy)

The Wolverhampton Wanderers have not gotten their paws on English soccer's premier trophy since 1960. But their vice president has. Robert Plant with the FA Cup in 2010. (David Bagnall/Alamy)

Raising sand on the road—Robert Plant and Alison Krauss at the Bonnaroo Music Festival in June 2008. (Kristoffer Tripplaar/Alamy)

Priory of Brion in 2000 (*left to right*): Andy Edwards, Paul Wetton, Robert Plant, Paul Timothy, and Kevyn Gammond. (Dave Peabody/Redferns/Getty Images)

Plant performing with the Strange Sensation at the Sziget Festival in Budapest, Hungary, on August 9, 2006. (Northfoto/Shutterstock.com)

Gathering Grammys: Plant, Alison Krauss, and T-Bone Burnett savoring their wins for *Raising Sand* at the 51st annual Grammy Awards in Los Angeles, 2009. (s_bukley/Shutterstock.com)

President Barack Obama meets (*left to right*) John Paul Jones, Robert Plant, and Jimmy Page at the Kennedy Center Honors on December 2, 2012, in Washington, DC. (White House Photo/Alamy)

Plant performing with the Sensational Space Shifters at the Adelaide Entertainment Centre in April 2013. (WENN Ltd/Alamy)

the wall-to-wall weirdoes who affected every sinister demeanor from Charlie Manson to Morgana Le Fey; on the other, a band of would-be warlocks and witches who found themselves fighting for browsing space with an army of teenaged Led Zeppelin fans, snuffling through the books on display in the hope of answering the questions that most bedeviled their nights: What is the meaning of the horned goat lurking to the left of John Paul Jones on the third album's inner wheel? The ankh that floats beneath him, or the UFOs on the gatefold?

And had Jimmy Page really sold his band's soul to the Dark Lord?

Even today, there's a lot of folk who believe all this. In a March 2014 report on Crowley's continued attraction to a host of latter-day seekers (the late Peaches Geldof among them, apparently), Britain's *Daily Mail* newspaper straight-facedly reported, "Led Zeppelin's Jimmy Page, for example, routinely took part in occult magical rituals and was so intrigued by Crowley he bought his former home."

If Page had concluded his own Faustian pact, however, Peter Grant suggested that he might want to consider asking for a refund. Though one would scarcely call *Led Zeppelin III* a failure by most artists' standards, by those to which Grant held Led Zeppelin, it was a long way from justifying their self-proclaimed status as the biggest band in the world. There was only one remedy. Return to the studio and get another album out quickly. And this time, make sure it had some rockers on board.

The band agreed. Headley Grange was available again, with its peculiar atmospheric mix of calm and cold spots; the Rolling Stones Mobile was back on the lawn; and though the band warmed up for the sessions by simply jamming, even their improvisations appeared golden. Both "Black Dog" and "Rock and Roll," two of the most assertive rockers the band would ever compose, developed out of jams, old Little Richard rockers that morphed magically into something else.

Other songs were shaped by the mood of the musicians; it was a drunken John Bonham, for example, who conjured up the final feel of the mighty "Four Sticks," a rolling, free-skating blur thoroughly underpinned by drums that skitter like giant insects. And it was the Grange itself, with its vast halls setting up acoustic patterns that no studio could ever have replicated, that lent its ambience to "When the Levee Breaks."

All four musicians were sparking. Past chroniclers have credited the month spent with Page at Bron-Yr-Aur the previous year with finally erasing any doubts in Plant's mind that he was his bandmates' equal in terms of what he brought to the band, and the confidence certainly bubbled over now, both in his vocal performances and his lyric writing.

"Going to California," a song whose acoustic bed could easily have slipped onto *Led Zeppelin III*, may or may not have been intended as a paean to the land that inspired so many of Plant's late 1960s dreams—just as it may or may not have reflected on the state's vulnerability to earthquakes. What it did do was offer up a love song to a state of mind he had never hitherto been able to put into words: the mystic peace-and-love vibe that permeated the San Francisco music scene that he had adored as a teen, but whose own creators had long since moved on.

The corollary to this, very deliberately, was "Misty Mountain Hop": "Walking in the park . . . crowds of people . . . with flowers in their hair" sitting around and getting stoned, losing track of time, and sinking into a sea of such apathy that they didn't even seem to care when the police arrived to break it all up—and all delivered in a wordy monotone that almost defied the track to be described as a song, just a looped riff and Plant's droning recital, as pancake flat as the minds it was condemning.

These songs alone marked the new album out as something remarkable. Two songs, however, dominate what became *Led Zeppelin IV*—one, "Stairway to Heaven," rising to such heights that more than forty years later, it is still routinely regarded among the greatest compositions of the rock 'n' roll era; the other, "The Battle of Evermore," though firmly cast in the shadow of the former by its understated arrangement, deserving acknowledgement among Plant's finest-ever lyrics.

"Stairway to Heaven" was originally built around a melody that Page was toying with during the Bron-Yr-Aur respite and only slowly took on its final shape, after the guitarist declared that the new album required an all-pervading anthem, a new "Whole Lotta Love," and set about deliberately marshalling his bandmates into creating one.

Plant wrote as his bandmates played, his lyric building in response to what they were creating at the same time as developing his own themes. The popular modern vision of the song's mystical meaningfulness was, of course, easily punctured when Page admitted, to writer Brad Tolinski, that when he asked Plant to explain the line about there being "a bustle in your hedgerow," the singer simply cackled, "That'll get people thinking." But it could also be argued that it is the intrinsic redundancy of some of the lines that has led to the song's popularity and importance. If every lyric was self-explanatory, there would be no room for the listener's own imagination to take flight, and that was "Stairway to Heaven"'s primary goal.

"It was a milestone for us," Jimmy Page told *Rolling Stone* in 1975. "Every musician wants to do something of lasting quality, something which will hold up for a long time, and I guess we did it with 'Stairway.'"

A pagan love song that became the most played and most requested song in the history of American rock radio, the ultimate youth-club slow dance, the best-selling single piece of sheet music in the world—it was the absolute zenith of Led Zeppelin's folk-rock hybrid. Yet Plant himself was never as impressed with the song as either his bandmates or his audience seemed to be. The lyrics were naive, and sometimes even clumsy. There was no more significance to some than the fact that they rhymed. And, of course, like "Moby Dick" on *Led Zeppelin II*, it became the parent of any number of later sins, as imitator after imitator flocked to create their own "Stairway to Heaven" and ultimately forged an entire new musical genre from it, in the power-ballad boom of subsequent nightmarish infamy.

Nevertheless, "Stairway to Heaven" did pack a punch—a building, soaring edifice that started soft and sweet and rose, precisely as Page had envisioned, to baroque magnificence. And if it was gargantuan on vinyl, it quickly became even vaster on stage, the cue for the entire audience, it seemed, to hold cigarette lighters up in the air and sing along swaying to an anthem they all adored. It is refreshing, then, to listen to the performance Led Zeppelin gave for the BBC in April 1971, six months before the album was released, where the audience doesn't simply not know the words, it doesn't even know the song.

With Plant having apologized for postponing the broadcast the previous week ("We'd done eighteen shows in about six days and my voice just gave out," he explained), he introduces the song as "another thing off the fourth album," and the audience is silent as the grave. Even with a lengthy silence while Jones is "tuning in his bass pedal," leaving Plant "time for a quick swill of tea . . . hold on," and Page toys with the opening melody, the crowd remains quiet. A far cry indeed from the multiple orgasms with which even the opening note would be greeted on later performances.

"The Battle of Evermore" delves into similar pseudo-mystic territory as "Stairway to Heaven," but it does so from a far more concrete base. Inspired by his decidedly non-rock-star-ish studies of the semi-mythological tribal warfare that once raged through his beloved borderlands, shot through with a healthy sprinkling of Tolkien lore, "Battle of Evermore" was conceived less as a song than as a musical narrative. To that end, it is set against the simplest of accompaniment, and buoyed not only by Plant's own repertoire of vocal styles, but also with the addition of Sandy Denny, an old friend of Page's and a former member of Fairport Convention.

Possessed of one of the loveliest voices in British rock and capable of penning some of its most eloquent songs as well, Denny quit Fairport following 1969's *Liege and Lief* album, amid the shattering that opened the door for Dave Pegg to join. A new band followed, Fotheringay, but they broke up during the sessions for their second album, and by 1971, Denny was at work on her first solo LP, *The North Star Grassman and the Ravens*. With its contents ranging from a playful cover of Brenda Lee's "Let's Jump the Broomstick" to the traditional "Blackwaterside" (the root of Zeppelin's early staple "Black Mountain Side"), the so-evocative title track, and the melancholy "Late November," *North Star Grassman* was single-mindedly designed to raise Denny free of the folk bracket into which her Fairport years had placed her.

So was her appearance on "The Battle of Evermore," where her voice hangs as a chilling counterpoint to Plant's, so effortlessly contradicting and dovetailing with his aural panegyrics that it was like they had been singing together for years. All setting up a scenario that may not, in musical terms, have proved as influential as "Stairway to Heaven," but certainly spawned more notable offspring. Side two of Queen's second album, *Queen II* in 1974, was cast firmly in the shadow of "The Battle of Evermore," while Heart not only reprised the musical light and shade of the battle across their second (and most courageous) album, *Little Queen*, they also acknowledged its importance by including the song in their live set.

"Sandy always called that one session of her favorites of all the ones she did," her husband Trevor Lucas later said. "Not because it was the one that probably gave her the biggest audience she ever had, but because it was so easy for her to sing with Robert. But it did introduce her to people who might never have listened to her in the past, and there were always a few Zeppelin fans at the gigs from then on."

From Headley Grange, the sessions moved up to London, where Led Zeppelin took up residence at Basing Street Studios to iron out any last kinks in the mix and to wrap a few songs that were still deemed unfinished — "Stairway to Heaven" for instance, which had yet to be gifted with its guitar solo. Then it was back onto the road, through the US and onto their first-ever trip to Japan, after which Plant and Page celebrated a few weeks' break by taking the tourist route home, via Thailand, India, and Morocco.

It was a relaxing journey, a far cry from the increasingly taut and airless bubble that the last tour had plunged them into. With Bonham descending more and more into his role as Led Zeppelin's party animal, and Peter Grant's paranoia that everyone was out to rip off his charges reaching epic proportion, tours felt less like a journey into the heart of their audience than they did a hostile military incursion, the band rolling into each new city as an armored phalanx, setting up a defensive perimeter around hotel and venue and then preparing to repel all boarders.

"Their security were pigs," says the West Coast lawyer who wanted to get close to Plant in 1969. "I saw kids beaten up just for knocking on the stage door before the show, while we were also hearing these terrible stories about girls being taken back to the band's hotel and left bleeding in the room when the show moved on the next day. It didn't stop more girls from trying to get back to meet the band, of course, but there was always that sense of . . . well, other bands might knock you round a bit, but Led Zeppelin would really put you through hell." A response which does cause one to wonder why anybody would even want to go backstage in the first place, but the fact is, they did. Irrelevant to the Zeppelin story, but apropos regardless, was testimony given at a court case in the UK in 2013, a fan alleging she was sexually assaulted by a top TV soap star several decades before. He raped her the first time she visited his house, she said . . . and he did it again, the second time she visited.

The fact is, certain rock bands had certain reputations, whether brought on by genuinely depraved sexual appetites or by the sheer boredom of life on the road and the constant search for something new to break the cycle, and they had fans who wanted to find out if they were true, perhaps for many of the same reasons. Led Zeppelin simply had an even darker reputation than most—and a publicity machine around them that loved nothing so much as to broadcast it.

Led Zeppelin IV was released in November 1971, delayed by what now seems a quite absurd squabble between Jimmy Page and Atlantic Records. The legend is that Page, tiring of rumors that Zeppelin's success was as much media and promotion driven as it was derived from genuine audience appreciation, wanted to release the new LP with absolutely no mention of the band's name—or any other information, come to that—on the cover. No name, no title, no label identification, no catalog number, no track listing, no credits. A completely blank canvas, both inside and out. Only once you opened the shrink wrap and took out the vinyl would you know what it was. It was a notion that Atlantic Records was apparently swift to shoot down. The delay in the album's release, it is said, was the result of the ensuing standoff.

Or not, as a veteran Atlantic insider recalled. "Atlantic were fine with it. The only reason the album was delayed was because they wanted it out as close to Christmas as they could, knowing everybody would want the new Led Zeppelin as a Christmas present. The story about the sleeve being rejected was just something to tell the press, so that when it came out, everybody would be on the lookout for this amazing revolutionary cover. They didn't even need to hear the record; they bought it for the sleeve." In other words, while claiming to be battling the accusations of hype, the entire thing was conceived to take the hype to a whole new level. Brilliant. And yes, everybody did get it for Christmas.

Further mysteries lurked within. At Page's instigation, the band's name on the album's inner sleeve was replaced by four symbols, each one hand-picked by each individual band member—and each one (plus a fifth for Sandy Denny) destined to send certain elements of the fan club delving deep into all manner of arcane and obscure lore and litany in search of their actual meanings.

In fact, Plant and Page alone seem to have given the matter any thought; both Jones and Bonham essentially delved into what the modern world would call clip art for their symbols. But Page created a distinctively scripted "Zoso," which he has since refused to expound on any further, while Plant chose a feather surrounded by a circle, representations of courage and truth.

Ultimately, it was all just an artistic fancy. But it fed deeper into the sense of mystery and magic that now permeated the Led Zeppelin legend, a sense that they were in league with forces that mere mortals might never understand. But which they strove to, with a fervor unseen in rock since the late 1960s' insistence that Paul McCartney was dead and the Beatles had spent the years since then posting coded obituaries across their lyrics and sleeves.

Neither were Zeppelin (and the Beatles') fans alone in attempting to decode these messages. With growing force and influence across the United States, the evangelical movement was taking its hatred of the devil's music into a new sphere of research, with the unveiling of a horrific new trend in rock 'n' roll.

"Backward masking," it was revealed, was the art of recording subversive messages on vinyl, and then twisting them so they could only be deciphered if the record was played backwards. Which in these days of defiantly forward-playing CDs and mp3s does not seem that effective a method of getting a message across. Nor was it at the time, with many turntables stubbornly defying any attempt to reverse the natural order of their inner workings.

The Beatles were the first; if you play "Revolution #9" backwards, you can allegedly hear a voice repeating "Turn me on, dead man"—another reference to the late McCartney, allegedly. (At which point, one should point out that whoever they got in to replace him turned out to be a fairly good writer and musician in his own right.)

"Stairway to Heaven" was cruising for a righteous bruising from the moment the evangelicals clapped ears on it, from its very first mention of the pagan May Queen. Spinning it backwards just reinforced the horror. The lyric that begins "Yes, there are two paths you can go by," played backwards, apparently insists, "There's no escaping it. It's my sweet Satan. The one will be the path who makes me sad, whose power is Satan." Which really doesn't make much sense, but no matter.

A little later, when Plant asks, "Dear lady, can you hear the wind blow?" what he is really saying, we learn, is "Oh I will sing because I live with Satan." Which must have come as news to Maureen—now pregnant with the couple's second child, Karac Pendragon Plant. But of course there was more: Page's proprietorship of Equinox, and his admission that one of the main reasons he opened a bookshop of his own was so he wouldn't have to travel all over the place to pick up the books he wanted; his ownership of the old Crowley house and Plant's alleged refusal to visit it—not necessarily because he disapproved of its former owner, by the way, but because the highlands of Scotland are quite a trek to undertake if you're just dropping by to say hello.

Still, the controversy was just fresh grist to the mill in terms of publicity—and, Grant admitted, in terms of making sure he got what he wanted when he was issuing demands to promoters and distributors. He'd just mention Jimmy Page's reputation as a powerful and evil magician, he said, and it was astonishing how quickly people's resistance crumbled.

Led Zeppelin toured through the remainder of 1972 and into the new year as well, that same well-oiled machine setting down and then picking up again the following day, leaving a trail of rumors, inventions, distressed hoteliers, and debauched groupies in their wake. Jacob Aranza, author of an early 1980s book on rock 'n' roll's Satanic leanings, *Backward Masking*

Unmasked, reported, "[Led Zeppelin's] actions would cause many of us to question their popularity. In one Hollywood Hotel they destroyed a painting, submerged four stereos in a bathtub and ran motorcycle races in the hallways. Other tales include one rock magazine's account of a groupie they doused with a bucket of urine."

But they also put on some of the most scintillating rock 'n' roll shows of the era, events that eschewed the blatant theater that was edging into other bands' performances as glam rock took hold on the early 1970s, but were as breathless and breathtaking regardless. Released in 2003, the live album *How the West Was Won* captures Zeppelin at two stops during this epochal year, with Page certainly adamant that this was the height of the band at its fighting fittest, as he told the *Times* in 2010: "I think what we did on . . . *How the West Was Won*—that 1972 gig—is pretty much a testament of how good it was."

But the drive for it to get better had still to be curtailed. Almost as soon as they were off the road, the band was back in the studio, this time moving into Mick Jagger's Stargroves mansion to cut what became *Houses of the Holy*—the one Led Zeppelin album whose ambition and sense of humor does not seem to have been forgiven by history.

There was, in the aftermath of *Led Zeppelin IV*, and particularly in the wake of "Stairway to Heaven," a very real sense that Led Zeppelin's next album would follow that same train of thought, continuing into the realms of grand symphonics and overarching verbosity. Instead, they looked toward simple pop and jocular parody, with most cynics turning the full weight of their wrath upon "D'Yer Mak'er," a song that had already been benighted with what even its admirers confess is one of the most hamfistedly punning titles ever conceived.

It was a mock-reggae number at a time when reggae itself was still largely being mocked by the average rock cognoscenti. Bob Marley was two years away from a breakthrough; Eric Clapton's genre-bending "I Shot the Sheriff" was twelve months off in the future. Though Page and Plant both adored the music privately, even taking Marley tapes with them as they holidayed together, Zeppelin, riding a lyric that rhymed

"You don't have to go" with "Oh oh oh oh oh," were apparently taking reggae no more seriously than anybody else at that time. So why did they bother recording it?

Because it was fun. Because, in the midst of all the madness that devoured Led Zeppelin, and the absurdly high standards to which their audience now demanded they aspire, it was good to just kick back and relax and remind people that, after all, they were in this game to enjoy themselves as well. Which is not easy when you're playing a three-hour concert every night, and your every last word or action is being analyzed by half the watching world.

The treadmill upon which Led Zeppelin found themselves in the early 1970s was not unique. Accustomed as we are today to even brand-new bands taking years between albums, and filling the interim with nothing more exhausting than a quick tour around the summer festivals, it seems incredible that there was once a time in which even a few months' silence could sound an act's death knell, no matter how popular they were. Album–tour–album–tour, interspersed with no more vacation time than the average office worker might expect to be granted. Indeed, Zeppelin were considered positively sluggish by some band's standards—a mere album a year when many others were pumping out one every nine months or so, and in fact, David Bowie was virtually on a six-monthly cycle between late 1971 and early 1975.

The tours were grueling too—months-long assaults that hit every town that could be shoehorned into the itinerary, until every show blended into one another, to be highlighted in the mind only by the memory of anything weird that might have happened. Another reason, of course, for the boys to start behaving badly, but another reason too for them to wonder what it was all actually for.

Was this it—was this their life? A never-ending succession of ever-cheaper thrills punctuating the boredom of travel, hotel rooms, and studios—"a force of nature," some writers claimed, so powerful that when they did get a break, the four musicians could scarcely stand to even be in one another's company? Off the road, all four would split for their private estates, return home to family in the knowledge that even their friends would expect to hear all about the adventures from which they'd returned. And they could not understand how those adventures now seemed scarcely more exciting than those friends' own jobs in shops and offices.

It was this sense not of "job done" but "requirements fulfilled" that permeated the writing and recording of *Houses of the Holy*, with Plant in particular feeling the need to remarshal his forces. For all his onstage strutting and superhuman confidence, Plant—like the permanently withdrawn John Paul Jones—had little interest in living the rock-style life, or maintaining the rock-style image, when he was off duty.

Jimmy Page, courtesy of the imagery he so painstakingly drew around him, could guarantee deference and respect whenever he showed his face in public. Because, if he didn't receive it, people worried, he would turn them into something ceramic and place them on the Boleskine House mantelpiece.

John Bonham, thanks to his reputation as a wild man, remained a wildman wherever he was, to the point where, even after he bought the property next door to Jennings Farm, he was seldom a welcome visitor around the place. Especially when he'd been drinking for a few days, which was becoming more and more his default setting.

Plant, on the other hand, knew when to switch off. He told writer Cliff Jones (*Rock CD*, April 1993), "I reasoned that I could sing about misty mountains and then chip a football into the back of the net on my days off. That felt like the good life to me back then. It wasn't all-consuming for me in the way it was for the others."

On the road, he acknowledged, it was easy to "get caught up in all that hotel room and drug binge kind of thing, because it was part of the experience, almost expected." But as he told *Circus* in 1973, and also as he reminds people to this day, "I'm a family man, and I thought it was all a bit hysterical. Without sounding a real killjoy, it was all rather silly. I could only go out after a gig and piss about for a short amount of time or else my voice would pack up." Even when he did pick up a girl on the road, he was more likely to simply disappear to his room with her than share her largesse with bandmates and crew. As though he was seeking a sense of stability within one of the most unstable environments around.

He never lost sight of the fact that once his front door (or hotel room door) closed behind him, he was a husband, a father, a farmer. He bought another property, a sheep farm in Dolgoch, in his old family-vacation stamping grounds, and was as happy mooching around with the flock and a sheepdog as he could ever be on the road. If he felt the need to make music, he'd call in some friends from his very first bands, or the acquaintances that they had introduced to him, and everyone would just sit around the barn, singing and playing.

He'd go to the pub, or go to the soccer; spring 1972 saw Wolves reach the final of the UEFA Cup, one of the major pan-European tournaments, and though they lost (ironically, to another English team, Tottenham Hotspur), it was clear that the side had turned the corner after the dark days of the 1960s. For the first time in a long time, being a Wolves supporter did not mean that fans of other, better-known sides would glance sympathetically over and softly ask, "Why?"

Now if only that same question did not feel equally pertinent to his day job.

For the first time, nobody seemed distressed, or even particularly surprised, that *Houses of the Holy*—the first Led Zeppelin album to be given an official title—was received with less than unalloyed joy by the critics or public alike. Even Peter Grant's expected display of outraged umbrage felt forced as he realized that the best album his exhausted charges had in them at the time was not necessarily the best album they had ever made.

Of course it had its highlights: "The Song Remains the Same," "The Rain Song," and the third-album offshoot "Over the Hills and Far Away." "No Quarter" was a fine, lengthy, and atmospheric epic, steeped in mystery and misty suspense—a second cousin of "Immigrant Song" in its invocation of Norse mythology and destined to grant John Paul Jones an onstage showcase at least as virtuosic as Page's "Dazed and Confused" and Bonham's "Moby Dick."

Against those, however, could be balanced the songs that any other album might have left on the cutting room floor: "D'Yer Mak'er," "The Crunge" (another of the songs that, sharp-eyed gossips murmured, might well have been about Plant's sister-in-law Shirley), the lightweight "Dancing Days," and "The Ocean," a song whose lyrical punchline placed it midway between Chuck Berry's "Memphis, Tennessee" ("Marie is only six years old . . .") and the Brotherhood of Man's "Save Your Kisses for Me" ("even though you're only three").

But they had also stockpiled a large amount of material toward their next, sixth, album, including what would otherwise have been this current set's title track; and perhaps unwittingly, but very effectively all the same, they had released an album that was actually their most perfectly timed ever. 1973 was the year in which Pink Floyd unveiled *The Dark Side of the Moon* and Mike Oldfield debuted with *Tubular Bells*, two albums set to dominate both the charts and the critics on both sides of the Atlantic for much of the next year. No record released in their shadow could ever have been granted more than a cursory inspection before attention returned to those two all-conquering Goliaths. If Zeppelin *had* to release a low-key record, this was precisely the right time to do it.

Besides, if *Houses of the Holy* was destined for a lifespan scarcely more comfortable than that of *Led Zeppelin III*, the tour that Grant had lined up for them that summer was the largest and most lavish they, or anybody else for that matter, had ever undertaken. A coast-to-coast scouring of the United States that was already being described as the most successful tour of the decade—and that would also spawn the next installment of the group's intended conquest of the world.

A feature film, *The Song Remains the Same*, was to be shot at Madison Square Garden, a massive concert movie that would be further flavored by extravagant fantasy sequences, each member of the band interspersing their personal showcase with a glimpse into his own innermost personal vision. And Plant had already decided upon his sequence. Taking over Raglan Castle in Wales for the shoot, he would be an Arthurian knight, riding to the rescue of a damsel in distress.

Rock movies were in a peculiar place in the early 1970s. Fast outgrowing their initial manifestation as comedic vehicles for top pop stars, but daring not follow Mick Jagger into the psychodrama of *Performance*, the genre had elected the concert film as the most likely to succeed. Yet it rarely did. Few, if any, of the music movies released in the early 1970s, from Emerson, Lake & Palmer's *Pictures at an Exhibition* to T. Rex's *Born to Boogie*, did business anything like that which record sales might have predicted, while other expected blockbusters—DA Pennebaker's capture of David Bowie's 1973 "farewell" performance, for example—did not even wind up being released for close to another decade.

Occasionally, something would break the mold. The Rolling Stones' *Gimme Shelter* document of their 1969 show at Altamont Speedway was a hit, but it was Altamont, already a byword for the souring of the '60s dream, that was the star of the show—that and the on-camera murder of an audience member. Not the Stones themselves.

The *Woodstock* movie was enormous by virtue of the sheer ubiquity of the festival's name, but two British *Woodstocks*, at Glastonbury and the Isle of Wight, faded into cinematic obscurity almost as soon as they were released. And when Neil Young tried to breathe fresh life into the genre with the willful conceptual obscurity of *Journey Through the Past*, it vanished so quickly that most people never even knew it existed.

This, then, was the landscape into which Led Zeppelin intended releasing their movie, and they too had what they thought was a solution to the genre's ills. *The Song Remains the Same* was not intended solely to enshrine the band's performance, nor to visualize the musicians' private fantasy lives. It was also to serve as a ninety-minute primer into the sheer magnitude of the Zeppelin experience: the private plane that flew them between cities; the massive crowds that oversold every venue on the tour, setting fresh attendance records in almost every city; the giant PA; the lasers and mirror balls.

The cameras did not linger on the so-called perks of the job—cocaine being snorted through rolled-up $100 bills, fresh girls being lined up so the musicians could take their pick—but the grapevine filled in those gaps, to be joined in later years by the memoirs of crew and passing journalists alike. According to some of those remembrances, Led Zeppelin's 1973 American tour was the absolute apex of on-the-road debauchery. Yet they are remembrances from which the band members themselves have unflinchingly distanced themselves—according to Grant, with good reason.

"What happened was, the Stones did that American tour in 1972, which was filmed, and a print came out called *Cocksucker Blues*, because of one short sequence that took place on their plane. Nobody saw it, it was never released, but a bootleg copy went around and the tour picked up a lot of notoriety. The fact that you know what I'm talking about now, all these years later, proves that. So I said to Richard [Coles], 'We need to top that. We want this tour to be talked about even more than the Stones tour.' And that's what happened."

It's a comparison that was backed up by the words of a member of the film crew that awaited the band in New York: "You know what that movie's working title was? *Fishfucker Blues*. Because of the mudshark story."

Of course.

The madness boarded the Zeppelin. Following the show at the LA Forum, all concerned were invited to a party in Laurel Canyon, thrown to mark John Bonham's twenty-first birthday. Music blared, people drank, and a video player looped *Deep Throat* into the room. Was anybody even watching it? It doesn't matter. Any journalists present would still have had their Zeppelin Porno Party anecdotes delivered.

Besides, and once again, the band was not entirely blameless. As Bonham's oldest friend within the band, and closest too, Plant often found himself on the scene when one of the drummer's legendary furies kicked off, sometimes attempting (but generally failing) to act as peacemaker, other times content to remain a mute witness on the sidelines. Neither would he turn up his well-coked nose at the amount of female flesh that was permanently on offer, although it is interesting to note that the vast majority of kiss-and-tell narratives that have spilled out from the tour are provided by male witnesses to the initial seduction, as opposed to female participants in whatever developed.

So the groupie grapevine reverberated with memories of the night Plant led a Zeppelin deputation along to Rodney Bingenheimer's English Disco when the tour hit Hollywood in summer 1973, but anyone who followed him back to the hotel seems not to have immortalized their impressions in any public forum—unlike devotees of so many of the Disco's other superstar visitors. It is the nature of the Disco and the temptations it offered that is remembered—beginning with the distinctly under-age but voraciously precocious clientele that called the venue home—as if it is sufficient simply to document the temptations and assume that the succumbing naturally followed.

Three years earlier, recording *Led Zeppelin III*, Led Zeppelin turned their attention to "Gallows Pole," a variant on the folk ballad "The Maid Freed from the Gallows," as collected by the folklorist Francis J. Child. Eleven different versions of the song appear in his *English and Scottish Popular Ballads* collection. Were some future chronicler to attempt a similar scholarly enterprise with the purported adventures of Led Zeppelin, any single tale you have heard of their antics could probably run to just as many variants.

Off the road, the band's attention turned to the movie. But it was slow going. *The Song Remains the Same*, shot across all three of the Madison Square shows (the musicians carefully wore the same outfit each night to allow for seamless editing) would take close to three years to be realized, and when it did finally make it out, it was to a sea of condemnation. Bloated and pretentious, complained the critics. The fantasy scenes were pedestrian and boring; the live footage had already been exceeded by the scale and majesty of the band's next tour in 1975. The soundtrack had been so remixed and overdubbed that it scarcely felt like a live recording any longer, and the band members themselves were sick of it as well, so long had it taken and so fraught was the process.

By 1976, however, a lot had happened in the Led Zeppelin camp. The birth of their own record label, Swan Song, to mark the renewal of their contract with Atlantic Records. A new double LP, *Physical Graffiti*, to renew their claim on the acclaim that had hung fire since *Led Zeppelin IV*.

And a brace of tragedies that came close to crashing the Zeppelin once and for all.

"The name 'Led Zeppelin' means a failure," Plant told *Rolling Stone*'s Lorraine Alterman in 1975. "And 'Swan Song' means a last gasp—so why not name our record label that?"

15

Season of the Witch
(1999–2004)

I f any single project can be said to epitomize everything that Robert Plant has ever represented in the course of his career, it is Priory of Brion.

Received history and a depleted rain forest's worth of "best song"/"best album"/"best band" retrospectives can toot the horn for their own private favorites. Disgruntled fans, complaining decades later that Plant doesn't still play with his old friends, can bitch about his refusal to tread again the trampled stairway to evermore. But in terms of taking the songs that best suited his vocal, matching them to the vocal that best suited the music, and then delivering an entire package with flawless attention to feel and flavor—as opposed to detail, virtuosity, and grandeur—Priory of Brion leaves the rest at the starting post. In the same way that the career renaissance that it inaugurated in 1999, and the fifteen years that have elapsed since then, represent the truest and most honest manifestation of Robert Plant the artist.

Not simply because he had stopped worrying about how it looked to other people or stopped competing with other bands, although that is certainly a part of it. It is because he stripped away all the pressures, and all the people, who felt their interpretation of his talent was the one he should be kowtowing to, and listened to himself alone.

It wasn't the first time he'd done that, of course. The original, glorious Honeydrippers shows radiate precisely the same qualities that he would be returning to in 1999. So did the albums *Now and Zen* and *Fate of Nations*.

Those, however, would ultimately be revealed as mere brief flowerings, tentative moments of self-realization before he returned to the industry treadmill once again. This time around, he was doing it for keeps, and the fact that he did not even bother leaving behind a record of all that Priory of Brion achieved cannot dim its glory. It lives on in everything he has accomplished since then.

He had already burned one bridge, informing Page and manager Curbishley that they would not be making another record together, no matter how successful *Walking into Clarksdale* had been. Neither was he thinking about making another album under his own steam. For the first time since 1967, he didn't even have a recording contract. Instead, he just wanted to get out and have some fun, in exactly the same way as he had in 1981 and under precisely the same code of semi-secrecy.

With Kevyn Gammond and Andy Edwards again by his side, Plant set about building a band, adding bassist Paul Wetton and keyboard player Paul Timothy, members of a jazz trio that Edwards played around with. Plant's garage became their rehearsal space, and his bandmates quickly grew accustomed to the silver, gold, and platinum discs that lined the walls. Just as they grew accustomed to some of Plant's other peculiarities: his insistence that his own entire back (and, indeed, future) catalog was off limits, and his decision only to play shows in Wales, the border counties, and his own midlands stamping ground.

Plant played rhythm guitar through the rehearsals, introducing his new bandmates to the songs they needed to learn—oldies one and all, numbers that might once have been a part of Band of Joy's live set, or could have been had the group lasted longer. The highlight was, and remains, Donovan's "Season of the Witch," a number whose inclusion so thrilled its author that his autobiography credited the cover to Led Zeppelin, and that prompted Plant to remember the time, long before, when a man in a brown corduroy cap sold him a car in Lowestoft. The car had a burned-out clutch, and the seller was Donovan.

More songs followed. "Morning Dew." "If I Were a Carpenter." "Darkness, Darkness," an old Youngbloods number that had seen service in the hands of everyone from Mott the Hoople to Solas. "Early in the Morning." "We're Gonna Groove," a Ben E. King number that Zeppelin did record, but left unreleased until the 1982 *Coda* collection of odds-and-sos.

"Evil Woman." "Baby Please Don't Go." "Gloria," the glorious growler that Van Morrison wrote while he was with Them, which had since become an integral component within garage rock's DNA. "No Regrets," an aching Tom Rush ballad that gave the Walker Brothers a comeback chart topper in 1976. James Brown's "Think." "Girl from the North Country." Hendrix's "If Six Was Nine," and another Tim Rose song, "Hey Joe," to be prefaced onstage by the observation that it was "a desperate song, for desperate people in desperate times. A dangerous story of everyday country folk . . . a bit like 'Gallows Pole' with a New Searchers introduction."

Walk unawares into one of the band's rehearsals and you could be forgiven for thinking you'd stepped back in time, with even Timothy's keyboards set to pipe a '60s Hammond aura into the air.

Plant came up with a band name, Priory of Brion, a combination of two of popular culture's greatest spoofs and hoaxes. The Priory of Sion was created in 1956 by French scholar Pierre Plantard and then granted a fictional history that traced its origins back to the Crusades; the bloodline was expounded (as fact) in the book *The Holy Blood and the Holy Grail*. Monty Python's third movie, *The Life of Brian*, had as its subtext people who are so desperate to find something to believe in that they end up believing in something utterly absurd. This, in turn, suggested that the whole affair should not be taken *too* seriously. But that it was not intended as a joke, either. Because when they performed, there was no sense that this was anything but Plant's heart's desire.

"I don't see it as a bold move at all," Plant told *Folk Roots* magazine in 2000. "I'm just having fun." He didn't want the Priory of Brion to "get any bigger" because that was not the point. He had nothing to prove to anybody, and he would have had no desire to do so even if they asked.

Priory of Brion's first show, on July 23, 1999, took place at the band's local pub, the Three Tuns Inn in Bishop's Castle, in front of a crowd of around three hundred people. Even without an ounce of advertising, word got around that something special was occurring. A month later, Priory of Brion were playing in nearby Oswestry; the following night at the unequivocally named Jazz & Roots Club in Shrewsbury. A larger crowd awaited them at the Bridgnorth Folk festival at the end of August, a smaller one at the King's Hotel in Newport.

With the Honeydrippers' old ally Roy Williams again arranging their schedule, steps further inland to Sheffield, Dudley, and Ludlow, saw the last remaining cloak of secrecy fly away from the band's identity. But still Plant stuck to his guns. Halloween brought an appearance at the National Forest Folk festival in Leicestershire; November saw them hit the Red Lion Folk Club in King's Heath Birmingham. Other shows as the century faded away caught him almost retreading the footsteps he'd first taken back in the days of the Crawling Kingsnakes and Listen, town halls and village pubs that even the Honeydrippers might have looked twice at.

Plant did not claim to know the words to every song. Many shows, he spent his time seated on a stool, lyric sheets on a music stand beside him, wearing a pair of reading spectacles. Cynics, and of course there were many, argued that he was simply slumming it, going out with a show that had no bearing whatsoever on his career as a superstar, in the knowledge that he could stop it whenever he wanted and dash out a million-seller instead. Nothing hinged upon the success of Priory of Brion, they said; there was no reputation at stake or ego to be bruised.

This is true. But those things are not necessarily negatives. For Plant, they were also cathartic: an opportunity not to humble himself in front of an audience that was more accustomed to see him bare-chested and screaming, but to show them the human behind the deity—and, by doing so, to remind himself of it as well. To prove that his onstage and offstage personas did not need to be so different from one another, and that the talent and showmanship the universe expected from him was always there, whichever role he was playing.

No less than in 1981, not everybody who came to see Priory of Brion necessarily recognized that fact. Several shows attracted audiences that still hoped against hope that Plant might throw in an unscheduled oldie. He never did, though, even as Priory of Brion marched into the new millennium with a rapidly filling date sheet and gigs that took them even further afield, north to Liverpool, south to Reading, and across the sea to Norway, where they appeared at the Ole Blues festival in Bergen. Another run of gigs saw them opening for Van Morrison on a short tour of Ireland, while June 2000 took them to the Glastonbury Festival for a riotously received set in the Acoustic tent.

Always, however, Priory of Brion returned to their roots: barely publicized shows in towns and venues far off the traditional beaten track, the whole band crammed into a single Transit van. "I don't want all that rock 'n' roll hoopla," Plant continued during that *Folk Roots* interview. The important point, he insisted, was that "the audience don't agitate for 'Stairway to Heaven,' which must mean that they get it. . . . People come with an interest and then the craft of the songs carries the night." He would, he admitted, have enjoyed trying to move things to "the next level," but he acknowledged that it couldn't be done. Not without "reintroducing the rock 'n' roll madness."

Slowly, however, it started to feel like work again. At the end of July, Priory of Brion appeared at the Cambridge Folk Festival, an event that—like Glastonbury in the rock world—hung at the very apex of the British folk scene. On either side of it, they played a string of festivals in Europe—across Italy, Portugal, Switzerland, France, and Belgium, with local promoters completely ignoring entreaties to keep Plant's name out of the advertising. Now it was Priory of Brion whose identity was the surprise.

Venue sizes increased. When they started, Plant was happy to face a couple of hundred people. Now, a couple of thousand was becoming the norm. Isolated gigs in out-of-the-way locations were slipping off the radar, replaced by virtual tours. Crowds were growing rowdier, PAs were growing louder.

There were still highlights, of course. On August 11, 1999, Priory of Brion appeared at the Cropredy Festival, the annual get-together organized by Dave Pegg and Fairport Convention, which dated back with so much serendipity to what was meant to have been Fairport's last-ever concert . . . but turned out to be one of Zeppelin's instead.

Fairport had already announced their decision to fold, and were going out with a bang, first playing Zeppelin's August 1979 Knebworth bonanza and then helicoptering back to their home turf for a final farewell party there. Which proved so successful that it became a tradition. Once a year, Fairport would come back from the grave and put on a show for the faithful. It was Zeppelin, for whom Knebworth was intended simply as an overture to another year of gigging, who never came back from that August afternoon. So now the boot was on the other foot. It was Plant who was performing at Fairport's show.

But Cropredy was an exception, a night of excitement and triumph, shared with friends as well as bandmates. More often, and increasingly as the summer turned to fall, Plant would come offstage feeling as though he was back on the same carousel that Priory of Brion was supposed to have freed him from, and he acknowledged that it would have been easy to fall back into enjoying the ride as well.

He would not, after all, be the first '70s megastar to undergo what his audience called a complete musical transformation and then ride the waves back to the top. Three years earlier, Ritchie Blackmore turned his back on his reputation as the rock god behind Deep Purple and Rainbow to form a new group with his wife Candice, dedicated almost exclusively to the folk and renaissance music that had always hung so heavily in his personal musical background. Like Plant, he eschewed the conventional live circuit, preferring Renaissance fayres and romantic ancient castles; like Plant, he refused to give in to the hordes that descended to demand "Smoke on the Water" and "Strange Kind of Woman." Now, two or three albums into their career, Blackmore's Night were establishing themselves as a solid, reliable draw.

And that was the difference. Although they did go into Rockfield to cut a handful of demos, Plant had no intention of making albums with Priory of Brion. And he had no wish for them to become a solid, reliable draw. So he began to withdraw instead.

Priory of Brion saw out most of their scheduled dates: a short Greek visit in late November followed by a final burst of concerts at home. But a string of Scandinavian shows were written off in early December, and when Priory of Brion convened for their last three gigs of the year—in Crewe, Derby, and Wolverhampton (Plant resplendent in his Wanderers "Pride of the Black Country" scarf)—it was with the knowledge that these were the last gigs they'd ever play. Other shows, penciled in for the following spring, would be handled by another band entirely: Plant's next project, Strange Sensation.

It would be easy to argue that Priory of Brion were very hard done by. Strange Sensation—reunions with Charlie Jones and Porl Thompson, plus drummer Clive Deamer and keyboard player John Baggott—played their first shows in Scandinavia, making up for the Priory of Brion gigs that were wiped out in December. And the new band's first album was essentially comprised of the old band's core repertoire.

All three of Plant's fellow bandmates had had to give up their day jobs in order to undertake the adventure, and while not one of them would have done things differently given the choice, still they were effectively out on their ears, abandoned before the project could reach the next level. But they also knew what they were in for when the ride began. The fact that it was just a ride—that Plant had no intention of building his career around them and that Priory of Brion had always had a very finite existence. That it had even lasted as long as it did, and risen as high on the live circuit as it did, was an eventuality that none of them had expected—and that Plant had never desired, either.

Still label-less, despite manager Curbishley's insistence that he could walk into any record company in the world, Plant decided to finance the new record himself. He would make it, Curbishley would shop it. That way, nobody would be under any misapprehensions about what they could expect from him. Nine years had elapsed since his last solo album, and he had no intention of rolling them back at the behest of a label that still wanted Led Zeppelin. Or even "Big Log." There was a reason why, when the album was released in July 2002, Plant called it *Dreamland.*

There would be some new compositions on board—four in total, all written with his new musicians: "Win My Train Fare Home," "Dirt in a

Hole," "Last Time I Saw Her," and "Red Dress." But their form would be dictated by the rest of their surroundings: "Morning Dew," "Hey Joe," and "Darkness, Darkness"; Bob Dylan's "One More Cup of Coffee"; Tim Buckley's "Song to the Siren"; Bukka White's foreboding "Funny in My Mind (I Believe I'm Fixin' to Die)"; and Skip Spence's eerie eulogy "Skip's Song," a tribute to the artist who, via Moby Grape, had proven such an inspiration to the teenaged (and, indeed, the adult) Plant.

It was a downbeat album, featuring songs of loss and reflection, of the blues in all their guises. None of the songs were especially obscure. "Song to the Siren," indeed, had become something of a touchstone for an entire generation that would still have been kids when its composer passed away in 1975; rediscovered a decade later by the Cocteau Twins, in the guise of the This Mortal Coil collective, "Song to the Siren" now epitomized sorrow and shadow, mourning and melancholy, and the challenge for Plant as he went back to the song was to conjure a version that could stand alongside not the original but its reinvention. He succeeded, for the same reason that he was likewise able to breathe new life into "Hey Joe," another song that had been hammered so definitively into place (by Hendrix) that anything but a photostat would leave the purists howling. Because he was content to let them howl.

Plant chose his collaborators wisely. Both Baggott and Deamer had emerged within the Portishead collective that all but singlehandedly blueprinted the trip hop scene of the early 1990s, a swampy ocean filled with slow beats and shifting shadows that stripped melody back to its sparsest rhythms and then rebuilt from there. Plant did not want to travel in that direction. But still his "Hey Joe" was a reinvention, sonically and stylistically—shards of sound and shattered chords crashing above and beyond familiarity, half-heard echoes that shivered in the mix and then retreated back before others came to take their place.

"Song to the Siren" went the other way entirely. A guitar that echoed nothing so much as the Spartan picking with which Jon Mark once accompanied the '60s Marianne Faithfull was Plant's sole accompaniment through the first verse. And when strings rose up to serenade the second, still Plant's vocal felt isolated, alone, as though he sang with no awareness whatsoever of the musicians that soared around him.

Other players slipped in: BJ Cole on the pedal guitar that added its voice to "Song to the Siren" and guitarist Justin Adams, who loaned gimbri and darbuki to the sound of the sessions. Plant also forged one more link in his long and still utterly coincidental habit of revisiting the Adverts' family tree. Backing vocalist Ginny Clee had recorded and toured with their singer, TV Smith, in the '80s—and was a major *Lord of the Rings* fan as well. "It was my Bible," she told her website. "Acid can do that."

Together, this was the team that breathed yearning desperation into "One More Cup of Coffee" (always one of the most foreboding moments on Dylan's *Desire* album back in 1976, but restated now by the sheer fragility of Plant's vocal), the team that ensured that the fear and resignation with which Priory of Brion imbibed "Darkness, Darkness" was at last cast in stone. "That was a very influential song way back in the old days," Plant used to say as he introduced it live, and clearly it still was.

Once again, Plant was striking out afresh from within the cocoon of his distant past, discovering and rediscovering tensions within his own musical tastes, then following them. He fell in love with Emmylou Harris's *Wrecking Ball* album, and certainly elements of that album's unique Daniel Lanois–produced styling found its way into Plant's own collaboration with co-producer Phill Brown (yet another TV Smith veteran—he produced 1983's *Channel Five* album) as *Dreamland* came together. He started listening to bluegrass—the sonic polar opposite of the symphonic pastures that Lanois created, but a match for the hybrid that was coalescing in his mind, a lush soundtrack gouged through with the sounds of rural Appalachian folk. He discovered, too, a new voice that worked within that particular field—an Illinois singer named Alison Krauss—and she was not the only fresh sound to be turning his head.

Promotion for the new album got off to a rocky start, however. On May 1, 2002, Plant and the band were scheduled to appear at the Primo Maggio Festival in Italy on a bill with Oasis. That same day, Wolverhampton Wanderers were playing Norwich City in one of the most decisive matches of their recent history, the semifinal of the end-of-season play-offs, to determine whether or not Premiership football would come to Molineux next season. Wolves were down 3–1 from the first leg; nothing less than three unanswered goals would see them through. And Plant knew where he needed to be. The festival date was cancelled and he took his regular place at the stadium instead.

Wolves won, but the 1–0 was not enough. And as Plant told *FourFourTwo* in 2002, he was so enraged that he spent great swathes of the match screaming abuse at Norwich player Iwan Roberts. "I started shouting, 'Roberts, you prick!' almost as if I was saying, 'Come on—eject me!' You can get banned for using language like that now." Reflecting on half a century spent following the team through hell, high water, and every other obstacle that history has thrown at him, he admitted, "That might be my only way out."

Worse was to come. In the other play-off game, local rivals Birmingham emerged triumphant, while West Bromwich Albion, too, had a successful season. "Seeeething," Plant hissed when it was all over. "That's how I've been these past few weeks." Of course he got over it; soccer fans have a built-in resilience that allow them to forgive all manner of failings, even those committed in the wake of a season that Wolves should have walked. They were ten points clear at the top at one point. They ended up thirteen points behind the eventual leaders, in third.

But there's always next year, and in May 2003, Wolves did finally make it, beating Sheffield United 3–0 in the play-off final. Plant, of course, was there to watch them, and there too for the adventure that followed, as Wolves mixed it with the big boys for the first time in twenty years.

Five months before that momentous afternoon, however, Plant took his own journey into the unknown. In January 2003, off the road from a tour that had consumed much of the past six months, he and Justin Adams joined the crew of the BBC children's show *Blue Peter* on a flight to what was popularly referred to as the most isolated music festival in the world: the Festival au Desert in Essakane, near Timbuktu, Mali.

A celebration of North Africa's musical heritage, set deep within the desolate splendor of the Sahara Desert, the festival was into its third year, although this was the first in which it received more than cursory attention from the West; aside from Plant, the French band Lo'Jo were also on the bill, with their percussionist Matthieu Rousseau, bassist Nicolas Meslien, and guitarist Skin Tyson lined up to accompany Plant and Adams. Yet his own performance was not even close to the forefront of Plant's mind or imagination. The Sahara, the most breathtaking backdrop to any concert he had ever played or attended, and the music of its people, the most haunting, personal sound he'd ever heard, swept all of his own thoughts out of his mind.

Plant was mesmerized—so much so that he returned home obsessed with the idea of relating all he experienced there in the form of his next album. Timbuktu had exposed him to some of the most captivating, vibrant, and affirming music he had ever experienced. In every sense of that word. Music that affected his every sense, every thought, every dream. And that was the sensation and the effect that he and Adams were now working to combine with their own music. Some of it was their own variation on remembered themes, some borrowed directly from rhythms and patterns that he had encountered in Africa. All, however, would be imposed onto and into his rock 'n' roll, to create a fusion that, he confessed to writer Barney Hoskyns in *Tracks* magazine, left him "a little lost for words."

Home was now a farm close to the favorite vacation spot of his childhood, the town of Machynlleth in Snowdonia. It was close, too, to Bron-Yr-Aur, the cottage that alchemized *Led Zeppelin III*, and it was there that this new project was breeding and brooding. "It's a beautiful place," he assured Hoskyns, and the atmosphere that it engendered had certainly proven conducive to the music. A new album, he was sure, would be released the following year. In the meantime, to follow the success of *Dreamland* and pave the way for the new sounds, at least in titular terms, there was *Sixty Six to Timbuktu*, a two-CD selection that was half conceived as a journey through what he considered the best of his solo career, and half as a stamp collection filled with gems and rarities. "There was so much stuff of mine that had never seen the light of day. If anyone were to say to me, 'Well, your solo career has been a bit patchy, and you've been a bit schizoid with the way it's danced around,' I would say, 'Absolutely so, and merrily so.'"

He likened himself to a cultural dervish, simply whirling from place to place, a New York punk rocker one week, an Arthur Alexander tribute the next; Africa in one breath, Ibiza in another. And that is the impression that he wanted people to take from the new CD, because it's the impression that he himself took. "I know that historically, and in quality of material, there's no way I could ever touch the legacy of Led Zep. However, I am having a good time with my life, and these are the sorts of things that I think were quite a hoot."

Early singles, Band of Joy demos, odd collaborations, outtakes, and oddities—*Sixty Six to Timbuktu* then ended in Timbuktu itself, with a soaring "Win My Train Fare Home," recorded live at the festival. The new album, meanwhile, continued to gestate, taking on the stately shape that would emerge as 2005's *Mighty Rearranger*. And already, Plant was looking even further ahead.

His investigation of his new-found fascination with bluegrass received a major fillip when he headed off on vacation, hiring a car and traveling through the regions that called the music home with a pile of CDs to keep him company. So when he received a call from the music cable network VH1, inviting him to appear on *CMT Crossroads*, he agreed . . . on one condition.

Plant was no stranger to VH1. Back in June 2002, he appeared on the network's *Storytellers* program, an hour-long concert in which performers interspersed a set of favorite songs with stories about each song. Ray Davies and David Bowie were among the artists who had previously turned in excellent installments, and Plant's contribution matched either of them. *CMT Crossroads* was a very different proposition. Aired on VH1's country music affiliate, it offered the opportunity for top country stars to perform alongside rock 'n' rollers—sometimes to devastatingly hybrid effect, other times to mute embarrassment—and when Plant's involvement was first announced, more than a few outsiders shuddered and considered this the most poorly schemed-out proposal yet. Particularly when his collaborator was named. It was Alison Krauss.

Their first conversation was not promising. Plant called, and was surprised at how quiet she was, even as he waxed rapturously about her music and his hopes. What he didn't realize was that she was putting her three-year-old son to bed, lying alongside him as quiet as she could be. Which is difficult when you have a rock god ranting eighteen-to-the-dozen in your ear. "Alison wasn't really saying anything and I thought, 'Fucking hell, she's got those Quaaludes I've been looking for!'" Plant laughed later, in Q magazine. "I've been married before, so I know what it's like to have a woman mumbling at me." Even when he suggested she write down his phone number, Krauss demurred. She didn't have a pen, she told him, and she couldn't get up to find one.

Plant persevered, however, and once she told him the reasons for her silence, he knew he'd learned his first lesson. Never call her at bedtime. Because the rest of the time, she was as excited at the proposal as he was, and when he suggested they think about making a record together, she leapt aboard that notion too.

On November 3, 2004, with Plant and Justin Adams intending to fly to Cleveland to appear at a tribute to Lead Belly at the Severance Hall, Krauss agreed to appear alongside them to perform "In the Pines" (a song granted a fresh lease on life a decade previous, when Nirvana included it in the *Unplugged* performance) before they both took the stage with Los Lobos for "Pretty Little Girl with the Red Dress On." Plant and Adams alone performed "Alabama Bound"; he and Los Lobos aired "Gallows Pole." But it was his union with Krauss that made the greatest impression on him. "It was an amazing night," he recalled for the BBC documentary *By Myself.* "I'm stood next to a beautiful woman who can sing like an angel and knows exactly what she wants. I thought, 'That's got to come back again.'"

Other witnesses agreed. "The ex-Led Zeppelin frontman was at the center of some of the evening's greatest moments," declared the Cleveland *Plain Dealer's* review the following day, while Plant's own emotions surrounding the event were made very clear as he stood onstage, surveying the two thousand or so souls in attendance: "This is a great way of saying some kind of protracted thank you for all those great songs."

16

Like I've Never Been Gone
(1974–1977)

R obert Plant entered the twenty-first century without a record label. Twenty-five years earlier, he'd had two. Atlantic, to which Led Zeppelin was signed, and Swan Song, to which they swore their own allegiance—because it was, indeed, their own.

By 1974, it was no big deal for a band to have their own label. The Beatles, as usual, were the first to demand their own identity away from the typography of their parent company when they launched Apple in 1968. The Rolling Stones' eponymous setup followed in 1971 as part of their own newly inked deal with Atlantic; the Moody Blues, Deep Purple, T. Rex, and Emerson, Lake & Palmer numbered among those who had followed suit. If Zeppelin really were, as they claimed, the biggest band in the world, then they too needed their own label identity and a stable of genuine stars to accompany them, the latter being the one side of the entire business to have largely evaded the efforts of their label-owning predecessors.

Early signings to the label were impressive: Bad Company, the supergroup formed by Free's Paul Rodgers and Mott the Hoople's Mick Ralphs; '60s veterans the Pretty Things; and one-time Stone the Crows singer Maggie Bell, one of the most impressive female blues singers the UK had ever produced. Indeed, Bad Company immediately repaid Zeppelin's faith by becoming one of the biggest rock bands of the mid-1970s, at the same time as Ralphs and Plant spent many hours recalling their shared apprenticeship on the Black Country circuit. Originally from Hereford, Ralphs had replaced Kevyn Gammond in the Shakedown Sound when Gammond quit for the Band of Joy. There, he linked up with organist Verden Allen and, shortly before the end of the band, drummer Dale Griffin—who in turn became the roots of Mott the Hoople.

Of all of Led Zeppelin, Plant was Swan Song's biggest cheerleader. For his bandmates, having a label was simply another piece of business, another way of keeping Led Zeppelin's name in the public eye. All four band members were credited as executive producers (Peter Grant was president, their US publicist Danny Goldberg and Atlantic Records veteran Abe Hoch were vice presidents), and all four expressed an interest in the label's signings. For Plant, however, it was personal. He told *Rolling Stone* in 1974:

> A long time ago in England with Bonzo, I was playing a very contemporary form of music and at the time the accepted music to be playing was all the cliché music—the Beatles, the hit parade stuff. Anybody who was a little bit out of the ordinary or trying very hard was always ignored by the record companies, because they wanted to play it safe.
>
> We thought it would be really nice to get a company together where it's run by the people who really understand. I mean you can't get any closer to the artist than being a fellow artist.

But there was more to it than that. For Plant, Swan Song filled him with the same kind of joy that he used to feel as a kid, leafing through the vinyl in a local record store and coming across label imprints that he'd never seen or heard of before—imprints that, though they operated from offices on the other side of the world in the hands of media moguls of whom he had never heard, became *his* labels. Parlo! Instant!! Laurie!!! Names that could still make his heart race. Now he envisioned Swan Song having the same effect on other people.

In fact, Swan Song enjoyed only a modicum of success beyond Led Zeppelin's marquee attraction. Bad Company blazed brightly but briefly, and Dave Edmunds enjoyed a couple of golden years. But never was Swan Song regarded as anything other than Led Zeppelin's label, with no less

than seven of its twenty-seven LP releases being either Zeppelin or Zeppelin related (Jimmy Page's *Death Wish II* soundtrack and Robert Plant's
Pictures at Eleven were both Swan Song releases). And while both Bad
Company and the Pretty Things had albums out on the label before its executive producers deigned to stir, they could still be regarded as little more
than appetizers in the face of the main attraction's next offering.

Work on Led Zeppelin's follow-up to *Houses of the Holy* kicked off at
Headley Grange in the spring of 1974, with Plant still ecstatic over Wolverhampton Wanderers' latest feat. On March 2, goals from their two latest
heroes, Kenny Hibbitt and John Richards, were sufficient to dispose of the
much-fancied Manchester City in the final of the League Cup tournament,
having already knocked out Norwich, Exeter, and the favorites, Liverpool,
en route to the final. It was the club's first major trophy since 1959, and not
only was Plant at Wembley for the game, it also took him three days to get
home from there, as he revealed to *Record Collector* in 2007. He remembered that the Mayor of Wolverhampton officially received the team, and
that he himself was there briefly. He also admitted, "It played havoc with
my marriage for a while."

Headley Grange had not changed since the band's last visit, although
this time, they had Ronnie Lane's mobile studio parked outside. In testament to Jimmy Page's legendary eye for cost cutting, it was a cheaper op-
tion than the Stones' setup they had hitherto employed, although any sav-
ings were probably eaten up by the decision of all but the guitarist to move
into a nearby hotel for the duration of the band's stay. Where, incidentally,
their behavior was impeccable.

The notion that this next album would be a double had been floating
around for some time, and was confirmed as the band worked through the
backlog of material they had accumulated over the years. The overabun-
dance of songs that emerged during the *Houses of the Holy* sessions was
naturally the cornerstone of this trove, but "Custard Pie" dated as far back
as the band's third album, while seven new songs included "Trampled Under Foot," Plant's funky tribute to rock's long tradition of girl-as-car; "Sick
Again," a weary worm's-eye view of the underage groupies who had haunt-

ed the band in Hollywood; and another number drawn from his and Page's trip to Marrakech in 1972, "Kashmir."

Another time-honored tradition—of taking an out-of-copyright blues and making it one's own, both musically and in terms of songwriting credits—arose with the band's epic take on "In My Time of Dying," an old Blind Willie Johnson number that Bob Dylan repopularized in the early 1960s and that, quite coincidentally, was a lengthy centerpiece in folk duo John Otway and Wild Willy Barrett's live set of the day. Coming to Zeppelin's version after recent exposure to that, and reading the songwriting credits that they claimed for themselves, was an intriguing experience.

What really set the new material aside, however, was the production, and the way it was translated onto vinyl. For all that medium's (post-digital) reputation for sounding warmer and more alive than compact disc, vinyl nevertheless suffered one major drawback. The more music that was packed into the grooves, the more its ultimate reproduction suffered. Forty-five minutes, spread over two sides of a disc, was generally considered the optimum; exceed that and not only would the sound begin to suffer but the actual size of the physical grooves would narrow too, rendering even the smallest scratch a lengthy succession of annoying clicks or worse.

Page had always born this failing in mind—both in terms of an album's length and, while mixing the music, the dynamics he wanted to emphasize. Even in full acoustic mode, Led Zeppelin albums sounded loud. Neither was he willing to reveal the tricks of his trade—when 10cc's 1975 *The Original Soundtrack* album tried, but failed, to capture that Zeppelin bombast, *NME* reviewer Charles Shaar Murray simply observed that Jimmy Page's production secrets "remain a secret." *Physical Graffiti* was to be the apogee of Page's production, fifteen tracks spread across four slabs of wax, released in February 1975 and given further granite-like substance by a sleeve design that slipped both discs into a New York City tenement block.

The band was on the road again, thirty-five dates across the United States that placed them in some of the largest venues in the country and kept them there for two or three nights at a time. It was the biggest tour of the year, in terms not only of ticket sales and logistics, but also the sheer larger-than-life presence of the four musicians onstage. At home in the UK, the band was now so huge that they couldn't even tour—there were no venues in the country large enough to hold them. Instead, they block-booked the eighteen-thousand capacity Earls Court Arena for five days, knowing that ticket demand could have kept them there for a month. According to the *Financial Times* newspaper, Zeppelin were on course to earn $40 million in 1975 alone.

The new material, and in particular "Trampled Under Foot" and "Kashmir," translated as effortlessly as any past classic to the stage but exceeded them too—which itself was a remarkable achievement as the 1970s moved on and too many bands rested content on the laurels they'd laid down on earlier discs. For Led Zeppelin to be six albums into their career and still capable of turning out new material as good as, and even better than, that which made their name was a remarkable achievement. Indeed, with the exception of the inevitable "Whole Lotta Love" and "Stairway to Heaven," it is unlikely whether any Led Zeppelin song can outrank "Kashmir" in the popularity stakes.

Plant's lyrics and vocals were as integral to this accomplishment as any other player's contribution. Yet still he felt as though he were being treated like a junior member of the team, the one who simply got up there and sang while his bandmates did the real work.

He'd long grown accustomed to Peter Grant essentially treating the band as Jimmy Page-plus-three, and reviews often followed a similar track. Audiences focused on Plant because he was the front man, and that in itself was gratifying. But it was so easy for his bandmates to upstage him: Jones, with the ever-more-inventive solos with which he could expand "No Quarter" to close to thirty minutes; Bonham, with the ruthless battery he laid down onstage and the ruthless thuggery with which he behaved off of it; and Page, with his violin-bow guitar solo, and the knowledge that the moment he drew the bow across the strings, he'd be rewarded with one of the loudest roars of the evening.

It was sheer gimmickry, of course—a visual hook no more or less stage-managed than Roger Daltrey swinging his mike above his head or David

Bowie going down on one knee to give head to Mick Ronson's guitar. It didn't always even sound that good. But of all the images that people associate with Led Zeppelin in their pomp, Page's violin bow was up there with the best of them. Which, if you're already feeling a little insecure and a little undervalued in your role within the band, was not something you'd want to be reminded about. Especially when your own parents, as was the case with Plant's, continued to look askance at their son's choice of career, regarding it as no better than the time he had wasted as a teenager and still wondering when he would settle down to a responsible job.

Nothing was ever said to deliberately make Plant feel bad—or not much, anyway. Occasionally, he might feel excluded during a rehearsal or soundcheck as his musicianly bandmates lost themselves in an instrumental jam that may or may not have been purposefully designed *as* an instrumental. But really, what he felt was a general sense of dissatisfaction, a nagging feeling that no matter what he brought to the band, it was never enough to raise him to equal status with his bandmates in the estimation of those whose opinion he valued the most. His bandmates.

He didn't complain. But observers were aware regardless—through the petty disagreements that Plant and Page, in particular, seemed more prone to than before, through the singer's increasingly visible distaste for the circus that surrounded the band, through the influx of hard drugs into their circle, and through Page's unblinking acceptance of his own personal legend. "There was a lot of unspoken rivalry," Plant admitted in a *Rolling Stone* interview. In the beginning, Page "employed a very democratic approach to the whole thing. He encouraged me a lot. Then, suddenly, we were side by side, and he didn't quite like that." Little put-downs that pecked at petty vulnerabilities, little instances of one-upmanship. "[If] we were both sitting in the same bar, and a woman walked by and we both liked her. Then it was, 'Oh no, here we go.'"

One clear sign of the divisions that festered within the camp was broadcast when the band arrived in Los Angeles in March. Everybody was accustomed to Jones distancing himself as quickly as possible from whichever hotel the band had deemed Madness Central, which in Hollywood was the

Riot House. This time, however, Plant too chose to rent a private house for himself, leaving Page and Bonham alone to hold court. Which, according to multitudinous sources, they proceeded to do with fine abandon.

Plant, on the other hand, stayed in his rental and listened to records.

Lee Brilleaux, the powerhouse vocalist with Dr. Feelgood, ran into the band at the conclusion of their London concerts. Rising fast through Britain's pub circuit, the Feelgoods were among the most talked about new group in the country at the time, with a repertoire that modeled wholly on the R&B bands of the early-'60s blues boom. They performed at Zeppelin's after-show party, and Brilleaux recalled, "Plant was the one who asked for us, and he was the one who paid attention while we playing, bopping about in front of the stage, just getting into the music." He seemed oblivious, Brilleaux marveled, to everything else going on in the room. "He just wanted to listen to us play. Looking back, even though I wasn't ever impressed by the stars who came to watch us, because I knew most of them were only there because someone said it'd be good if they were seen in the crowd, Plant did impress me. He cared about the music."

The London shows were Led Zeppelin's last for the moment. More American dates were scheduled for later in the year, but for now, in May 1975, the band members' time was their own.

Plant promptly scooped up Maureen and the kids, and two days after the final concert, they flew out to Agadir, a small town on the Moroccan coast. Later in the trip, they would hook up with Page, his girlfriend Charlotte, and their daughter Scarlet for an excursion to Marrakech—a working holiday in a way, as the pair mused again about recording some of the ethnic music that surrounded them.

The travels continued. There was a band meeting to attend in Montreux, Switzerland, and the same town's annual jazz festival to take in, and then the party moved on to Rhodes, where the numbers were swollen by the arrival of Maureen's sister Shirley and her husband. Page himself would be staying just a few days; one of Aleister Crowley's former homes on the island of Sicily had come onto the market, and the guitarist was considering its purchase. But Charlotte and Scarlet remained behind, and the day after Page's departure, the entire contingent—Plant and Maureen, Carmen and Karac, Charlotte and Scarlet, Shirley and John Bryant—divided themselves across two cars, all three of the kids in the back seat of the Plants' rented Austin Mini sedan, for a scenic drive across Rhodes.

They never completed the journey. Driving, Maureen lost control of the vehicle. It veered off the road and smashed hard into a tree. All five aboard were injured: Scarlet received cuts and bruises, Carmen's wrist was fractured, Karac's leg was broken. Maureen suffered a broken leg, pelvis, and skull; Plant a broken wrist, leg, and ankle.

A passing fruit truck transported them to the nearest hospital, the rest of the party following close behind. There, while Maureen was rushed into surgery, Plant was taken to a room that he would be sharing with another patient, a drunken soldier who had fallen and banged his head. "As he was coming around," Plant told *Melody Maker*, "he kept focusing on me, uttering my name. I was lying there in some pain, trying to get cockroaches off the bed, and he started to sing 'The Ocean.'"

It was not Plant's first highway accident. Five years earlier, driving home from a Spirit concert in February 1970, he wound up in Kidderminster Hospital with broken teeth and facial lacerations after a collision with another motorist left both cars as total write-offs. On that occasion, he was up and about the next day. This time, he would not be so fortunate.

Maureen was the most seriously injured; indeed, had her sister not been there, she might have died. She had lost a lot of blood, and Shirley was the only person in the hospital, perhaps even on the entire island, who shared her blood group. Back in London, as news of the accident reached headquarters, a Harley Street orthopedist was summoned and flown to the island aboard a private plane, loaded down with medical supplies. Then all five casualties were loaded aboard the same plane and flown back to London.

For all the local doctors' good intentions and expertise, there was no way they could tend to the full extent of Maureen's injuries, while everybody was also well aware that once word spread of the hospital's superstar patient, it wouldn't be just one concussed soldier who was singing Plant's music. The entire island would be under siege from journalists and fans alike.

Confined to a wheelchair for the first weeks of recovery and unable to walk unaided for a time after that, Plant turned to soccer for his physical therapy. Wolverhampton Wanderers opened their treatment to him, where he came under the care of club physio Kevin Walters (brother of actress Julie) and manager Sammy Chung. "They helped me walk again," he revealed.

The injuries he sustained in that accident bother him to this day. He still has difficulty with the damaged arm, and trouble with his back as well—a pain that he would exacerbate when he took to traveling with his bandmates in a van during the Honeydrippers and Priory of Brion excursions.

For now, however, his greatest challenge was that he was unable to remain in the UK. As the incumbent Labour government battled to halt the country's final decline into the financial abyss that was already consuming it, a new wealth tax had been instituted, a staggering 83 percent levied on the nation's highest earners. Already, all but the most stubborn musicians, artists, actors, and businessmen had announced their intention to go into tax exile; many already had. At Peter Grant's insistence, Zeppelin were now following, although Plant would not travel too far. He opted for the Channel Island of Jersey, a part of Britain that handled its own tax arrangements and wanted nothing to do with the supertax.

Settling into a guesthouse belonging to businessman Dick Christian (whose insurance broker godson was a friend of roadie Richard Cole), Plant was close enough to London that Maureen, so slowly recuperating from her injuries, was in reach, but far enough away that the taxman couldn't touch him. Which was probably not much solace to Maureen herself, particularly after she discovered that John Bonham had decided to just bite the financial bullet and remain at home. In June, he and wife Pat celebrated the birth of their second child, daughter Zoë. For now, at least, they were staying put.

In any case, neither remained still for long. Although Plant's injuries saw both the next American tour cancelled and a string of European and Far Eastern shows too, there would be no break in the routine. Rather, with at least one eye on the money lost from the concerts, Peter Grant called all four musicians to Los Angeles in September to outline his revised plans for the next twelve months—beginning with the recording of a new album.

Plant did not necessarily follow his doctors' orders. An intense regime of physiotherapy was the first to fall by the wayside, alongside the recommendation that he not mix his prescription drugs with any recreational compounds. He rented a beach house in Malibu, which swiftly developed a reputation as a nonstop party, described by local scenester Kim Fowley as being decorated with wall-to-wall women.

Another visitor, however, suggests that the extent of Plant's injuries, and the strength of the drugs he was taking to combat the pain, had a rather unexpected effect on the young man whom Hollywood groupiedom perceived as sex on legs: "The girls were there for company and color. Anybody who was expecting a nonstop orgy was very quickly disappointed." Indeed, Fowley told biographer Paul Rees that his own attempt to entertain the fallen god with a wild lesbian freak show was dismissed by Plant's insistence that instead Fowley find him one particular record he wanted, one that he was willing to pay $25,000 for.

He might have been talking about the next Led Zeppelin album. With over a year's worth of live work lined up in the aftermath of *Physical Graffiti*, the band had scarcely given even a thought to the album after that, and had certainly not started gathering material. Grant's insistence that they start *recording* it a full six months before they even intended writing it placed them in a very sticky position, all the more so since *Physical Graffiti* had devoured everything they had previously set aside.

To which difficulty could be added Plant's injuries and—despite the appearances that other sources like to paint—his continued concerns about Maureen. And to that can be added his continued resentment at the way in which he felt he was being treated, and maybe he did have a point there. One cannot help but wonder whether Grant would have hurried Page back into action so soon after an accident.

Then pile on Page's own apparent disinterest in doing anything beyond drawing tight the curtains of his rented home and apparently sitting in the dark. It is little wonder that work on the new album was more or less at a standstill. Nor that when it did finally get under way, the majority of the material would be substandard by almost any band's standards. Five songs, one epic (the swirling atmospheres of "Achilles Last Stand") and one studio jam (the sole band composition, "Royal Orleans") were somehow pulled together in time for the band's arrival at SIR Studios in Hollywood, and from there, at the end of October, the sessions moved to Musicland Studios in Munich, where further difficulties arose in the form of the Rolling Stones.

They were due at the same complex just eighteen days after Zeppelin booked in, to commence the marathon sessions that would ultimately emerge as their *Black and Blue* album. Ultimately, Plant was able to strike some kind of deal with Mick Jagger and postpone Zeppelin's eviction for another three days. Nevertheless, twenty-one days in which to wrap up an album that had barely got off the creative starting blocks yet was just one more pressure that Led Zeppelin didn't require. And the album that emerged from it all echoed its desultory birth.

Presence was not the work of a cohesive, or even functioning, rock band. The best melodies sounded forced, the worst were barely present. It was as if Page was still shut away in his house, Plant was still in pain, Jones was off doing whatever he did when he was not onstage, and Bonham was too bound up with his own chemical demons, a recent taste for smack included, to do more than go through the motions. Even that one widescreen epic, "Achilles Last Stand," was impressive only if one had never wondered what might happen if "Immigrant Song" was grafted onto "Kashmir" and affected not to notice that Plant's vocal, here and throughout the album, was barely a ghost of its customary wild howl. His injuries and recuperation had taken their toll there as well.

None of which seemed to matter as *Presence* hit the record stores at the end of March 1976, and its cover art—a nuclear family gazing blankly at an obsidian obelisk of no apparent purpose—became as much of a talking point as any past runes ever had. Simply the fact that there was a new Led Zeppelin album was sufficient to send sales through the roof. But as is so often the case when a superstar disappoints, that only meant that it would stop selling the moment people started hearing it. And this time, Peter Grant himself was too distracted to react. A cocaine habit had spiraled out of control, his marriage was collapsing, Swan Song was turning into a one-trick pony, and Led Zeppelin had already achieved everything Grant had even dreamed might be possible. There simply was nothing left to dream about.

Eight years old—that is, the same age as the classic John-Paul-George-Ringo Beatles were when they finally called it a day—and Led Zeppelin, too, appeared to have reached the end of the line. Unfortunately, nobody was willing to pull the plug on them. So the fates, be they the dark forces that Jimmy Page allegedly gathered around him or the natural energies that Robert Plant drew from the misty myths of Celt and Viking, set about pulling it for them.

Plant's continued recuperation placed any touring plans on hold for the time being; in lieu of a full-scale Zeppelin flight, the long-gestating *The Song Remains the Same* movie was finally given a release that fall. And it bombed.

Not necessarily through any fault of its own. True, the fantasy sequences would have been fairly preposterous no matter when the movie was released. But issued at any time within the two years after it was shot, *The Song Remains the Same* would have offered the world precisely what it intended: the sight and sound of the biggest band in the world as they approached their musical peak. Three years after it was filmed, however, and two albums on from its most recent inclusions, there was a distinct aroma of yesterday's news to the entire affair; plus, with *Presence* having both underdelivered and underperformed, there was even a stink of desperation about it. As though the band was admitting, "Yes, our last album was a turkey. But do you remember when we were good?"

One other factor influences memories, and historical recounting, of Led Zeppelin's first *annus horribilis*. Late 1976 was also the season that marked the first stirrings of punk rock, a musical force that hindsight insists rose up to purge the rock scene of its sainted dinosaurs and replace them all with purple-haired teenagers with buzz-saw guitars and Mach 3 amphetamine habits.

A modicum of this is true. Certainly no examination of the year 1977 would be complete without reference to the Sex Pistols taking the British imagination by the throat and painting themselves as the ultimate *enfant terribles*, and 1976 was the year in which the band first started moving on to the establishment and mainstream media's radar. It is true, too, that the punks quickly learned that the best way to get their names in the papers was to slam the bands that preceded them—to call them tired and irrelevant, and laugh at their jets and pretensions and drum solos. But hindsight, in this case, is as blinkered as the kids who made those remarks—and the journalists who believed them. Firstly, punk was almost wholly a British experience throughout the most potent months of its lifespan, and secondly, even within those excruciatingly narrow parameters, it was never the all-consuming passion that historians like to claim it to have been.

Outside of the pub and club scene where punk flourished, and the singles chart where its best efforts were concentrated, the dinosaurs browsed on as unperturbedly as they ever had in the past. Genesis, Pink Floyd, Fleetwood Mac, Yes, and Emerson, Lake & Palmer all released albums during 1977 that proved to be among their biggest British hits yet, and most spun off equally monstrous hit singles too. And why? Because the vast majority of people who bought and listened to their music didn't care a damn for punk rock. It was a minority pursuit for a minority of kids, and it was only later in the decade that it became apparent just how crucially punk rock had changed the way things were done. Meaning, when fans and critics alike rejected *The Song Remains the Same* in fall 1976, or *Presence* six months before, it was *not* because they were all lining up to stick the first safety pin through their eyeballs. It was because they expected more from Led Zeppelin than either of those.

Led Zeppelin were not immune to punk's impact, though. Plant and Page's unscheduled viewing of an early Adverts rehearsal, as Led Zeppelin themselves rehearsed upstairs from the band, was their first introduction to the band responsible for some of the new movement's most enduring anthems: "Bored Teenagers," "One Chord Wonders," and "Gary Gilmore's Eyes." And the following month, February 1977, Plant, Page, and Bonham stopped by the Roxy in Covent Garden to catch another of the movement's pacesetters, the Damned, and professed themselves fans.

Well, Plant did, anyway. "I was really impressed by them," he enthused after their set. "I like to see new bands, see what they're doing, how good they are."

Bonham, too, was impressed, and that despite being thrown off the stage by the club's security, a fat, bearded drunk whom the musicians failed to recognize and whose bandmates were too busy laughing at to intervene. His final words as he tumbled back onto the floor were "This is a fucking great band."

Unlike Led Zeppelin, who were a fucking tired band.

Nobody in the group welcomed the announcement of a fifty-one-date American tour that was initially scheduled to begin in February 1977. Therefore, nobody shed a tear when Plant made it clear that he had still to recover sufficiently from his injuries and the dates would have to be pushed forward, a point that he reinforced when he then contracted laryngitis. The tour was rescheduled for March, but the portents remained ominous. The show was barely on the road when a gig at the Riverside Coliseum in Cincinnati was scarred by a near riot, as ticketless fans rushed the arena. Sixty were injured, seventy were arrested. Another gig, another riot—when thunderstorms forced the cancellation of the band's Tampa show, another slew of injuries were laid at Zeppelin's doorstep.

There would be time for some relaxation, but even that was scarred by paranoia. Arriving in Los Angeles for their shows at the Forum, Plant quickly hooked up with some other English ex-pats, and clad in a gold Wolves shirt and a pair of multicolored striped speedos, delighted passers-by when he joined in with an impromptu game of soccer at a park in Encino. Of course he was spotted and recognized, and photographer Brad Elterman later recalled the star's reaction on his own website: "He came up to me (with his surly roadies acting as bodyguards) and demanded my business card. 'I want your business card,' he screamed and then threatened me that I would never work again in Los Angeles; but hey, it was my town. It is an incredible rush when a major star tells you that you will never work again."

The arrival in the band's inner circle of former gangster John Bindon dampened spirits even further, as he set about alienating almost everybody he came in contact with, friend or foe. As a kid, Bindon had been known to one and all as "Biffo" on account of his penchant for what he called "biffing" people—a comical-sounding euphemism for some really rather deadly assaults. Later in life, Bindon won a police award for bravery after leaping from Putney Bridge to save a man from drowning in the Thames. "The funny thing is," he later told a friend, "I didn't get anything for throwing the bastard in, in the first place." Now he was working for Zeppelin, although mercifully his residency would not last long; he was sacked after the violent beating up of a member of Bill Graham's security team, Jim Matzorkis, landed Bindon, Peter Grant, Richard Cole, and John Bonham in an American court (they were handed suspended sentences).

Not that they were angels, either. The mood around the Zeppelin camp was so dark, so pregnant with paranoia and fear, and so strung out on several pharmacies' worth of illicit cocktails that simply looking at someone the wrong way was enough to merit a beating—and as the tour rolled on, the violence grew more and more palpable. The band members themselves were largely insulated from all that was being perpetrated in their name. But they were aware of it—and aware, too, that they were helpless to intervene. Conscious that after two less-than-stellar releases, the cachet that was once Led Zeppelin's by divine right had finally started to slip, their own fears becoming as real as the brutality taking place outside of the bubble.

Their private Bacchanalia had become a very public Babylon, and just to add an even sharper edge to the blade, Peter Grant was already talking about them returning to the studio as soon as the dates were over to begin work on another album. Not because they needed to, but because he couldn't think of anything else for them to do. And the band members were probably already counting down to this next day of reckoning when they checked in at the Maison Dupuy Hotel in New Orleans, at 6 a.m. on July 26, where Plant was greeted by a frantic call from Maureen. Karac had been taken ill. Thirty minutes later, while Plant was still sitting on his hotel room bed, already half decided that he needed to fly home immediately, another call came through. His son was dead.

17

Upon a Golden Horse
(2004–2013)

leveland notwithstanding, Plant was publicly silent throughout 2004, breaking surface only for another charity bash at the tennis club in January and when the statue of Owain Glyndŵr (to which he had contributed) was unveiled in September. The death of his father that year hit him hard, and much of his time was spent in mourning, or in sorting out the old man's affairs and estate.

Just as had happened when his mother passed away, however, the sadness also galvanized him back into action. A fresh burst of songwriting was followed quickly by a reunion with his Strange Sensation bandmates, and *Mighty Rearranger* was all but recorded by the end of the year, a sweeping vista of notion and nuance that *Word* magazine proclaimed "some kind of rebirth."

Elsewhere, writer Ed Vulliamy opined, "Plant and this exceptional group of musicians [have] arrived at that point that Bob Dylan reached when he added 'and The Band' to the official literature." A single unit comprised of two disparate parts, but so absolutely in tune with one another that it was suddenly difficult to imagine them ever living apart. The difference was, Dylan and the Band really didn't capture their chemistry on record, and *Mighty Rearranger* was neither as haphazard as *The Basement Tapes* nor as sterile as *Planet Waves*. (Although it would be great to hear Plant cover that album's epic "Dirge.")

Acoustic overall, but without ever losing sight of its electrifying destiny, *Mighty Rearranger* flows through similar veins that pump world music to the masses, but yes, it rearranges them, taking the impetus but not the influence, knowing the import but eschewing the impact in favor of taking other turns entirely.

A theme does run through the album, that of the worlds of man and higher spirit in constant—and constantly growing—opposition, Babylon rising on the bones of its citizens' crushed and broken dreams and beliefs. Maybe there never was a golden age during which men chose careers in politics because they truly believed they could improve the peoples' lot. But neither had there ever been one when so many politicians were just in it for their own greed and glory, and regarded the actual act of government as a grind that got in the way of making money.

"Freedom Fries," titled for post-9/11 America's attempt to rename French fries as such to protest France's reluctance to approve the Iraq War, was Plant at his most political, tearing imagery from the Bible to berate the rush to war. True, the United States was scarcely the first nation to set about rechristening things as a snub to a foreign enemy; during World War I, the British renamed everything from a breed of dog (German Shepherds became Alsatians) to the monarch's family name (Saxe-Coburg and Gotha was changed to the modern House of Windsor) in a bid to rid the land of the stench of the enemy Germans. And sauerkraut, a popular cabbage dish, was briefly revised as liberty cabbage. The difference was, France was never actually the Americans' enemy, just a nation whose leaders happened to agree with the sentiments of most of the citizens of the world. "Freedom Fries," like the band name Priory of Brion before it, condemned the knee-jerk rush to believe in *something*, no matter how utterly absurd it might ultimately be.

The album rolled on, through the beautiful "All the King's Horses," its chorus and melody so simplistically divine that they blanched every man jack of the competing pop aspirants when they made it to radio; the retro-rhythms of "Let the Four Winds Blow," purposefully cast in the same resonant key as Don Fardon's "Indian Reservation"; and the number that Ed Vulliamy describes as "one of the more important British songs of now." On ethnic strains and Western bombast, the musical equivalent of the Iraq War itself, "Takamba," mourns the Tony Blair government's headlong rush to sell its country's heritage down the star-spangled river for the sole sake of its leader's place in glorious posterity. At which point, we pause and ask: how many times can an old rock 'n' roller be credited with making his best album yet? Even Dylan had yet to gain a second breath as glorious as Robert Plant's.

It was time to go back out on tour, an outing that consumed much of 2005 as it swept across Europe and the US. The album itself was warmly received, earning kind reviews and a Grammy nomination, and while it's safe to say there was never any danger of it reestablishing Plant as a "front line" attraction, neither was there any risk of him actually wanting such an accolade.

The nostalgia boom that started rising in the 1990s, with all manner of grisly specters from the past relaunching themselves onto the boards, had only accelerated since then; there were weeks when a look at the local gig guide had you checking the date at the top of the page, for fear that you'd suddenly been swallowed up by a time storm and it really was 1974 all over again. Plant could not help the fact that his own presence on the live circuit only furthered that impression. But he could ensure that anyone going to see him and expecting the same kind of nostalgia show that so many other veterans were now churning out would either be disappointed or pleasantly surprised.

The oldies remained in the set, of course. "No Quarter" and "Black Dog" even rocked the opening salvo some nights, and his encore reappraisal of "Whole Lotta Love" now reached back to its early '70s incarnation, a vehicle for a wealth of improvisation and medleying, but only after emerging from a slow blues shuffle that was scarcely even recognizable until Plant dropped in a familiar lyric. Then the familiar riff kicked in, but this was no chest-beating anthem aggrandizing the past.

"Whole Lotta Love" in the twenty-first century has outgrown its own former status as dramatically as Plant has outgrown his. Especially when it drifts into an old classic Diddley beat, and suddenly it's "Who Do You Love" leaking out, big bad Bo's boast of cobra snakes, human skulls, and barbed wire fences that go on forever.

Around the old favorites, there were some nights when the set list suggested that the new album was going to get very short shrift indeed. But that was on paper. Onstage, the logic behind the CD's title, *Mighty Rearranger*, was laid bare for all to hear. For the oldies had indeed been rearranged, brought in line with the themes that the album brought to bear, but *not*, as is so often the case (and the Page-Plant collaboration was certainly guilty of this to an extent) for the sake of making them sound different.

Rather, like Dylan throughout his Never Ending Tour, and David Bowie during the late 1990s and early 2000s, the rearrangements were intended to make the songs feel comfortable; to transform them from obligations, if that is not too strong a word, into pleasures. Performances that Plant looked forward to, not only for the thrill of the audience, but also for his own joy at singing them again, in a manner that made perfect sense to him now. And so effectively did he achieve this that some nights the audience remained completely unknowing till Plant opened his mouth to sing. "No Quarter" as a stately blues march and the aforementioned "Whole Lotta Love" were merely the first and last of the surprises.

Amidst all the traveling, Plant and Alison Krauss remained in touch, and when fall 2006 finally brought an end to the tour, Plant was on the move again, flying to Nashville to meet up with her again—this time in the studio.

They had not agreed on everything. Plant had hatched the notion of recording in New Orleans, with local musicians and the distinct taste of the region's musical heritage pumping through the ether. Krauss preferred to stick with what she knew: a country-tinged album recorded at Sound Emporium Studios in Nashville, with T-Bone Burnett producing and a studio band built around guitarist Marc Ribot and Nashville sessioneers bassist Dennis Crouch and drummer Jay Bellerose. And when he thought about it, Plant knew it made sense. Before rock 'n' roll, it was country that rocked, and you only had to listen to the sides that Elvis and Johnny Cash cut for Sun Records to appreciate that.

Burnett himself was more of an Americana musician than a straightforward country player, one steeped in the blurred archaeological roots of the genres that seem to mean so much today, and it turned out that Burnett felt the same way about Plant. "The same darkness that you find in bluegrass and murder ballads, it is a darkness that is absolutely in Robert, in his voice and life," Burnett told *Rolling Stone's* David Fricke in 2008. "Alison understands that, and Robert worked hard to get it."

Their repertoire was arrived at more democratically, Plant and Krauss amassing a playlist of over fifty songs, ranging from pre-war blues to pre-rock standards, from Tom Waits (guitarist Ribot's regular employer) to Townes Van Zandt, and on into Plant's own songwriting stash, "Please Read the Letter" from *Walking into Clarksdale.* Just thirteen would make the final cut, and three of those were taped on the very first day. If Plant— or Krauss—had had any doubts beforehand about how they would actually gel in the studio, that opening session sent all of them packing. Along with any common assumption of what a "country" album should be. Plant's beloved bluegrass found a welcoming chime in Krauss's contributions; her roots likewise found fertile soil in Plant's open-mindedness.

Their vocals thread into one another, each instinctively locating the tone and the terms that the other demands, moving toward and sometimes even capturing the same natural nuance and sympathetic bows that hallmarked perhaps the greatest of all country-themed duets, Gram Parsons and Emmylou Harris. Their work together, across two deathless albums in the early 1970s, has never been surpassed. But *Raising Sand*, as Plant and Krauss called their record, at least equaled it, and did so with such assurance that it could not be termed a departure for either of them.

In 2007, Plant described the partnership to the *Los Angeles Times* as "a miracle," and admitted that "the easiest thing about anything that's happened in the last four or five years has been making this record." Even more impressive, he laughed, was when he discovered his sister Allison loved it. "My sister, who normally thinks that my music—well, she thinks that I should be sectioned, taken off somewhere and strapped down—she's texting me: 'It's so beautiful, I can't wait to meet Alison, she's made you sing properly.'"

She was correct. Plant had never shied away from exploring his own dexterity, not since Priory of Brion had freed him from the need to "rock";

Krauss had never allowed her reputation as a youthful prodigy daring enough to take unexpected twists to mask her sense of self. But still the pair were stepping into new territory, a musical landscape that Plant described as building up from "this juju sub-mambo thing" that Burnett laced into the percussive bedrock of the project, then forced the singers to work up from there. Indeed there were moments when their vocals all but exchanged roles, so that Krauss became the voice of hard-earned experience and Plant the comparative ingénue, learning at her feet.

But if there was one aspect to *Raising Sand* that saw it rise above all its other accomplishments, it was this. It lived through the next Led Zeppelin reunion, and it came out even stronger on the other side. Not even the roar of acclaim and publicity that reverberated throughout the entire music scene when the old mastodon declared it had thawed out once again could stop *Raising Sand* from raising its own understated variation of hell.

Amid so much other activity, and so many other triumphs, Plant could easily have been forgiven if he'd put Zeppelin firmly in the back of his mind. Priory of Brion never recorded an album, but if one counts the best of the circulating live tapes as one, and then adds *Dreamland, Mighty Rearranger,* and *Raising Sand* to Plant's twenty-first-century tally, he had now cut four albums in succession that rated among the best he had made. And certainly added up to his most consistent streak ever.

Which may be why this latest reunion idea appealed to him, when so many past suggestions and offers hadn't. Plus, like Live Aid and the Atlantic Records birthday party, it was intended only as a solitary one-off. Later, Jimmy Page would lead the chorus of voices demanding that they tour together, and promoters offered sums of money that made all their past earnings feel like small change. And Plant would be seen as the villain of the piece when he turned his back on all of them. For now, however, it was just one show: Plant, Page, and Jones back together, with Jason Bonham once again depping for his dad, and a staggering two million people sending in applications for tickets to a venue, the O2 in London, that could hold only eighteen thousand.

Only.

An online lottery would determine who the lucky applicants were, at a cost of £125 a pop. It's a mark of just how high anticipation had risen that many people considered that a bargain, admitted that they would have paid (and thanks to the touts, were able to pay) many times that for admission. Meanwhile . . .

With *Raising Sand* all but complete, Plant had returned home for Christmas and immediately set about revisiting his past, reforming the Honeydrippers with Robbie Blunt and Andy Sylvester, plus keyboard player Mark Stanway, and playing a couple of shows—a benefit at Kidderminster Town Hall in December, raising funds for a neighbor's life-saving operation, and a birthday party at JBs in Dudley in February to mark Roy Williams's sixtieth birthday on Valentine's Day. They rehearsed in the barn, relearned their rocking oldies, and even welcomed Jeff Beck onstage at JBs to add his own breed of magic to the night's entertainment.

What Plant's bandmates didn't know was that wheels were already in motion for Zeppelin to resume flight. On December 14, 2006, Atlantic Records founder Ahmet Ertegun died after taking a tumble backstage at a Rolling Stones show. Almost immediately, his widow, Mica, began planning some kind of memorial show, and just as Ertegun itself had done when Atlantic had its birthday party, she insisted it wouldn't be complete unless Led Zeppelin topped the bill.

By June 2007, the band was rehearsing, breaking for a few weeks while Strange Sensation played a clutch of shows, and then making the public announcement in September. The gig was set for the end of November, just weeks after *Raising Sand* was released—to a reception that reinforced Plant's conviction that if it hadn't been for Mica, and wanting to do something to remember Ahmet, he would have been spending his time far more profitably than this.

Raising Sand entered the charts on both sides of the ocean at No. 2, with sales that would hit the two million mark before the end of the year. The single, "Gone Gone Gone," put radio into a stranglehold from which nothing could release it. Television, radio, and concert halls were all crying out for Plant and Krauss to appear, but of course he'd known months in advance that the end of his year would be tied up in other pursuits. Although he would certainly miss a few rehearsals as he headed out to do some early promotion for the album, and more as he and Krauss recorded their long-awaited *CMT Crossroads* performance, the bulk of that stuff would need to wait till the new year.

In the meantime, he had a few arguments to fight. The proposed Zeppelin set list was forever the bone of contention; so were the now-rising specters of the future, and the unimaginable sums of money that Plant's stubbornness was withholding from everybody else. Jimmy Page had new management, and they weighed in, constantly buttonholing Curbishley to ask him to persuade his client to reconsider. And maybe he thought he could. But Plant was standing firm. He'd agreed to one show; he would perform one show.

The day grew closer; the mood grew blacker, as if the trio's very presence in one room together was sucking the joy out of being back together. Or maybe it was the venue where the show would take place. Prince Charles, the heir to the British throne, once described modern architecture as a figurative carbuncle. The O2 took him literally, and resembled one as well: a dead-flesh, off-white bubble rising on the banks of the Thames as a ghastly millennial monument to ex–Prime Minister Tony Blair's vainglorious attempts to make his mark on British society before his reign stumbled into discredit and disgust. It would be no surprise whatsoever to learn that a building that looked so much like a carbuncle should start behaving as one now, gorging itself on poison and pus.

But it was all that was available. With so many other of London's most storied major venues either scaling back or closing down (even Earls Court, home of Zeppelin's 1975 London marathon, looked like falling prey to the wrecking ball soon), the O2 was the best the city had available. And Zeppelin was the biggest it had ever hosted.

Dark clouds continued to gather. Early in November, Page fractured a finger. The gig was postponed, pushed back until December 10. Around the same time, Plant's assistant, "Big" Dave Hodgetts, was diagnosed with terminal cancer. The curse of Zeppelin had made it along to the reunion show as well.

In the end, all went well on the night itself. Sixteen songs in two hours kicked off with "Good Times Bad Times," swung into "Ramble On." "In My Time of Dying," "Trampled Under Foot"—they played the greatest-hits selection that everyone hoped to hear, the crowd's expectations raised and rewarded by the release, on the eve of the show, of *Mothership*, the latest in a now almost tiresome succession of Zeppelin's compilations. Later, both a movie and a box set of the gig itself would join it on the shelves, the band overcoming any reservations they might have felt regarding the efficacy of the concert to agree with the massed voice of the assembled hordes.

But it would be foolish, as many people did, to insist that this was Led Zeppelin at anything approaching their best. Because, first and foremost, it wasn't Led Zeppelin, and it wouldn't have been even if John Bonham were still alive. It was three guys who used to be in a band together, getting together to play the old songs again. There was none of the old chemistry, although there were certainly moments of camaraderie; there was no sense of urgency; and most of all, there was no need to raise the roof. Their reputation had already done that. They just needed to make sure they didn't mess up.

They didn't. But Plant still wasn't interested in carrying on, not even when he was formally presented with plans for a full-scale world tour, thirty shows around the globe and cash registers screaming in every one. According to Page, the rest of the band were so certain that their frontman would go along with the plans that Jason Bonham even resigned his current gig, playing with '80s soft rockers Foreigner's reunion. And when Plant continued to say no, they actually considered carrying on without him, seeking a replacement via a handful of top-secret auditions that everyone seemed to know about.

Maybe they genuinely were imagining that Zeppelin could fly without Robert Plant. Maybe they just wanted to make him think they were, so that he'd come running back to stop them. It had worked once before, after all, back in 1977. Either way, it didn't matter. Plant ignored them, and the auditions fizzled out.

Which is not to say that he had turned his back on the band. Two Led Zeppelin numbers, dramatic recastings of "Black Dog" and "When the

Levee Breaks," were included in the CMT Crossroads broadcast early in
the new year, both stripped of all bombast and weight to be reconfigured
in the manner of the music that surrounded them—and that had inspired
them in the first place. But the rest of the set, built around Raising Sand,
was equally impressive, and it was difficult not to watch the performance
and wish that Plant had undergone a similar, all-encompassing, musical
rebirth a decade earlier than he had.

The duo of Plant and Krauss set out on tour in April 2008, opening a
forty-four-date American outing in Louisville, Kentucky, and returning another Led Zeppelin classic to its roots, as "The Battle of Evermore" at last
crept out of the shadows of its better-known playmates on Led Zeppelin IV
to be revealed as the true jewel in Plant's songwriting crown. So sparse, so
spectral, Plant and Krauss not just singing but living the lyric, in the manner of the strolling minstrels who might have sung its equivalent when the
battle was still news. In a live show littered with spine-tingling moments,
"The Battle of Evermore" was one that raised the hair on the back of the
neck as well.

The tour would consume much of the spring and early summer, returning Plant to London for a show at Wembley Arena and making magical
haunts in Birmingham, Manchester, and Cardiff, as well as a run of shows
across the continent. At every halt, he and Krauss combined as though
they'd been singing together for years, not months; at every halt, any disappointment that Zeppelin had not docked there for a night or two was gently
salved by a performance that may not have been layered with so much
legend but was certainly a lot more real.

A milestone loomed during the outing's midsummer break—Plant's sixtieth birthday, celebrated with friends and family at his local pub. A series
of milestones, in fact.

Plant accepted the invitation to become a vice president at Wolverhampton Wanderers, as they battled once again to join the Premier League
(their last visit lasted just one season). And he was the utterly unexpected
special guest who made that year's Cropredy festival so memorable, the
secrecy surrounding his appearance so tight that he did not even appear

at the band's warm-up show earlier in the week. "We [did] one very low-profile run-through . . . two weeks earlier, in a village hall not far from where he lives," Fairport's Simon Nicol told his band's biographer Nigel Schofield. "He came along unannounced, [which] was considered unremarkable because of him living locally. He got up on stage and joined us for [a] song, which gave everybody the opportunity of playing it together."

The song they chose to play was "The Battle of Evermore." The year 2008 marked the thirtieth anniversary of Sandy Denny's death, and band member Jerry Donahue's daughter Kristina was already preparing to step into Sandy's shoes for the evening. Now there was an even greater aspect to the proposed tribute, as Dave Pegg informed the audience during a short break in Fairport's set.

He was remembering Sandy, how "she was in the Strawbs, then she helped out Fairport for a bit . . . but there was one other band she helped out, she was the only female singer to sing on a Led Zeppelin track." Then, with the audience still wondering where the monologue was leading, he concluded, "and we're really honored to have Robert Plant here."

"I'll tell ya, singing with Sandy was never as serious as that!" Plant, meandering onto the stage, joked. "It was great fun. It worked out good."

Then, with the audience howling in surprise and excitement, and Chris Leslie's mandolin setting out the familiar opening, "The Battle of Evermore" spun eerily out, Plant and Donahue following the recorded version but expanding it somehow, giving fresh nuance to lyric, fresh emphasis to tones.

Behind them, Fairport played as though they did this every night—as though the Zeppelin song was a staple in their repertoire and not a song they'd only ever played together once before. And when it was over, Plant remained on the stage alone, just talking to the crowd about his own memories of Sandy, before turning to the giant screen at the back of the stage and remaining in place to watch the video tribute that had been prepared for the evening. It was, writer Schofield later mused, "pure stagecraft."

By September 2008, Plant was back on the road with Alison Krauss, and in February he was in Los Angeles, as *Raising Sand* was awarded the

Grammy for Album of the Year and then picked up four more: Record of the Year for "Please Read the Letter," Best Pop Collaboration with Vocals for "Rich Woman," and Best Country Collaboration with Vocals for "Killing the Blues." "I'm bewildered," Plant admitted at the end of the evening. "In the old days, we would have called this selling out. But it's a good way to spend a Sunday."

It was not Plant's first-ever Grammy triumph; that honor went to a *Walking into Clarksdale*'s "Most High," which won for Best Hard Rock Performance in 1998. Krauss, on the other hand, was probably running out of places to put the things. As CNN remarked, "The win adds to Krauss' eye-popping Grammy total of twenty-six awards—more than any female artist in history and third only to conductor Sir Georg Solti . . . and producer-arranger-mogul Quincy Jones." And as if to round off twelve months of achievement, July 2009 brought Plant to Buckingham Palace, to be dubbed a Commander of the British Empire (CBE) for his services to music.

Any suggestion that he might now sit back on his laurels, however, simply to absorb the strides that he had made over the decade he'd just passed through, were swiftly disavowed. Plans for a second album with Krauss, with Daniel Lanois mooted as its producer, were abandoned; it was Krauss who called the halt, but Plant knew she was right, that their plans for a follow-up would fail for precisely the same reasons as the original album worked so well: they'd already done it and there was nowhere else they needed to go. A lesson that Plant might not have taken on board ten years before, and certainly wouldn't have in the '70s and '80s, but which now was the clarion that guided his career.

Instead, Plant turned his mind toward another burgeoning collaboration, with guitarist Buddy Miller, a member of the *Raising Sand* band. Still keen to explore the roots of Americana—and to work with the band that he and Miller had constructed around singer Patty Griffin, bassist Byron House, guitarist Darrell Scott, and drummer Marco Giovino—Plant effectively relocated himself to Nashville, and they went into rehearsal. "We each have similar places we come from as singers," Griffin explained to *Billboard*. "He inspires me. He goes far and deep."

It was, in many ways, a return to the Honeydrippers/Priory of Brion situation, building a repertoire of favored oldies. This time, however, Plant drew from the wealth of music that preceded the '50s and '60s that those bands recreated. He delved into the annals of song marked out by folklorists who lived before he was even born, old-timers like "Cindy, I'll Marry You Someday" and "Satan Your Kingdom Must Come Down." Having set the parameters, the group began inching them forward, now seeking songs that retained those same spirits or writing fresh numbers that tugged the same chords: Plant and Miller's "Central Two-O-Nine"; "Highway Song," another song penned with Griffin, which was destined for her own next album; Richard Thompson's "House of Cards"; Townes Van Zandt's "Harm's Swift Way."

And barely had they settled upon an album's worth of songs to play than they were in the studio itself—Gillian Welch and Dave Rawlings's Woodland first, then the House of Blues—recording an album that was a successor to *Raising Sand* only in that it also ranked Plant alongside a powerful female vocal (from Griffin) and in that it was just as honest, just as open, and ultimately, just as good. Even Plant's decision to move fully into the modern age by taking two songs from the Minnesota band Low that might have seemed better suited to *Dreamland*, "Silver Rider" and "Monkey," was proved the right move in the end, as their Spartan ethos and wide-open arrangements loaned both numbers the space to shift into Plant and Miller's vision.

According to engineer Mike Poole, talking to Soundonsound.com, Miller and Plant "talked a lot" about their intentions, but nothing whatsoever was nailed into place beforehand. Rather, they shared CDs of various songs; talked about influences, inspirations, and ideas; and made certain that everybody knew that it was the mood of the music, not the mechanics, that they were concerned with capturing. Even the final arrangements were left until the last minute, hashed out in the studio, and "if they worked, great . . . [but] if there was no magic, we simply moved on."

Plant purposefully eschewed any but the most essential technological timesavers. They recorded live, with as few overdubs as possible, with Plant purposefully limiting them to recording on just sixteen analog tracks, as opposed to the infinite possibilities of digital recording. "This meant that we had to make decisions early and we couldn't mess around with laying down many different drum scenarios, or whatever, which you tend to do when you have tons of available tracks. It's easy to get lost in a world of endless options."

These same attitudes were in view as the group prepared to hit the road, and other songs squeezed into the show. For they, too, would undergo that same magical transformation: Zeppelin's "Misty Mountain Hop," "Rock and Roll," and "Houses of the Holy"; Plant's own "In the Mood" and "Tall Cool One"—all rubbing noses with both the familiarity of the album and some other surprises too: an "In My Time of Dying" stripped back beyond even Dylan's masterful retelling and a magical "Wade in the Water," a Pentecostal spiritual that was a highlight every night it was included in the set. Plant didn't even need to scramble for a name for this new enterprise. Digging deep into his past—but into his frame of mind as well, for he and Griffin were now a couple together—he called it the Band of Joy.

Through the next year, the band toured around, neither slacking nor slackening as the months merged together until their final show together at the Hardly Strictly Bluegrass festival on September 30, 2011, in Plant's old spiritual home town of San Francisco. And when the shadow of the Zeppelin loomed over him again, Plant listened to what Page laid on the table, but remained ultimately unmoved. As he told Australian television's *Today Tonight* show early in 2013, "I'm up for anything that's new. Just give me a hint of something that's good fun."

So he rejoined his old bandmates for their second movie premiere, the *Celebration Day* chronicle of the carbuncle concert, and he was with them when President Barack Obama presented Led Zeppelin with a Kennedy Center Honor for their contribution to American culture and the arts. He even cracked a smile when the president thanked them for not trashing any hotel rooms during their stay in the nation's capital, and later in the evening, he was reported to have blinked back a tear as Heart's Ann and Nancy Wilson, accompanied by Jason Bonham and a choir and string section, regaled guests and honorees with a version of "Stairway to Heaven."

But tears were all that he would shed. Reports of Strange Sensation's demise had already proven premature as he relaunched them as the Sensational Space Shifters, touring their asses off once again and astonishing all comers with an all-covers set that felt, every night, like it had only just been written. He had relocated to Austin, Texas, and it would be easy, as one considers the fate of most artists of Robert Plant's age, to imagine it as one of the final moves of his life, to think that he might now be considering slowing down—maybe even settling down—and growing old and brown in the Texas sun.

And then it all changed. He returned to England, to a new home in Ludlow. He parted with Griffin and announced a new album. He was not slowing down, and he was not settling down, either. What he was doing was taking full advantage of the fact that time itself has ceased to have any meaning, at least as far as his career is concerned, and the career has ceased to have meaning either, at least as far as his music goes.

True, he did once say that he had no intention whatsoever of fading out gracefully, playing ever more disheveled oldies shows to decreasing audiences on the Black Country pub circuit. But even if he found himself trapped in that position, one has the feeling that he'd soon leap out of it. Either that, or he'd deliberately put himself there in the first place, just for the challenge and the fun he might have.

It took him a long time to realize that those factors are what he needed, and even longer to put that knowledge into practice. But carve Plant's career into ten-year-or-so increments, and erase everything but the music that he made at each junction—*Led Zeppelin I*, those first Honeydrippers shows, *Manic Nirvana*, Priory of Brion, and most recent of all, *Band of Joy*—and one common factor rebounds through them all.

He has never started anything he cannot complete, and (though he may, as we all do, get distracted every so often), he's never done anything he doesn't want to do, either.

Except once.

The time he went back to Led Zeppelin, when he really should have quit.

18

Let Your Loss Be Your Lesson
(1977–1980)

His son's face the only thing in his mind, Plant returned to England on the same day that he learned of the boy's death, the complacency of the vast machinery that surrounded Led Zeppelin stunned into action by the news. It wasn't easy piecing the flights together, but they managed it, flying him first to Newark, New Jersey, and then a shuttle to New York's JFK for an international flight to London. A car waited there to take him home.

He barely left the house, or Maureen's side, for months to come—for almost a year, in fact, before he was finally lured to that band meeting at Clearwell Castle in May 1978. And even then the wound was still fresh, the grief still palpable, and the blame still tightly focused—on himself for not having been there either at the time of Karac's death or for the majority of his life as well, and on the band for having assured that in the first place.

All those months, all those years. He had questioned in the past the need, instilled into each of them by Peter Grant, for the band to continue churning, one album after another, one tour after another. He had asked on so many occasions why it was that Led Zeppelin needed to work like a horse when other bands that could conceivably have been placed on a similar plateau to them, Pink Floyd and Emerson, Lake & Palmer among them, were already falling into far more leisurely routines. Two years had separated each of Floyd's last three albums, and while touring had devoured at least half of the interim, still the band operated to a regime that felt luxurious compared to Zeppelin's. ELP had enjoyed an even longer

break, leaving the road behind in 1974 and not even considering recording a new album (1977's *Works*) until they'd had close to two years during
which to recharge their batteries.

Grant would counter in the same way as he always countered. By pointing out that Led Zeppelin were bigger than either Pink Floyd or ELP, and
the reason for that was because they kept going. Nobody could overtake
them, nobody could outgross them. Now Plant was realizing the price
they—no, not "they," *he*—had had to pay for that.

Only one member of the band was welcome at Jennings Farm throughout this long, ghastly exile; the only one who even attended Karac's funeral.
John Bonham, Plant's nearest neighbor, dropped by whenever he could,
and was allowed to stay whenever he was sober. The friendship the pair
had ignited so many years before, and that had remained on track despite
all Plant's misgivings about the drummer's excesses, remained strong—perhaps grew even stronger now, as Bonham hid his own demons from view as
he fought to pull Plant back on track.

Occasionally, Bonham would invite Plant along to watch the band that
he was jamming with, led by the Move's old bassist Trevor Burton, but
there was never any pressure to do more than watch. But it did inspire Plant
to take a similar route, teaming up with another local singer, Melvin Git-
tus, in a band that they saddled with the most unbecoming soubriquet they
could think of, the Turd Burglars—a popular English expression reflecting
upon the propensity of strangers to walk into a public restroom just as one
is about to release one's cargo. The sphincter closes, the turd has been
burgled. Childish, yes. But a great band name, all the same.

Cherry picking members from Plant's other hobby, the soccer team that
turned out for the local Queen's Head pub, the Turd Burglars gigged when
the soccer team played, pitching up at venues the night before a game for
a pre-match sing along to sundry favorite oldies. Plant even took the Turd
Burglars into the local Old Smithy studio to record a brace of favorites,
"Buzz Buzz A-Diddle It" and "Three Months to Kill," and just maybe he
detected a slice of irony in that latter title, because he did indeed have just
three months left before the Zeppelin siren call finally lured him back.

He heeded the call and regretted it instantly. He found he still resented his bandmates' coldness when he needed them the most, with Page, Grant, and Jones's avoidance of the funeral only the most hurtful of the thoughtlessness they exhibited. A few phone calls, a note, a "How are you, mate?" That was all they needed to do. Instead, they left him to his solitude and heartbreak, maybe reassuring themselves that what Percy needed was peace and quiet, and they didn't want to intrude. But as Plant's father later growled, "All this success and fame . . . what is it worth? It doesn't mean very much when you compare it to the love of a family."

How serious was Plant about leaving Led Zeppelin? Very. And how was he brought back on board? Gently. He had already had his application to a teacher training school accepted when the first overtures were made, and his initial inclination was to ignore them.

It wasn't as if there was unfinished business; Led Zeppelin had set out to become the biggest band in the world, and they had succeeded. They had dreamed of creating music that would survive for all time, and it looked like they'd achieved that as well—at least as far as anything can last that long. There was nothing left to prove, nothing left to do. It was the end.

Except it wasn't. Among the rumors that percolated around the music industry, and made their way to Plant as whispers and "Did you hears," was the most peculiar notion that Jimmy Page and Roy Harper were working together again. In fact, it was more than a rumor.

According to journalist Chris Welch, Harper had recently been interviewed by a farming magazine—no surprise, as he was also a farmer—and in the course of the conversation, he mentioned that he might be joining Led Zeppelin. Plant "subscribed to the same farming magazine and read the interview," recalled Welch in *Peter Grant: The Man Who Led Zeppelin*.

It was a trick that the band would play again thirty years later, when Plant proved so reluctant to continue the latest Led Zeppelin reunion. On that occasion, it didn't succeed. This time, though, it apparently did. "Horrified that Harper might be taking his place," Welch continued, "he contacted Page for the first time in months."

Harper plays the story down. "Me as Robert Plant doesn't work!" he avows. He'd already tried to front a rock group once, a couple of years earlier with his *HQ* album, and he'd sworn off band work for good as a consequence. "When I have a band onstage, I'm not as focused on the audience as I should be, I'm more concerned about the democracy of the band. In order to maintain your quasi-leadership of the democracy, you have to give everyone their head, and give every instrument its due in the performance, and I always found myself diluted."

Whatever the reasons behind Plant's change of heart—and likely it was simply the passing of time, the opportunity to heal, and the tug of a lifestyle that he had generally enjoyed—he agreed to go back, and immediately had second thoughts. But having committed, there was no honorable way out. A new album was called for; a new album would be delivered. And once again, Grant didn't even seem to care that, with a chilling echo of *Presence*, there was no new material, meaning whatever they intended recording would move straight from conception to realization as fast as it could be hustled.

Page appeared to have written nothing during the band's long layoff, tinkering instead with various soundtrack projects; Jones had a few ideas, but was intending them for his own solo album; and Plant, whose attention was understandably far from the business of songwriting, had just one thing to offer, a piece he had written for Karac titled "All My Love." It is no coincidence that of all the songs that would eventually be pulled together for what became *In Through the Out Door*, that song alone dripped with anything close to genuine passion.

Elsewhere, and this is where the now eighteen-month-old ramifications of punk rock did turn around and bite the band, it was as if Led Zeppelin had remained in both a creative and sonic bubble since *Physical Graffiti*, neither advancing on the sounds and textures that established that album as the epitome of their craft nor even particularly seeming to care to try.

Punk, and its new wave mutation, had spurred many other artists to try something new, to at least have a go at updating their signature sound to match the bands that were exploding all around them. Not all succeeded, and some perished trying. Others went rocketing off on fresh tangents that rendered them all but unrecognizable to their core following. But a handful (led by Pink Floyd, who commenced work on *The Wall* around the same time as Led Zeppelin began *In Through the Out Door*) had absorbed all the lessons that punk could teach them, and emerged all the more successful as a result.

Five years earlier, Led Zeppelin would have been consumed with curiosity, ravenous to restake their claim on their position as the world's No. 1. Now it was as if they didn't even care. Sequestered in the Polar Studios in Sweden, from whence ABBA had masterminded their own superstardom, Led Zeppelin went through motions that were as tired as any that had contributed to *Presence*—and just as fraught. Page, for the first time, abdicated his production duties in all but name. It was Plant and Jones who shepherded the album to completion; Plant and Jones, too, who became the album's lead composers; and Jones alone who seemed to have noticed that music had moved on since the last time they were together. The studio was loaded with a clutch of the latest synthesizers, and Jones set himself the task of mastering them. Always the most adventurous of the band members when it came to grasping technology, Jones at least attempted to bring fresh pastures to the music.

Plant remained wracked by doubt regardless. As he told *Uncut* in 2005, one evening, out on the town with one half of ABBA, he found himself pondering death, and very sincerely asking himself, "If I go tomorrow, is this where I want to find myself? In a sex club in Stockholm, being silly with Benny and Bjorn from ABBA, while Agnetha and Frida are driving around trying to find which den of iniquity Led Zeppelin had taken their husbands to?"

The answer, for all the distractions that Stockholm could offer, was no.

In later years, Plant could find some justification for the album. "*In Through the Out Door* wasn't the greatest thing in the world," he admitted to *Q* in 2007, "but at least we were trying to vary what we were doing, for our own integrity's sake. Of all the [Led Zeppelin] records, it's interesting, but a bit sanitized because we hadn't been in the clamor and chaos for a long time. In '77, when I lost my boy, I didn't really want to go swinging around—'Hey hey mama say the way you move' didn't really have a great deal of import anymore. *In Through the Out Door* is more conscientious and less animal." The problem was, that conscientiousness was all too often ditchwater dull.

With the album complete, Plant flew home in time for the birth of his third child. Logan Romero was born in January 1979, and Plant knew he had the next six months free. Peter Grant had desperately tried to force a fresh American tour into the calendar, but Plant was adamant. He was still in pain from the accident; Maureen too. They had a new child. He would not tour; he would not even leave the country.

He acceded to just one request: to announce the release of *In Through the Out Door* with a single festival appearance, at Knebworth House in August, topping a bill that would also include Todd Rundgren, Southside Johnny and the Asbury Dukes, the Marshall Tucker Band, and, playing what they intended to be their last-ever public performance before breaking up for good, Fairport Convention.

As it turned out, ticket demand was so vast that a second performance was added for the following weekend as well, with Led Zeppelin's total earnings from the two performances widely touted as the largest single fee ever paid to a rock band at that time. Then, on the largest stage ever constructed for a concert, at a volume that received noise complaints from as far away as seven miles, Led Zeppelin played the last two British concerts of their life.

It was, Plant mourned in its aftermath, two he wished they had never given. He was "racked with nerves." Aside from a warm-up in Brondby, Denmark, a few days earlier, the first Knebworth performance was Led Zeppelin's first concert in two years—and their first British gig in four. The sheer weight of expectation from the four hundred thousand people who turned up for the two shows was simply too great. "[It] was useless. It was no good at all. It was no good because we weren't ready to do it, the whole thing was a management decision. It felt like I was cheating myself because I wasn't as relaxed as I could have been. There was so much expectation there, and the least we could have done was to have been confident enough to kill."

They weren't. So they didn't.

In Through the Out Door was released immediately following the second Knebworth show, and though its sales were certainly respectable (four million sold in the United States before the end of the year), cynics (and there were plenty now) murmured that it only sold as well as it did because of a remarkable gimmick attached to the release. Delivered to the stores in a sealed brown paper bag, with just the band's name and album title stamped on the front, the LP boasted no less than six different covers. And while nobody seems to have calculated how many people purchased multiple copies in the hope of acquiring all six, the fact is, many did.

Knebworth over, Plant retreated once more. He would surface once, to perform Elvis Presley's "Little Sister" alongside Dave Edmunds' Rockpile at the Concert for Kampuchea gig in London, and he mused on the possibility of launching a record label of his own, named like his studio for daughter Carmen's Palomino horse, and specializing in hard-to-find oldies. But a year would elapse before he finally said yes to Peter Grant's constant requests to reconsider his reluctance to tour again with Led Zeppelin. He agreed to a three-week European tour that would eschew the vast auditoriums and marathon performances of the past in favor of smaller venues and a tighter, more concise set. His bandmates even agreed to forgo their solos.

The shows that followed were, by no means, legendary Led Zeppelin performances. Which is maybe why Plant enjoyed them so much. A smaller stage and lesser dynamics allowed him to work as the front man in a rock 'n' roll band again, as opposed to a preening sex god on an unreachable dais. As long as Grant could guarantee similar-sized venues, and his bandmates would agree to a similarly paced set, Plant was prepared to tour again.

Grant got to work, putting together a month's worth of American dates, beginning in October 1980. Logistically, he knew that the tour would inevitably run into trouble, simply because the demand for tickets was destined to swamp every one of the venues they played. But it was enough to have gotten the band back on the road. In late September, the band set up their new headquarters in the small town of Bray, close to Windsor on the outskirts of London, with Plant and Bonham commuting daily from their roost at the Blakes Hotel in London, while Bonham opted to live at Page's house.

Live there and, on the night of September 24, die there.

Led Zeppelin died with him.

Acknowledgments

The roots of this book, if I were to really dig deep, lie in an idea that I had thirty years ago for a dozen or so of rock's most legendary entrepreneurs to reveal the deepest tricks of their managerial trade for a book I wanted to title *Hype: How to Make (or Break) a Band in 1970s Rock 'n' Roll.* Within which Led Zeppelin would take pride of place, because an interview with Peter Grant suggested they deserved it.

The book was titled, but it has not yet been written. One day. . . . My first thank you, nonetheless, goes to Peter Grant, Led Zeppelin's manager throughout their career, and the first person I ever spoke to who acknowledged that a lot of the things we believed about that band might never actually have happened. A chip in a solid foundation that has continued to fascinate ever since, at the same time as the foundation itself has only grown thicker and stronger—to the point, today, where it is virtually impossible to place Led Zeppelin's achievements into any kind of context, because their legend created the context in the first place.

It is to those people who assisted me in reevaluating that context that my next round of thank-yous go. Particularly those who, speaking under condition of anonymity, shed light on those areas that had hitherto lurked in the realms of supposition alone—and those others with whom I enjoyed conversations that frequently had nothing whatsoever to do with this book, but whose memories, thoughts, and opinions appear within it regardless: Jorgen Angel, Carmine Appice, Long John Baldry, Jeff Beck, John Bindon, Deborah Bonham, Lee Brilleaux, Jack Bruce, Richard Byers, Lee

Black Childers, Neil Daniels, Tony Defries, Donovan, Judy Dyble, John Entwistle, Mick Farren, Roy Harper, Nicky Hopkins, Tony Iommi, John Paul Jones, Simon Kirke, Alexis Korner, Trevor Lucas, Phil May, Brian May, John Mayall, Jim McCarty, Mickie Most, Simon Napier-Bell, Dave Pegg, Cozy Powell, Tony Secunda, TV Smith, Chris Townson, Dave Walker, Chris Wood, and the myriad other Zeppelin peers, pals, disciples, and dreamers whose words and thoughts join mine in telling this story.

To everyone at Backbeat Books, but in particular, Marybeth Keating, John Cerullo, Jessica Burr, and Joanna Dalin Sexton; and finally, to the usual cast of characters, suspects, and fictional beings for their assistance, advice, and enthusiasm as this book came to life, including: Amy Hanson; Jo-Ann Greene; Oliver, Toby, and Trevor; Karen and Todd; the Mortensen family; Rita and Eric; Linda and Larry; Gaye and Tim; Dave and Sue; Bateerz and clan; sundry gremlins; Barb East; Geoff Monmouth . . . and many more.

Discography

Robert Plant Singles

(With Listen) You'd Better Run/Everybody's Gonna Say (CBS 202456—UK)—1966

Our Song/Laughing, Crying, Laughing (CBS 202656—UK)—1967

Long Time Coming/I've Got a Secret (CBS 202858—UK)—1967

Burning Down One Side/Moonlight in Samosa (Swan Song 7 99979)—1982

Pledge Pin/Fat Lip (Swan Song SS 99522)—1982

Big Log/Far Post (Es Paranza 7 998447)—1983

In the Mood/Horizontal Departure (Es Paranza 7 998207)—1983

(The Honeydrippers) Rockin' at Midnight/Young Boy Blues
(Es Paranza 7 99686)—1984

(The Honeydrippers) Sea of Love/I Get a Thrill (Es Paranza 7 99701)—1984

Little by Little/Trouble Your Money (Es Paranza 7 99644)—1985

Too Loud/Kallalou Kallalou (Es Paranza 7 99622)—1985

Ship of Fools/Billy's Revenge (Es Paranza 7 99333)—1988

Tall Cool One/White, Clean and Neat (Es Paranza 7 99348)—1988

Heaven Knows/Walking Towards Paradise (Es Paranza 7 99373)—1988

Hurting Kind/I Cried/Oompah (Es Paranza 96483-2)—1990

29 Palms/Whole Lotta Love (Es Paranza 98388-2)—1993

Led Zeppelin Singles

Communication Breakdown/Good Times Bad Times (Atlantic 2613)—1969

Whole Lotta Love/Livin' Lovin' Maid (Atlantic 2690)—1969

Immigrant Song/Hey Hey What Can I Do (Atlantic 2777)—1970

Black Dog/Misty Mountain Hop (Atlantic 2849)—1971

Rock and Roll/Four Sticks (Atlantic 2865)—1972

Over the Hills and Far Away/Dancing Days (Atlantic 2970)—1973

D'Yer Mak'er/The Crunge (Atlantic 2986)—1973

Trampled Under Foot/Black Country Woman (Swan Song SS70102)—1975
Candy Store Rock/Royal Orleans (Swan Song SS 70110)—1976
Fool in the Rain/Hot Dog (Swan Song SS 71003)—1980
Travelling Riverside Blues (Atlantic PRCD 37627-2)—1990
Baby Come On Home (Atlantic PRCD 5255-2)—1993
Whole Lotta Love/Baby Come On Home/Travelling Riverside Blues
(Atlantic 7567-84014-6—UK)—1997
The Girl I Love She Got Long Black Wavy Hair/Whole Lotta Led Medley
(Atlantic PRCD 8376-2)—1997

Led Zeppelin Albums
LED ZEPPELIN I (1969)
Good Times Bad Times; Babe I'm Gonna Leave You;
You Shook Me; Dazed and Confused; Your Time Is Gonna Come;
Black Mountain Side; Communication Breakdown; I Can't Quit You Baby;
How Many More Times

2014 Bonus tracks, live at the Paris Olympia, October 10, 1969
Good Times Bad Times/Communication Breakdown; I Can't Quit You Baby;
Heartbreaker; Dazed and Confused; White Summer/Black Mountain Side;
You Shook Me; Moby Dick; How Many More Times

LED ZEPPELIN II (1969)
Whole Lotta Love; What Is and What Should Never Be; The Lemon Song;
Thank You; Heartbreaker; Livin' Lovin' Maid (She's Just a Woman);
Ramble On; Moby Dick; Bring It On Home

2014 bonus tracks
Whole Lotta Love (alternate mix); What Is and What Should Never Be (alternate mix);
Thank You (backing track); Heartbreaker (alternate mix);
Livin' Lovin' Maid (She's Just a Woman) (backing track);
Ramble On (alternate mix); Moby Dick (alternate mix); La La

LED ZEPPELIN III (1970)
Immigrant Song; Friends; Celebration Day;
Since I've Been Loving You; Out on the Tiles; Gallows Pole;
Tangerine; That's the Way; Bron-Y-Aur Stomp;
Hats Off to (Roy) Harper

2014 bonus tracks
Immigrant Song (alternate); Friends (alternate);
Celebration Day (alternate); Since I've Been Loving You (alternate);

Bathroom Sound (early instrumental—Out on the Tiles);
Gallows Pole (alternate); That's the Way (alternate);
Jennings Farm Blues (early instrumental—Bron-Y-Aur Stomp);
Keys to the Highway/Trouble in Mind

LED ZEPPELIN IV (1971)

Black Dog; Rock and Roll; The Battle of Evermore;
Stairway to Heaven; Misty Mountain Hop; Four Sticks;
Going to California; When the Levee Breaks

HOUSES OF THE HOLY (1973)

The Song Remains the Same; The Rain Song;
Over the Hills and Far Away; The Crunge; Dancing Days;
D'Yer Mak'er; No Quarter; The Ocean

PHYSICAL GRAFFITI (1975)

Custard Pie; The Rover; In My Time of Dying; Houses of the Holy;
Trampled Under Foot; Kashmir; In the Light; Bron-Yr-Aur;
Down by the Seaside; Ten Years Gone;
Night Flight; The Wanton Song; Boogie with Stu;
Black Country Woman; Sick Again

PRESENCE (1976)

Achilles Last Stand; For Your Life; Royal Orleans;
Nobody's Fault but Mine; Candy Store Rock;
Hots On for Nowhere; Tea for One

THE SONG REMAINS THE SAME (live 1976)

Rock and Roll; Celebration Day; Black Dog (bonus track);
Over the Hills and Far Away (bonus track); Misty Mountain Hop (bonus track);
Since I've Been Loving You (bonus track); The Song Remains the Same;
The Rain Song; The Ocean (bonus track); Dazed and Confused;
No Quarter; Stairway to Heaven; Moby Dick;
Heartbreaker (bonus track); Whole Lotta Love

IN THROUGH THE OUT DOOR (1979)

In the Evening; South Bound Saurez; Fool in the Rain; Hot Dog;
Carouselambra; All My Love; I'm Gonna Crawl

CODA (compilation 1982)

We're Gonna Groove (live); Poor Tom; I Can't Quit You Baby (live);
Walter's Walk; Ozone Baby; Darlene; Bonzo's Montreux;
Wearing and Tearing

LED ZEPPELIN (box set 1990)

Whole Lotta Love; Heartbreaker; Communication Breakdown;
Babe I'm Gonna Leave You; What Is and What Should Never Be;
Thank You; I Can't Quit You Baby (live); Dazed and Confused;
Your Time Is Gonna Come; Ramble On; Travelling Riverside Blues (live);
Friends; Celebration Day; Hey Hey What Can I Do;
White Summer/Black Mountain Side (live);
Black Dog; Over the Hills and Far Away; Immigrant Song;
The Battle of Evermore; Bron-Y-Aur Stomp; Tangerine; Going to California;
Since I've Been Loving You; D'Yer Mak'er; Gallows Pole;
Custard Pie; Misty Mountain Hop; Rock and Roll; The Rain Song;
Stairway to Heaven; Kashmir; Trampled Under Foot;
For Your Life; No Quarter; Dancing Days;
When the Levee Breaks; Achilles Last Stand;
The Song Remains the Same; Ten Years Gone; In My Time of Dying;
In the Evening; Candy Store Rock; The Ocean; Ozone Baby;
Houses of the Holy; Wearing and Tearing; Poor Tom;
Nobody's Fault but Mine; Fool in the Rain; In the Light;
The Wanton Song; Moby Dick/Bonzo's Montreux;
I'm Gonna Crawl; All My Love

LED ZEPPELIN REMASTERS (vinyl compilation 1990)

Communication Breakdown; Babe I'm Gonna Leave You;
Good Times Bad Times; Dazed and Confused;
Heartbreaker; Whole Lotta Love; Ramble On;
Since I've Been Loving You; Celebration Day;
Immigrant Song; Black Dog; Rock and Roll; The Battle of Evermore;
Misty Mountain Hop (CD bonus track); Stairway to Heaven;
The Song Remains the Same; The Rain Song (CD bonus track);
D'Yer Mak'er; No Quarter; Houses of the Holy; Trampled Under Foot;
Kashmir; Nobody's Fault but Mine; Achilles Last Stand;
All My Love; In the Evening

LED ZEPPELIN BOXED SET 2 (box set 1993)

Good Times Bad Times; We're Gonna Groove; Night Flight;
That's the Way; Baby Come On Home;
The Lemon Song; You Shook Me; Boogie with Stu;
Bron-Yr-Aur; Down by the Seaside; Out on the Tiles;
Black Mountain Side; Moby Dick; Sick Again;
Hot Dog; Carouselambra; South Bound Saurez; Walter's Walk; Darlene;
Black Country Woman; How Many More Times; The Rover;
Four Sticks; Hats Off to (Roy) Harper; I Can't Quit You Baby;
Hots On for Nowhere; Livin' Lovin' Maid (She's Just a Woman);
Royal Orleans; Bonzo's Montreux; The Crunge;
Bring It On Home; Tea for One

THE COMPLETE STUDIO RECORDINGS (box set 1993)

Disc One—Led Zeppelin I
Good Times Bad Times; Babe I'm Gonna Leave You; You Shook Me;
Dazed and Confused; Your Time Is Gonna Come; Black Mountain Side;
Communication Breakdown; I Can't Quit You Baby; How Many More Times

Disc Two—Led Zeppelin II
Whole Lotta Love; What Is and What Should Never Be; The Lemon Song;
Thank You; Heartbreaker; Livin' Lovin' Maid (She's Just a Woman);
Ramble On; Moby Dick; Bring It On Home

Disc Three—Led Zeppelin III
Immigrant Song; Friends; Celebration Day; Since I've Been Loving You;
Out on the Tiles; Gallows Pole; Tangerine;
That's the Way; Bron-Y-Aur Stomp; Hats Off to (Roy) Harper

Disc Four—Led Zeppelin IV
Black Dog; Rock and Roll; The Battle of Evermore; Stairway to Heaven;
Misty Mountain Hop; Four Sticks; Going to California; When the Levee Breaks

Disc Five—Houses of the Holy
The Song Remains the Same; The Rain Song; Over the Hills and Far Away;
The Crunge; Dancing Days; D'Yer Mak'er; No Quarter; The Ocean

Disc Six—Presence
Achilles Last Stand; For Your Life; Royal Orleans; Nobody's Fault but Mine;
Candy Store Rock; Hots On for Nowhere; Tea for One

Disc Seven—Physical Graffiti (1)
Custard Pie; The Rover; In My Time of Dying; Houses of the Holy;
Trampled Under Foot; Kashmir

Disc Eight—Physical Graffiti (2)
In the Light; Bron-Yr-Aur; Down by the Seaside; Ten Years Gone; Night Flight;
The Wanton Song; Boogie with Stu; Black Country Woman; Sick Again

Disc Nine—In Through the Out Door
In the Evening; South Bound Saurez; Fool in the Rain;
Hot Dog; Carouselambra; All My Love; I'm Gonna Crawl

Disc Ten—Coda
We're Gonna Groove (live); Poor Tom; I Can't Quit You Baby (live);
Walter's Walk; Ozone Baby; Darlene; Bonzo's Montreux;
Wearing and Tearing; Baby Come On Home (bonus track);
Travelling Riverside Blues (bonus track);
White Summer/Black Mountain Side (bonus track);
Hey Hey What Can I Do (bonus track)

BBC SESSIONS (live compilation 1997)

You Shook Me; I Can't Quit You Baby; Communication Breakdown;
Dazed and Confused; The Girl I Love She Got Long Black Wavy Hair;
What Is and What Should Never Be; Communication Breakdown;
Travelling Riverside Blues; Whole Lotta Love;
Somethin' Else; Communication Breakdown; I Can't Quit You Baby;
You Shook Me; How Many More Times; Immigrant Song;
Heartbreaker; Since I've Been Loving You;
Black Dog; Dazed and Confused; Stairway to Heaven; Going to California;
That's the Way; Whole Lotta Love medley; Thank You

BEST OF LED ZEPPELIN—VOLUME ONE: EARLY DAYS (compilation 2000)

Good Times Bad Times; Babe I'm Gonna Leave You;
Dazed and Confused; Communication Breakdown; Whole Lotta Love;
What Is and What Should Never Be; Immigrant Song; Since I've Been Loving You;
Black Dog; Rock and Roll; The Battle of Evermore;
When the Levee Breaks; Stairway to Heaven

BEST OF LED ZEPPELIN—VOLUME TWO: LATTER DAYS (compilation 2000)

The Song Remains the Same; No Quarter; Houses of the Holy;
Trampled Under Foot; Kashmir; Ten Years Gone; Achilles Last Stand;
Nobody's Fault but Mine; All My Love; In the Evening

HOW THE WEST WAS WON (live 2003)

LA Drone; Immigrant Song; Heartbreaker; Black Dog;
Over the Hills and Far Away; Since I've Been Loving You; Stairway to Heaven;
Going to California; That's the Way; Bron-Y-Aur Stomp; Dazed and Confused;
Walter's Walk; The Crunge; What Is and What Should Never Be; Dancing Days;
Moby Dick; Whole Lotta Love (medley); Rock and Roll; The Ocean;
Bring It On Home; Bring It On Back

MOTHERSHIP (compilation 2007)

Good Times Bad Times; Communication Breakdown;
Dazed and Confused; Babe I'm Gonna Leave You;
Whole Lotta Love; Ramble On; Heartbreaker; Immigrant Song;
Since I've Been Loving You; Rock and Roll; Black Dog;
When the Levee Breaks; Stairway to Heaven; The Song Remains the Same;
Over the Hills and Far Away; D'Yer Mak'er; No Quarter;
Trampled Under Foot; Houses of the Holy; Kashmir;
Nobody's Fault but Mine; Achilles Last Stand; In the Evening;
All My Love; We're Gonna Groove (DVD—live);
I Can't Quit You Baby (DVD—live); Dazed and Confused (DVD—live);
White Summer (DVD—live); What Is and What Should Never Be (DVD—live);
Moby Dick (DVD—live); Whole Lotta Love (DVD—live);
Communication Breakdown (DVD—live); Bring It On Home (DVD—live);

Immigrant Song (DVD—live); Black Dog (DVD—live);
Misty Mountain Hop (DVD—live); The Ocean (DVD—live);
Going to California (DVD—live); In My Time of Dying (DVD—live);
Stairway to Heaven (DVD—live); Rock and Roll (DVD—live);
Nobody's Fault but Mine (DVD—live); Kashmir (DVD—live);
Whole Lotta Love (DVD—live)

DEFINITIVE COLLECTION MINI LP REPLICA CD BOX SET (2008)

Disc One—Led Zeppelin I
Good Times Bad Times; Babe I'm Gonna Leave You; You Shook Me;
Dazed and Confused; Your Time Is Gonna Come; Black Mountain Side;
Communication Breakdown; I Can't Quit You Baby; How Many More Times

Disc Two—Led Zeppelin II
Whole Lotta Love; What Is and What Should Never Be; The Lemon Song;
Thank You; Heartbreaker; Livin' Lovin' Maid (She's Just a Woman);
Ramble On; Moby Dick; Bring It On Home

Disc Three—Led Zeppelin III
Immigrant Song; Friends; Celebration Day; Since I've Been Loving You;
Out on the Tiles; Gallows Pole; Tangerine; That's the Way;
Bron-Y-Aur Stomp; Hats Off to (Roy) Harper

Disc Four—Led Zeppelin IV
Black Dog; Rock and Roll; The Battle of Evermore; Stairway to Heaven;
Misty Mountain Hop; Four Sticks; Going to California; When the Levee Breaks

Disc Five—Houses of the Holy
The Song Remains the Same; The Rain Song; Over the Hills and Far Away; The
Crunge; Dancing Days; D'Yer Mak'er; No Quarter; The Ocean

Disc Six—Physical Graffiti (1)
Custard Pie; The Rover; In My Time of Dying; Houses of the Holy;
Trampled Under Foot; Kashmir

Disc Seven—Physical Graffiti (2)
In the Light; Bron-Yr-Aur; Down by the Seaside; Ten Years Gone; Night Flight; The
Wanton Song; Boogie with Stu; Black Country Woman; Sick Again

Disc Eight—Presence
Achilles Last Stand; For Your Life; Royal Orleans; Nobody's Fault but Mine;
Candy Store Rock; Hots On for Nowhere; Tea for One

Disc Nine—The Song Remains the Same (1)
Rock and Roll; Celebration Day; Black Dog; Over the Hills and Far Away;
Misty Mountain Hop; Since I've Been Loving You; The Song Remains the Same;
The Rain Song; The Ocean

Disc Ten—The Song Remains the Same (2)
Dazed and Confused; No Quarter; Stairway to Heaven;
Moby Dick; Heartbreaker (bonus track); Whole Lotta Love

Disc Eleven—In Through the Out Door
In the Evening; South Bound Saurez; Fool in the Rain; Hot Dog;
Carouselambra; All My Love; I'm Gonna Crawl

Disc Twelve—Coda
We're Gonna Groove (live); Poor Tom; I Can't Quit You Baby (live);
Walter's Walk; Ozone Baby; Darlene; Bonzo's Montreux;
Wearing and Tearing; Baby Come On Home (bonus track);
Travelling Riverside Blues (bonus track);
White Summer/Black Mountain Side (bonus track);
Hey Hey What Can I Do (bonus track)

CELEBRATION DAY (live 2012)

Good Times Bad Times; Ramble On; Black Dog; In My Time of Dying;
For Your Life; Trampled Under Foot; Nobody's Fault but Mine;
No Quarter; Since I've Been Loving You; Dazed and Confused;
Stairway to Heaven; The Song Remains the Same; Misty Mountain Hop;
Kashmir; Whole Lotta Love; Rock and Roll

Robert Plant Albums
PICTURES AT ELEVEN (1982)

Burning Down One Side; Moonlight in Samosa; Pledge Pin;
Slow Dancer; Worse Than Detroit; Fat Lip; Like I've Never Been Gone;
Mystery Title; Far Post (bonus track); Like I've Never Been Gone (live)

THE PRINCIPLE OF MOMENTS (1983)

Other Arms; In the Mood; Messin' with the Mekon; Wreckless Love;
Thru' with the Two Step; Horizontal Departure;
Stranger Here . . . Than Over There; Big Log; In the Mood (live);
Thru' with the Two Step (live); Lively Up Yourself (live); Turnaround

THE HONEYDRIPPERS VOLUME ONE (1984)

I Get a Thrill; Sea of Love; I Got a Woman; Young Boy Blues; At Midnight;
Rockin' at Midnight (live)

SHAKEN 'N' STIRRED (1985)

Hip to Hoo; Kallalou Kallalou; Too Loud; Trouble Your Money;
Pink and Black; Little by Little; Doo Doo A Do Do;
Easily Lead; Sixes and Sevens

NOW AND ZEN (1988)

Heaven Knows; Dance on My Own; Tall Cool One;
The Way I Feel; Helen of Troy; Billy's Revenge; Ship of Fools;
Why; White, Clean and Neat; Walking Towards Paradise

MANIC NIRVANA (1990)

Hurting Kind (I've Got My Eyes on You); Big Love; S S S & Q;
I Cried; She Said; Nirvana; Tie Dye on the Highway;
Your Ma Said You Cried in Your Sleep Last Night;
Anniversary; Liars Dance; Watching You

FATE OF NATIONS (1993)

Calling to You; Down to the Sea; Come into My Life;
I Believe; Palms; Memory Song (Hello Hello); If I Were a Carpenter;
Colours of a Shade; Promised Land;
The Greatest Gift; Great Spirit; Network News

(Robert Plant/Jimmy Page) NO QUARTER (1994)

Nobody's Fault but Mine; Thank You; No Quarter; Friends;
Yallah; City Don't Cry; Since I've Been Loving You;
The Battle of Evermore; Wonderful One; Wah Wah; That's the Way;
Gallows Pole; Four Sticks; Kashmir

(Robert Plant/Jimmy Page) WALKING INTO CLARKSDALE (1998)

Shining in the Light; When the World Was Young;
Upon a Golden Horse; Blue Train; Please Read the Letter;
Most High; Heart in Your Hand;
Walking into Clarksdale; Burning Up; When I Was a Child;
House of Love; Sons of Freedom

DREAMLAND (2002)

Funny in My Mind (I Believe I'm Fixin' to Die); Morning Dew;
One More Cup of Coffee; Last Time I Saw Her; Song to the Siren;
Win My Train Fare Home (If I Ever Get Lucky); Darkness, Darkness;
Red Dress; Hey Joe; Skip's Song; Dirt in a Hole

SIXTY SIX TO TIMBUKTU (compilation 2003)

Disc One

Tie Dye on the Highway; Upside Down (previously unreleased);
Promised Land; Tall Cool One; Dirt in a Hole (from UK *Dreamland* CD);
Calling to You; Palms; If I Were a Carpenter; Sea of Love;
Darkness, Darkness; Big Log; Ship of Fools; I Believe;
Little by Little; Heaven Knows; Song to the Siren

Disc Two
You'd Better Run (original Listen 45, 1966);
Our Song (Robert Plant solo single, 1967);
Hey Joe (Band of Joy demo, 1967); For What It's Worth (Band of Joy demo, 1967);
Operator (Alexis Korner, 1968); Road to the Sun (outtake, 1983);
Philadelphia Baby (the Crawling Kingsnakes, *Porky's Revenge!* soundtrack, 1985);
Red Is for Danger (live with Robin George, 1988);
Let's Have a Party (*The Last Temptation of Elvis* compilation, 1990);
Hey Jayne (B-side, 1993); Louie, Louie (*Wayne's World 2* soundtrack, 1993);
Naked If I Want To (B-side, 1993); Years (B-side, 1993);
If It's Really Got to Be This Way (*Adios Amigo: A Tribute to
Arthur Alexander* compilation, 1994);
Rude World (Robert Plant and Jimmy Page, *The Inner Flame:
A Rainer Ptacek Tribute*, 1997); Little Hands (*More Oar:
A Tribute to Skip Spence*, 1999);
Life Begin Again (Afro Celt Sound System, 1991);
Let the Boogie Woogie Roll (Jools Holland, *Small World, Big Band—
More Friends Volume Two*, 2002);
Win My Train Fare Home (Live at the Festival in the Desert,
for the compilation *Le Festival au Desert Live*, 2003)

MIGHTY REARRANGER (2005)

Another Tribe; Shine It All Around; Freedom Fries;
Tin Pan Valley; All the King's Horses;
The Enchanter; Takamba; Dancing in Heaven; Somebody Knocking;
Let the Four Winds Blow; Mighty Rearranger; Brother Ray

NINE LIVES (box set 2006)

Disc 1: **Pictures at Eleven**
Burning Down One Side; Moonlight in Samosa; Pledge Pin; Slow Dancer;
Worse Than Detroit; Fat Lip; Like I've Never Been Gone; Mystery Title;
Far Post (bonus track: B-side); Like I've Never Been Gone (bonus track: live)

Disc 2: **The Principle of Moments**
Other Arms; In the Mood; Messin' with the Mekon; Wreckless Love;
Thru' with the Two Step; Horizontal Departure; Stranger Here . . . Than Over There;
Big Log; In the Mood (bonus track: live); Thru' with the Two Step (bonus track: live);
Lively Up Yourself (bonus track: live); Turnaround (bonus track: outtake)

Disc 3: **The Honeydrippers Volume One**
I Get a Thrill; Sea of Love; I Got a Woman; Young Boy Blues; Rockin' at Midnight;
Rockin' at Midnight (bonus track: live)

Disc 4: **Shaken 'n' Stirred**
Hip to Hoo; Kallalou Kallalou; Too Loud; Trouble for Money; Pink and Black;
Little by Little; Doo Doo A Do Do; Easily Lead; Sixes and Sevens;
Little by Little (bonus track: remixed long version)

Disc 5: Now and Zen
Heaven Knows; Dance on My Own; Tall Cool One; Way I Feel; Helen of Troy;
Billy's Revenge; Ship of Fools; Why; White, Clean and Neat;
Walking Towards Paradise; Billy's Revenge (bonus track: live);
Ship of Fools (bonus track: live); Tall Cool One (bonus track: live)

Disc 6: Manic Nirvana
Hurting Kind (I've Got My Eyes on You); Big Love; S S S & Q; I Cried;
She Said; Nirvana; Tie Dye on the Highway;
Your Ma Said You Cried in Your Sleep Last Night; Anniversary; Liars Dance;
Watching You (bonus track: B-side); Oompah (Watery Bint) (bonus track: B-side);
One Love (bonus track: B-side); Don't Look Back

Disc 7: Fate of Nations
Calling to You; Down to the Sea; Come into My Life; I Believe; 29 Palms;
Memory Song (Hello Hello); If I Were a Carpenter; Promised Land; Greatest Gift;
Great Spirit; Network News; Colours of a Shade (bonus track: UK CD);
Great Spirit (Acoustic Mix) (bonus track: B-side);
Rollercoaster (bonus track: demo); 8.05 (bonus track: B-side);
Dark Moon (Acoustic) (bonus track: B-side)

Disc 8: Dreamland
Funny in My Mind; Morning Dew; One More Cup of Coffee; Last Time I Saw Her;
Song to the Siren; Win My Train Fare Home; Darkness, Darkness; Red Dress;
Hey Joe; Skip's Song; Dirt in a Hole (bonus track: UK CD);
Last Time I Saw Her (Remix) (bonus track: B-side)

Disc 9: Mighty Rearranger
Another Tribe; Shine It All Around; Freedom Fries; Tin Pan Valley;
All the King's Horses; The Enchanter; Takamba;
Dancing in Heaven; Somebody Knocking;
Let the Four Winds Blow; Mighty Rearranger; Brother Ray;
Red White and Blue (bonus track: Japanese CD);
All the Money in the World (bonus track: B-side);
Shine It All Around (Girls Remix) (bonus track: B-side);
Tin Pan Valley (Girls Remix) (bonus track: B-side);
The Enchanter (UNKLE Reconstruction) (bonus track: B-side)

Disc 10: Nine Lives (DVD)
Nine Lives (documentary); Burning Down One Side (video); Big Log (video);
In the Mood (video); Rockin' at Midnight (video); Sea of Love (video);
Little by Little (video); Pink and Black (video); Heaven Knows (video);
Tall Cool One (video); Ship of Fools (video);
Hurting Kind (I've Got My Eyes on You) (video); Nirvana (video);
Tie Dye on the Highway (video); 29 Palms (video); Calling to You (video);
I Believe (video); If I Were a Carpenter (video); Morning Dew (video);
Darkness, Darkness (video); Shine It All Around (video)

(Robert Plant/Alison Krauss) RAISING SAND (2007)

Rich Woman; Killing the Blues; Sister Rosetta Goes Before Us; Polly Come Home;
Gone Gone Gone (Done Moved On); Through the Morning, Through the Night;
Please Read the Letter; Trampled Rose; Fortune Teller; Stick with Me Baby;
Nothin'; Let Your Loss Be Your Lesson; Your Long Journey

BAND OF JOY (2010)

Angel Dance; House of Cards; Central Two-O-Nine; Silver Rider;
You Can't Buy My Love; Falling in Love Again;
The Only Sound That Matters; Monkey;
Cindy, I'll Marry You Someday; Harm's Swift Way;
Satan Your Kingdom Must Come Down; Even This Shall Pass Away

LULLABY AND... THE CEASELESS ROAR (2014)

Little Maggie; Rainbow; Pocketful of Golden; Embrace Another Fall; Turn It Up;
A Stolen Kiss; Somebody There; Poor Howard; House of Love;
Up on the Hollow Hill (Understanding Arthur); Arbaden (Maggie's Babby)

Other Releases

Disc two of Plant's *Sixty Six to Timbuktu* and bonus tracks included in the *Nine Lives*
box (see individual entries) provide the strongest overview of solo Plant rarities.
The following cuts remain uncollected:

Adriatic Sea View (recorded 1967 with the Band of Joy, *In the Forest*, 1989)
Steal Away (recorded 1968 with Alexis Korner, *On the Move*, 1996)
Little Sister (with Rockpile, *Concerts for the People of Kampuchea* live album, 1979)
Dimples (live UK B-side, 1988)
The Only One (with Jimmy Page, *Outrider*, 1988)
Crazy Little Thing Called Love
(with Queen, Freddie Mercury Tribute Concert, 1992)
Innuendo (with Queen, Freddie Mercury Tribute Concert, 1992)
21 Years (UK B-side, 1993)
Whole Lotta Love (You Need Love) (UK B-side, 1993)
Hey Jayne (UK B-side, 1993)
Naked If I Want To (UK B-side, 1993)
Calling to You (remixes: Song to Kalsoum Mix, Shookran Sah-Abi Mix, Always,
My Heart Mix, Artist's Valley Mix, Per la Gente Mix) (UK B-side, 1993)
Down by the Seaside (with Tori Amos, *Encomium*, 1995)
The Window (Jimmy Page/Robert Plant B-side, 1998)
Whiskey from the Glass (Jimmy Page/Robert Plant Japanese CD bonus track, 1998)
Gonna Shoot You Right Down (Boom Boom) (with Jimmy Page, Eric Clapton,
Blues Blues Blues: The Jimmy Rodgers All Stars, 1999)

Selected Bibliography

Aranza, Jacob. *Backward Masking Unmasked: Backward Satanic Messages of Rock and Roll Exposed*. Huntington House Inc., 1983.

Case, George. *Led Zeppelin FAQ: All That's Left to Know About the Greatest Hard Rock Band of All Time*. Backbeat Books, 2011.

Cole, Richard. *Stairway to Heaven: Led Zeppelin Uncensored*. IT Books (reprint edition), 2002.

Combe, John. *Get Your Kicks on the A456*. John Combe Associates, 2008.

Cross, Charles R., and Erik Flannigan. *Led Zeppelin: Heaven and Hell*. Sidgwick & Jackson, 1991.

Daniels, Neil. *Robert Plant: Led Zeppelin, Jimmy Page and the Solo Years*. Independent Music Press, 2008.

Davis, Stephen. *Hammer of the Gods: The Led Zeppelin Saga*. IT Books (reprint edition), 2008.

Davis, Stephen. *LZ-'75. The Lost Chronicles of Led Zeppelin's 1975 American Tour*. Gotham Books (reprint edition), 2010.

Des Barres, Pamela. *I'm with the Band: Confessions of a Groupie*. Chicago Review Press (updated edition), 2005.

Farren, Mick. *Give the Anarchist a Cigarette*. Jonathan Cape, 2001.

Frame, Pete. *Pete Frame's Complete Rock Family Trees*. Omnibus Press, 1993.

Godwin, Robert. *Led Zeppelin: The Press Reports*. Collectors Guide Publishing, 1997.

Holder, Noddy. *Who's Crazee Now?—My Autobiography*. Ebury Press, 1999.

Hoskyns, Barney. *Led Zeppelin: The Oral History of the World's Greatest Rock Band*. Wiley, 2012.

Lewis, Dave. *From a Whisper to a Scream: Complete Guide to the Music of Led Zeppelin*. Omnibus Press, 2013.

Lewis, Dave. *Led Zeppelin: The "Tight but Loose" Files*. Omnibus Press, 2004.

Lewis, Dave, and Simon Pallett. *Led Zeppelin: The Concert Documentary*. Omnibus Press, 1997.

Mylett, Howard. *Jimmy Page: Tangents Within a Framework*. Omnibus Press, 1984.

Nicholls, Geoff, and Chris Welch. *John Bonham: A Thunder of Drums*. Backbeat Books, 2001.

Peters, Dan, and Steve Peters. *Why Knock Rock?* Bethany House Publishers, 1984.

Rees, Paul. *Robert Plant: A Life*. IT Books, 2013.

Rey, Luis. *Led Zeppelin Live: An Illustrated Exploration of Underground Tapes*. Hot Wacks Press, 1998

Schofield, Nigel. *Fairport by Fairport*. Rocket 88, 2012.

Somach, Denny. *Get the Led Out: How Led Zeppelin Became the Biggest Band in the World*. Sterling, 2012.

Thompson, Dave. *If You Like Led Zeppelin . . . Here Are Over 200 Bands, Films, Records, and Other Oddities That You Will Love*. Backbeat Books, 2012.

Thompson, Dave. *Truth: Rod Stewart, Ron Wood and the Jeff Beck Group*. Cherry Red Books, 2006.

Tolinski, Brad. *Light and Shade: Conversations with Jimmy Page*. Broadway Books, 2013.

Wall, Mick. *When Giants Walked the Earth: A Biography of Led Zeppelin*. St. Martin's Griffin, 2010.

Welch, Chris. *Led Zeppelin: The Stories Behind Every Led Zeppelin Song*. Carlton, 2011.

Welch, Chris. *Peter Grant: The Man Who Led Zeppelin*. Omnibus Press, 2003.

Welch, Chris. *Treasures of Led Zeppelin*. Carlton Books, 2010.

Westwood, Jennifer, and Jacqueline Simpson. *The Lore of the Land: A Guide to England's Legends from Spring-Heeled Jack to the Witches of Warboys*. Penguin Books, 2005.

Yorke, Ritchie. *Led Zeppelin: The Definitive Biography*. Underwood Books, 1994.

Index